NO STRUGGLE
NO PROGRESS

NO STRUGGLE
NO PROGRESS

A WARRIOR'S LIFE FROM BLACK POWER
TO EDUCATION REFORM

BY

Dr. Howard Fuller

with
Lisa Frazier Page

MARQUETTE
UNIVERSITY
PRESS

LIBRARY OF CONGRESS CATALOGING-IN-PUBLICATION DATA

Fuller, Howard, 1941-
No struggle, no progress : a warrior's life from Black power to education
reform / by Dr. Howard Fuller with Lisa Frazier Page.
   pages cm
Includes bibliographical references and index.
ISBN 978-1-62600-044-5 (hardcover : alk. paper)
1. Fuller, Howard, 1941- 2. School superintendents—United States—
Biography. 3. African American school superintendents—Biography. 4.
Educators—United States—Biography. 5. Education—United States. 6.
Educational change—United States. 7. Black power—United States. 8.
African Americans—Civil rights. I. Page, Lisa Frazier. II. Title.
LA2317.F94N6 2014
371.20092—dc23
[B]
                                                      2014007946

COVER PHOTO: *During a demonstration in Durham after the death
of Dr. Martin Luther King, I gazed up and spotted white men with rifles
on a bank building. Turns out the men were police officers. (photo courtesy
of Billy E. Barnes)*

COVER DESIGN BY ANGELO D. DEVIGAL

∞ The paper used in this publication meets the minimum requirements of the
   American National Standard for Information Sciences—
Permanence of Paper for Printed Library Materials, ANSI Z39.48-1992.

MARQUETTE UNIVERSITY PRESS
MILWAUKEE

The Association of Jesuit University Presses

CONTENTS

Illustrations follow Chapters 1, 2, 3, 4, 5, 6, 3, 9, 10, 13, 14, 15, 16, 17, & Acknowledgments.

"If there is no struggle, there is no progress.
Those who profess to favor freedom, and yet depreciate agitation,
are men who want crops without plowing up the ground.
They want rain without thunder and lightning.
They want the ocean without the awful roar of its many waters.
This struggle may be a moral one; or it may be a physical one;
or it may be both moral and physical; but it must be a struggle."

—Frederick Douglass

For my mother (Juanita Smith) and grandmother (Pearl Wagner)
and
My grandchildren (William Fuller Rhatigan and Zoe Cooper),

The past and the future

INTRODUCTION

My meeting with Texas Governor George W. Bush was supposed to last a half hour. That's what a colleague explained when she told me that we'd managed to get on his schedule to discuss school reform. This would give us a chance to make a strong pitch for programs that give low-income families more education options for their children, such as charter schools and state-financed vouchers to private schools.

The suggestion to meet with the governor had come out of the blue while I was in Austin that spring of 1999 to persuade the state's Black lawmakers to support a contentious school voucher proposal. I agreed to the meeting, though I was less than eager to participate. I'd been around politics long enough to know that these kinds of sessions were largely ceremonial. The politician would do most of the talking, I might get to say a thing or two about why school vouchers were good for poor Black children, and we'd be up and out of there. But when my colleague and I sat down with the governor, a surprising thing happened: I connected with the dude.

Bush, who by then had launched his presidential campaign, told us up front that he didn't know much about school vouchers and was still trying to formulate a clear education platform. I could tell that he was genuinely listening as we explained our position. I'd been among those pushing for "parental choice" in Milwaukee when state legislators in 1989 approved the first program in the country to provide state funds for poor children to attend private schools. Then, after my four-year tenure as Milwaukee Superintendent of Schools ended in 1995, I'd become totally immersed in the movement and a rare Black advocate. Bush was full of questions, and the conversation flowed easily. He was engaging. His policies aside, I found him quite likeable. Before I knew it, one-and-a-half hours had passed. Finally, he rose and extended his hand, signaling the end of the conversation.

"Hey, I'm going to be the next President of the United States," he said. "Would you be interested in coming to Washington with me?"

I was stunned. I wasn't quite sure what he meant, whether he had anything specific in mind, but I couldn't imagine a scenario that might work. Number one, I'm not a Republican, and number two, I'm not a loyalist. I'm not the kind of person who can just go along with the party line for the sake of politics when I disagree on matters of importance. So, I politely declined. I did eventually agree, though, to be part of a committee that wrote his first two speeches on education—speeches that he delivered in Los Angeles and New York.

The next year, Bush was declared the winner of a tight and controversial presidential race ultimately settled by the U.S. Supreme Court. Then, shortly after he took office, I was invited to join a group of parent choice advocates to meet with him in the Oval Office. I was actually worried that his security team would do the mandatory background check, call me back, and say, "Uh, never mind!" My work, dating back to the 1960s and '70s, had hardly been free of controversy. I'd worked as a community organizer in North Carolina in the mid- to late 1960s and had been hated by the white political establishment there. I'd also founded Malcolm X Liberation University in 1969 and was a Black Power advocate known by the African name that the university students bestowed on me: Owusu Sadaukai. I got involved in the African Liberation Movement in the early 1970s and later even studied Marxism as a union organizer. But there I was one day in 2001, sitting alongside the new President of the United States of America, George W. Bush. This time the meeting was in the Oval Office. My first thought was that the office was much smaller than I'd imagined, and there were a whole lot of doors. I couldn't help wondering what secrets the rooms behind those doors held.

Once the word spread that I was working with the Republican president on education, people immediately began making assumptions about me. Some former friends called me a sellout and Uncle Tom—charges that were not new to me. Even though I knew such accusations to be completely off base, I understood the perception. Others figured I'd become a Republican and changed my views and beliefs, which wasn't true either. Who knows what assumptions, if any, people like the President were making about me. But as I left 1600 Pennsylvania Avenue that day, it occurred to me: *This man has no idea who I really am. And neither do the people who've been so quick to pass judgment on me my entire life.*

At long last, this book is my answer. This is, as best I can tell you, who I am and how I got here, in the heart of the struggle to reform the nation's schools. I have always believed that it is important for poor and working class Black people to gain access to the levers of power controlling their lives. I also believe that those of us who are educated and resourceful have a moral and historical responsibility to help others, and that is what I have always tried to do. Early in my life, I found truth in the words of the great Frederick Douglass: "Power concedes nothing without a demand. It never did, and it never will." So struggle we must. That understanding of the relationship between struggle and progress is what propelled me down dark alleys and dirt roads in some of North Carolina's poorest communities in the 1960s, and pushed me into the bush, mountains, and war-torn villages of Africa nearly a decade later. It is what pushes me still in the fight over one of the most contentious education issues of this era: parental choice. I believe deep in my heart that giving low-income and working-class parents the power (and the money) to make choices about the schools their children attend will not only revolutionize education but provide the compass to a better life for the many poor, Black children stuck in failing systems. Make no mistake about it: Education reform is one of the most crucial social justice issues of our time, and I will spend the rest of my days fighting for my people, most especially those without the power or the resources to fight for themselves.

I

GRANDMA'S HANDS

When I was four or five years old, growing up in Shreveport, Louisiana, just the sight of a police car scared me. I lived with my mother and grandmother on Baxer Street in a raised, shotgun-style house on the Black side of town, and my favorite hiding spot was underneath the front porch. Every time I saw a police car rolling through the neighborhood, that's where I ran. I don't recall what I'd seen or heard that had caused such fear, but this was 1940s Louisiana. Black folks had no rights. Jim Crow policies and procedures made sure of that. Most Black families throughout the state were poor. The mothers and fathers were undereducated: In rural areas they worked from an early age in sugar cane and cotton fields; in the cities as domestics, cooking, cleaning, and caring for white children. Ridiculous poll taxes and literacy tests dissuaded many from trying to vote and kept them locked out of the political system. The Ku Klux Klan terrorized Black communities with their random cross burnings and clandestine acts of violence. Studies show that in the first three decades of the twentieth century, more Black men were lynched in the northern parishes of Louisiana, including Caddo, where Shreveport is located, than anywhere else in the state. It was no secret to Black folks that many of the same white officials running the cities and towns during the day rode with their hooded brethren at night.

Whatever the reason for my fear, my grandmother, Pearl Wagner, wasn't having it. Dignity meant something to her, and no grandson of hers was going to run at the sight of a white man. She happened to see me dash to my hiding spot when a police car rolled through one day, and she immediately called me out.

"Don't you ever let me see you do this again," she demanded.

I had done nothing wrong and had no reason to run and hide from the police, she explained. I think the bigger lesson she taught me that day, though, was that I shouldn't fear anyone, especially people with power, and that has stuck with me throughout my life. She lived that way, too—fearlessly. She was one of the toughest human beings I've ever known. There was nothing physically imposing about her—she was an average-sized woman with a kind face and gray hair, even in my earliest memories. She wasn't loud or mean, but everyone around us knew that she fiercely protected her family, namely my mother and me. Pearl Wagner wasn't afraid of anybody. One evening I ran inside the house from playing to report that a man down the street had hit me and, for no apparent reason, pushed me off his back porch. My grandmother headed outside and down the back alley to confront the culprit, who was standing among a group of men. She stopped in front of the group, inquired about the incident, and when the guilty one didn't respond to her liking, she picked up a large concrete brick from a pile stacked next to her, threw it at him, and walked away. Word had it the brick broke the man's arm. As far as I know, no one ever came looking for her, and I never had any trouble from him again.

My grandmother responded with the same tenacity one day when a white police officer, looking for a robber in the neighborhood, rushed up to our back porch, falsely accused my mother of hiding the suspect, kicked her, and pushed her aside to search the house. Someone called my grandmother at work to tell her what was happening. She came home right away, got her gun, and headed for the police station to demand some answers. I never knew what happened once she got there, but she made it back home safely. And that just confirmed what I already knew: My grandma was the baddest woman on earth.

Perhaps she was so strong because she had to be. She was the matriarch of a small family of missing men. All I know about my grandfather is that I must have had one. He wasn't a factor in our lives, and children back then knew better than to ask questions about grown folks' business. Likewise, I knew little about my father. My mother, then Juanita Carter, was eighteen years old when she married Tom Fuller in what I later learned was a typical shotgun wedding. I was born on January 14, 1941, and given the name Howard Lamar Fuller. Soon afterward, my parents split up. My father stayed away, and I was too young to remember anything about him. If not for a photo that my mother kept of him, I wouldn't even have known what he looked like.

But seeing that picture didn't stir up any particular feelings. It was like looking at the face of a stranger in a magazine; the image connected to nothing. I wasn't particularly bothered by the fact that my father wasn't around, though. While I understand the yearning that many boys have for a relationship with their missing fathers, I can honestly say that I don't recall a single moment of longing for him. Early in my life, I stopped even wondering about him. No one mentioned his name. He just wasn't part of my reality.

My childhood revolved around Baker Street and the two women who were determined to make sure I never had a real reason to hide from the police. I called both of them "Mama." Neither believed in sparing the rod, and they tore my behind up at the slightest hint of trouble. My grandmother even made me go outside and pick the switch she used for the whippings. I once figured out a way to get a slight reprieve while she was whipping me: I held my breath, closed my eyes, and let my body go limp. She thought she had hurt me, and it was one of the few times I actually saw her afraid. She dropped her switch and broke down, crying: "Oh, my baby!" When my eyes popped open, she held me close, greatly relieved. But I made the foolish mistake of trying that trick again. She was on to me, though, and just kept whipping me until I breathed.

Because she never finished school, she wanted to make sure I understood the necessity of education. She and my mother talked to me constantly about the importance of making good grades and making something of myself someday. They even enrolled me in preschool at a local Catholic school and somehow were able to pay the tuition. My grandmother worked as a domestic and at a local doctor's office, and when she got off work most evenings, I'd be playing in the front yard. I'd spot her in the distance, walking home slowly in her starched white uniform and flat "work" shoes. She always walked as far as she could to save on the bus fare. But even after she made it home, her workday was far from over. She stayed awake much of the night washing white men's shirts by hand, starching and ironing them, too. Her customers would drive up to our house, drop off a load of their dirty shirts, and return at an assigned time later in the week to pick them up. She spent hours bent over a huge tin wash tub, scrubbing each shirt on an old washboard until every stain was gone. Our house was always filled with shirts in various stages of the cleaning process—tubs of them soaking in soapy or clear rinse water. Outside on the clothesline, rows of the shirts hung under the scorching sun and flapped in an occasional warm wind until they were dry. My grandmother then brought them inside, where she starched and ironed them until they were stiff enough to practically stand on their own. It touches me when I think about the transformative power in my grandmother's hands—how she worked them to the bone, making old shirts like new to provide for her family, and how those same hands issued the harshest punishment and the sweetest love.

By the time I was five years old, my mother had remarried and become Juanita Smith. She and her new husband, John, took a trip to Milwaukee to help out her cousin Idella, who was ill. The visit was supposed to be temporary, but at some point they decided to stay in Milwaukee, likely for the opportunity to find better-paying jobs. This was during the "The Great Migration," the period during the first part of the twentieth century when millions of Black men, women, and children fled the legalized segregation and racism of their birthplaces and headed "up North" in a quest to improve their lives. Black Wisconsinites settled mostly in the state's southeastern corner—Kenosha, Racine, and Milwaukee—47, 60, and 90 miles, respectively, up Lake Michigan's shore from the Windy City. In Milwaukee, three rivers flowed into one another and into Lake Michigan, and many of the best blue-collar jobs were located in the plants, factories, and small shops near the rivers and railroads.

I had never been apart from my mother and missed her so completely that her time away felt like years. Actually, only a few months passed from the time she left, decided to stay in the Midwest, and returned to Shreveport for me. Then, suddenly, my mother and I were nearly 1,000 miles away from our matriarch, the one who had always made my life feel stable and protected. Life would change in some dramatic ways—some good, some bad. But other elders from my new community soon would step into my life with their wisdom.

My first home in Milwaukee with my mother and stepfather was a small cottage on 11th Street in a mostly poor and working-class Black neighborhood. My stepfather, who had dropped out of high school and served time in the Army, found a job at the Armour meat packing plant, where he spent his days shoveling cow and pig manure. The work seemed fitting for a man who was, to me, aloof and mean. He was also a heavy drinker, and once away from the watchful eyes of my grandmother, he began abusing my mother. Sometimes, I'd see her crying quietly, and I knew he had done something to cause her pain. Other times, I actually witnessed him hitting her. I felt helpless, and I always hated the man for what he did to my mother. As I grew older and bigger, it became even more difficult to watch. I was sixteen years old when I once tried to intervene, but my mother pushed me away. I'm sure she was afraid for me and didn't want the situation to escalate even more. When my stepfather drank, which was often, our house was not a pleasant place. I told myself then that I would never be like him. I would never hit a woman. I didn't think we needed him, and I could never understand why my mother—or any woman, for that matter—would stay with a man who beat her. One of my regrets is that I never asked my mother why she stayed, but, even now, I'm not sure it was my place to ask that question.

Nevertheless, my mother tried her best to make sure I had everything I needed. She became close friends with a group of four other mothers—Miss Mackie, Miss Delores, Miss Harriet, and Miss Virginia—whose families became part of ours. We rotated to each other's houses for big Sunday dinners and holiday meals. To lessen the load on the host, each of the mothers brought part of the meal. In a way those meals were symbolic of their bond. The women filled the gaps in one another's lives, sharing what they had, comforting and encouraging each other, and on some Friday or Saturday nights, partying together.

During the week, my mother worked at the local Kex factory, which produced batches of industrial towels, used back then by many businesses, such as gas stations, long before disposable paper products made them obsolete. Kex trucks drove around the city, picking up dirty towels and delivering batches of fresh ones. Meanwhile, my mother and an entire crew of women, most of whom were Black, worked inside the factory, feeding huge washing machines and dryers and folding towels to be packaged into bundles for delivery. By the end of the work day, the ladies would be covered from head to toe in lint, a work hazard that I am convinced caused serious health problems down the road for my mother. On weekends, my mother, who had graduated from cosmetology school, got to use her beauty school skills and earned extra cash by fixing other ladies' hair.

Though we were not Catholic, my mother clearly believed in Catholic schools and enrolled me in St. Boniface, located near the northern border of the area where most of the city's Black population

lived. Because of my family's low income, we did not have to pay tuition. To this day, I'm grateful that someone's philanthropy made it
possible for my mother to choose the education she believed was best
for me. I loved school, did well academically, and mostly stayed out
of trouble, except for talking too much. Back then, Catholic schools
had no problem dishing out corporal punishment, and I was sometimes on the receiving end for doing mischievous things. I once got
my hand slapped for pointing out the hair sticking from underneath
a nun's habit. But Juanita Smith wouldn't let me do much more than
talk. Every now and then, she would take me past the old Milwaukee
detention center for troubled boys and point to it with caution: "If you
don't do right, this is where you're going to end up." I'd imagine those
boys, separated from their friends and families, and I knew I didn't
want to wind up anywhere near there.

Early in my elementary school years, we moved into the new Hillside
Terrace, which was part of the first wave of public housing projects
in Milwaukee. With just two- and three-story walk-ups and no more
than six apartments to each building, though, Hillside was much different than the high-rise tenements that literally packed dozens of
poor families on top of one another in places like Chicago, New York,
and St. Louis. No one could have imagined the desperate, dangerous
places that some of these developments would become. But at the time
Hillside was a nice, safe place for families with limited means. It was
much more desirable than some of the adjacent rundown neighborhoods. Despite their well-intentioned purpose, though, public housing projects penalized poor people for working. Residents, who needed both their jobs and the rent break, were well aware that they could
be evicted if their incomes exceeded a certain limit, and they went to
great lengths to keep any evidence of their work a secret. The 1974
movie "Claudine," featuring Diahann Carroll as a hardworking welfare
mother, later highlighted this aspect of project life. A social worker's
knock on the door would send Claudine's six kids scurrying to hide
anything of value in the apartment that could provide a clue to outside
income or a man. I'm certain that Calvin Beckett, the resident manager at Hillside, knew that some of his tenants were working and that
some of the single mothers had men living there. When he dropped
by the apartments during the day for surprise inspections, he must
have heard a million different excuses from children about their parents' whereabouts. I told more than my share of creative tales. But Mr.

Beckett ignored what was going on because he was a Black man who understood what the mostly single women and their families were facing, and he was empathetic.

Although I was poor, I never felt deprived. Part of that had to do with the wealth of extracurricular activities the city provided through its parks, social centers, and recreation department. Throughout my childhood, I played baseball and basketball in leagues made up of neighborhood clubs that each had their own social center and playground. I played at Lapham Park, which had a huge asphalt playground with separate sections to play softball, volleyball, and basketball. On weekends and during the summer, my mother always knew where I was. When I didn't have to go to school, I'd wake up and head to the playground or the social center, hang out with my friends, and play ball until the sun went down. Then, instinctively, all of us would begin trickling out into the streets, trying to make it back home before the street lights came on.

Just before the start of eighth grade, I was ready to leave St. Boniface and go to school with my neighborhood friends. I persuaded my mother to enroll me in Lincoln Junior and Senior High, the public school where most kids from Hillside projects attended. Amongst my classmates and friends at Lincoln was a guy named Al Jarreau. I didn't even know that Al could sing. But after college, he got a gig singing at a local nightclub, where he became known around town as "the singing social worker." He would go on to earn international acclaim as a jazz singer.

At the end of my eighth-grade year, my family moved out of the projects back to 11th Street, in the same block of our original home. We lived in the rear of an old duplex that had been converted into four units. The move put me in the attendance zone for North Division High, a school that was located right next to St. Boniface, my old grade school. In my freshman year at North Division, white students made up about 65 percent of the population, but as white residents began fleeing neighborhoods with increasing Black populations, the number of white students began declining dramatically. Within four years North Division's student body would become mostly Black. Like most places in America, the specter of race was always there. I don't recall any racial incidents or overt racial issues. Black and white students often hung out together during school, but we all seemed to know the invisible boundaries. For the most part, we students didn't talk or think much about race. The things I cared about most were pretty basic—whether my team won, how I played, and if I had caught the attention of girls.

Every summer, though, I traveled back to Shreveport to visit my grandmother, and I had to deal with Jim Crow. I drank from "colored" water fountains, rode in the back of the bus, and felt anger rise inside me every time I had to enter the movie theater through the back door. Black patrons could sit only in the balcony, and my friends and I came up with a nasty scheme to get revenge: We dropped small balloons filled with urine and water on the heads of moviegoers below. We thought it was hilarious. It never occurred to me then what could have happened if we'd gotten caught. It didn't even register after I saw the *Jet* magazine photo of Emmett Till. Till was 14—the same age I was—in August 1955 when he was tortured and murdered by white men while visiting relatives in rural Mississippi. His crime: allegedly whistling at or flirting with a white woman. Till's mother, Mamie, insisted on an open casket and kept his body on display for five days so that all of Chicago and—with photos published by *Jet* and *The Chicago Defender*, the city's Black newspaper—the world could see her son's tortured body and the evil of racism. For Black mothers and fathers at the time, Till's brutal murder served as a terrifying reminder of what could happen to a smart Black boy who stepped out of what white folks deemed was his place.

At North, I began to focus more on basketball and decided to try out for the school team in my freshman year. I was already six feet tall and really enjoyed the sport. I just wasn't very good at it yet. I made the team, but barely. That was evident when Coach ran out of team shirts after handing everybody else a blue one, and I was the only guy on the team walking around in a green shirt. The only time I got to play was when the game was either already won or lost. Coach was taking no chances on me. I became determined to turn that around, though. At home, everything became a basketball—T-shirts, shorts, underwear, paper—rolled into a ball and shot across the room into a clothes basket or trash can. The rest of the time, I lived with a basketball in my hand, dribbling to and from school. I worked out more often to develop my muscles and even began running cross-country races to get in better shape. The summer after my freshman year, I worked harder than ever on the playgrounds to improve my game. There were a lot of really good ball players on those asphalt courts, and they pushed me to be better. We'd divide ourselves into teams of five and call "next,"

depending on when we got there. The next team always played the
winner. Of course, there was always arguing and sometimes fistfights
about who had next, but back then, you could walk away from a fight
knowing that whatever the beef was, you left it on the court. I never
worried about getting ambushed or shot, as many kids do today.

In my sophomore year, I was the leading scorer on the fresh-
man-sophomore team—the same team that had kept me warming
the end of the bench the year before. Near the end of my sophomore
year, I was allowed to practice with the varsity team. For me, there was
no more concrete example of what can happen when you focus on
a goal and work hard to achieve it. I continued getting better. In my
junior year, I started on the varsity team. We finished fifth in the City
Conference but went on to become the first team from Milwaukee
ever to play in the Wisconsin State Tournament for public schools.
We lost our first game, but we won the consolation championship. I
was the co-leading scorer for the tournament and named to the All-
Tournament Team. The next year, my senior year, I was named team
captain and selected for the All-City team. My name and picture began showing up in the local newspaper for making game-changing
plays. My mother always clipped the stories and photos out of the
paper and sometimes mailed them to my grandmother.

My teammates and I felt unbeatable, no matter whom we played.
Our coach, Vic Anderson, was also the ninth grade citizenship teacher
and an ex-Marine who didn't hesitate to get in our faces if we were
acting up. You didn't give Coach any lip because he would hit you, and
nobody—from the principal to the parents—would say a word. He
was white, but that wasn't an issue. We believed he cared about us and
about winning. He'd come and track us down in the neighborhood or
come to our houses to talk to our parents, if necessary. The fact that
most of us were poor, city kids motivated all of us to prove ourselves to
everybody else. One of the schools we played against was an exclusive
private prep school in the suburbs. Riding out there, we saw nothing
but green countryside, lakes, and trees. The campus was pristine, and
the classes were small, maybe five students in some of them. I just remember thinking: *We gon' crush these dudes!* Living in the city gave us a
harder edge, we believed, and if nothing else, poverty made us hungry
for victory. On the court, all things were equal, and we played as if our
lives were at stake. We were determined to earn our status and show
them that all the equipment in the world didn't necessarily make the

greatest ball players. We had all we needed: plenty of talent and heart. And, of course, we crushed them.

My mother was there every step of the way to support me. During a crucial game against Washington High School for the city championship, I was assigned to guard this tall, gangly center who, at six feet six inches, towered over everybody. But I managed to block his shot at the perfect time, picked it up, and dribbled all the way back down the court. I missed on the lay-up but got the rebound and put it in. As I was running back down the court, I happened to look up and spot my mother, who had jumped out of her seat. I'll never forget the look of pride and exhilaration on her face.

In 1958, my team went to the State tournament, undefeated for a second time. We made it to the finals, where we were matched with a team from Madison—Madison East. We played our hearts out, but in the final seconds we were down by three. When I went for the critical last shot, the ball actually rolled around the rim and spun out, as the horn sounded. Though I was fouled and got two free throws, I knew it didn't matter. With tears in my eyes, I just threw the ball up each time, and both missed. We lost 62 to 59. All these years later, I still remember that moment with surprising clarity.

Away from the basketball court, I developed into a solid all-round athlete. I ran cross-country and was one of few Black students in the city who played tennis on a high school team. I made it to the quarter-finals in my sophomore year, but, while there, I noticed people laughing and pointing at my racket. I'd bought the little racket at a local drug store and believed it was the real thing—until that competition. For the first time, I noticed how much smaller my racket was than the other competitors'. When I told my grandmother what happened, she was not amused. No grandson of hers would be ridiculed for not having the proper equipment. She sent me the money to buy my first real tennis racket. I'm not sure whether the new racket significantly improved my game, but it pleased my grandmother to know that I had all I needed not to be ridiculed.

In my senior year, I was elected president of the student body at North Division—an office I would hold at every school I would attend afterward. Because I made good grades, other opportunities outside school also opened up. I participated in an after-school program, called "Tomorrow's Scientists and Technicians," sponsored by the Urban League to encourage Black students to pursue careers in science. The Urban League's headquarters was located down the block from the social center where I played basketball, and I often stopped by the office for the organization's many youth activities. The group's executive director, Wesley L. Scott, was a World War II veteran who had earned a master's degree in social work after the war. Born the oldest of eighteen children in the mountains of West Virginia, he had clawed his way out of poverty, and whatever lessons he'd learned along the way, he was intent on sharing. He came to Milwaukee to work for the Urban League during my last year in high school and was named to the top post the next year, a position he would hold for the next twenty-three years. Mr. Scott was a brilliant man and a true visionary, who seemed to believe that he could change the future of his people by changing young lives, one by one. He took young people like me, who had demonstrated academic promise, under his expansive wings and tried to mold us into leaders. He offered advice, directed us to enrichment programs and opportunities, and always had encouraging words. When things got tough throughout my adult life, I turned to Mr. Scott. He'd listen, offer his take, and end with one of his favorite sayings: "Illegitimis non carborundum," a mock Latin phrase for "Don't let the bastards get you down."

My childhood was full of upstanding Black men like Mr. Scott who, because of segregation, usually lived and worked in close proximity to the city's poor. Black people of all incomes would interact on a regular basis in church, at the local YMCA, and through the Urban League and NAACP. I held summer jobs at the recreation department and worked under Black men like George Nash, who had graduated from Kentucky State University. I was extremely fortunate because there were always men in my life who encouraged me and set good examples for me. Men like community leader Nate Harris and YMCA directors Robert Starms and Lincoln Gaines, who were always there to boost my confidence. I had a sense that all of these men were not only looking out for me but counting on me to succeed. Because of them, I never felt that I was lacking anything. It didn't matter that at home my family drank out of old mayonnaise jars instead of glasses or that I had no connection to my father or lived with a stepfather that I hated. I had what I had, and that was that.

Whenever the need was great, somebody in the community always seemed to step up, like Dr. Charles Atkinson, a local Black physician who performed the physical exams required for me to play sports. He

treated me from then on without charging my mother a dime, and he
did the same for dozens of other promising youths and their families.
Dr. Atkinson lived in a huge house on the upper East Side in a neighborhood near the bluffs overlooking Lake Michigan. That place was
full of Old Milwaukee money, and it had been unheard of for a Black
family to live there. But Dr. Atkinson didn't shut himself off from his
people. In addition to the free medical care, he hired me and others to
do odd jobs around his house. Many of the Black physicians, entrepreneurs, and business people of his generation saw their own economic advancement tied directly to the upward mobility of our people. If
more Black people were educated and making good money, more of
them would be able to patronize Black banks and restaurants and go to
Black doctors. There was a strong sense that our fates were connected.

When the time came for me to think about college, I wasn't worried. I knew my mother couldn't afford to pay my way, but I figured
basketball would be my ticket. By my senior year, I was hearing from
several colleges and universities that were interested in my basketball
skills. But one school quickly rose to the top of my list: Carroll College
in Waukesha, Wisconsin. It was just eighteen miles away, though for
what little I knew of the place, it could have been on the other side
of the world. Admissions director Shirley Hilger was determined to
change that and actively pursued me. She arranged for me to visit, provided a tour, and discussed with me the financing options, including a
Trailblazer Scholarship, which would cover all of my tuition and living
expenses. I would also get to work on campus to earn extra money.
Though it was a basketball scholarship, the award had an academic
component. At a minimum, I'd have to maintain passing grades, improving to at least a "B" average by my junior year—requirements that
I figured would not be a problem. Even more important, I would get
to keep the scholarship if I got hurt and could no longer play basketball. I'd heard about ballplayers who had gone to some of the larger
schools and lost their scholarships when basketball injuries left them
unable to play. That possibility suddenly had become real to me after I
suffered torn ligaments in my ankle earlier in the year. The Trailblazer
award sounded like a great deal, but another thing left a lasting impression. Just before leaving, I was taken to a car dealership, and a salesman
handed me the keys to a brand new car to drive home for the weekend.
The only stipulation was that I return the vehicle on Monday. I was
also told that I would have a sponsor, a local doctor, who would provide

spending money and help with my expenses throughout my four years. All of that surely would be illegal today, but to a seventeen-year-old back then, this seemed like a dream. I was just about sold.

There was one major concern, though: I would be the only Black student on campus. As usual, I turned to Mr. Scott, who encouraged me to take the scholarship. Through its programs the Urban League tried to instill in young people a desire and a responsibility to give back to the community. The opportunity to integrate Carroll College was bigger than me, Mr. Scott said. This was my chance to make history, to help open doors that had been closed to our people for so long. Just one year earlier, the country had been riveted by grainy black-and-white television images of nine Black teenagers in Arkansas, walking up the steps of Little Rock Central High School under the protection of the U.S. military. They'd braved vicious white mobs, death threats, and even a recalcitrant governor to integrate the high school and demand the kind of education that the U.S. Supreme Court had said all Black children were due. Two years before that, Rosa Parks had refused to give up her seat on a public bus in Montgomery, Alabama. Her defiance had prompted Black people in that city to boycott the transit system—they carpooled, walked, and formed low-cost cabs to get around—for 381 days, and until the city finally repealed the law that had required segregation on the buses. Throughout the American South, my people were starting to fight back against Jim Crow. Now, in Waukesha, Wisconsin, Carroll College was swinging open its doors to me. I trusted Mr. Scott, and I needed the financial help. Also, one of my former basketball teammates at North, David Heinbuch, the only white starter in my junior year, was already at Carroll. He had enrolled there the year before to play basketball, and so I knew I'd have at least one friend. I decided to accept the Trailblazer scholarship.

For my high school commencement in May 1958, Mr. Scott was the guest speaker. As he talked about the times in which we were living, it was as if we all could feel the ground rumbling underneath our feet. With excitement. With possibilities. With hope. Change was coming. We could feel it long before Sam Cooke sang those words. We were far too young and idealistic to grasp how long it would take or what it would cost us as a people. All we knew in that moment was that the world was stretching out its arms.

And Mr. Scott urged us onward with his parting words: "Go, man, go!"

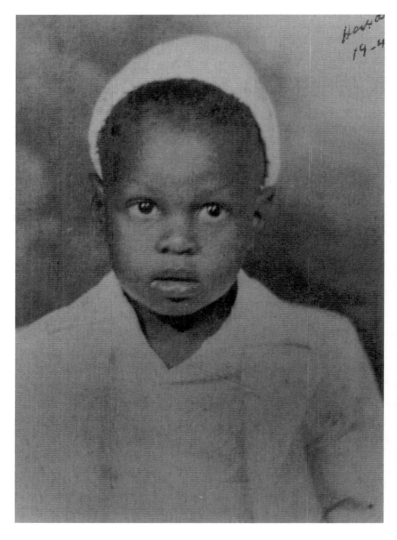

As a toddler, before moving with my mother to Milwaukee.

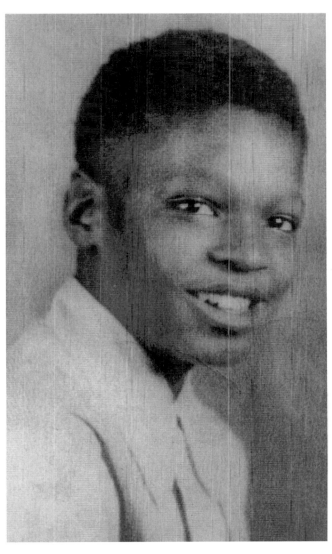

In my early years.

ST BONIFACE SCHOOL GRADE 3 OCT 1948 8

With my third-grade class at St. Boniface Catholic School.

My mother, then Juanita Carter, graduating from cosmetology school.

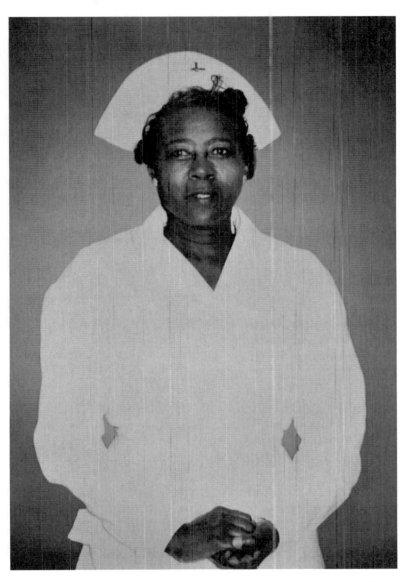

My grandmother, Pearl Wagner, in the uniform she wore to work.

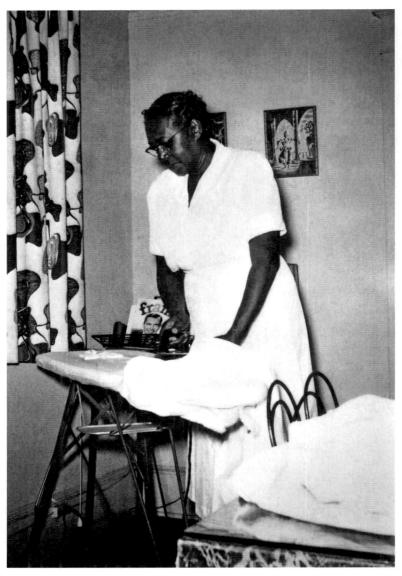

My grandmother, ironing white men's shirts
after getting home from her first job.

My grandmother, standing on ner porch on Bake⁻ Strᴣet in Sh⁻eveport.

With my mother after I had surgery for appendicitis
during my junior year in high school.

At age 15, playing basketball for Lapham Social Center
on the 1956 championship team,
sponsored by the Junior Optimist Club (I'm the tall one).

With my cross-country track team (in the back row, third from the left).

With the 1957 basketball team at North Division High School (third
from the right), the first team from Milwaukee ever to play in the
Wisconsin State Tournament for Public Schools, and Coach Vic
Anderson (far left), an ex-Marine who kept his players in line.

With the 1958 North Division basketball team (second from the left).

With a tennis teammate (I was one of few Black students in the city who played tennis on a high school team).

Team captain of the 1958 North Division basketball team.

With my friend Julius Wells on the night of my high school graduation.

2

BETWEEN TWO WORLDS

"One ever feels his twoness—an American, a Negro;
two souls, two thoughts, two unreconciled strivings;
two warring ideals in one dark body,
whose strength alone keeps it from being torn asunder."

—W.E.B. Du Bois, *The Souls of Black Folk*

My mother dropped me off at Carroll College in late summer 1958, and suddenly this trailblazer thing became real. There I was, one young Black man in a sea of white people. There wasn't another Black face for miles around. Not even the cafeteria workers, maids, and janitors were Black.

It's not that I was unaccustomed to white people. I'd been one of few Black students at St. Boniface, and my high school, North Division, had been predominantly white when I'd started in the ninth grade. Many of my high school friends were white. But at Carroll, I stepped into another world, where the culture that was familiar to me, the things that had always made me feel at home—the cool way my people walked, talked, dressed, danced, joked, sang, and even cooked—just vanished. I'd never even thought much about my culture until it was gone, and I was the anomaly. I stood out everywhere I went, and I felt as though all eyes were on me all the time. At first, when I talked—just everyday conversation, maybe describing a teammate as *my ace boon coon*, or bragging about the *bad* shot that won the game, or talking about the *fine* women back home—my new friends stared at me like I was speaking pig Latin.

"What are you talking about?" they'd ask.

For the next four years, I lived on a sort of stage, giving my white schoolmates and professors the closest view many of them had ever had into the life of a Black person. That came with the territory, I guess, but some days the pressure of it felt heavier than others. Some days, I didn't want to have to explain yet again that *bad* at times really meant good or that my mustache wasn't radical but simply the style where I came from. Some days I wanted to feel free enough to fall without anybody noticing and without worrying that any potential failure would lead to some unfair conclusion drawn about my people. I got tired of explaining myself, and I learned pretty quickly to turn off any cultural expressions that made me stand out more.

To their credit, many of my white schoolmates seemed to go out of their way to help me feel comfortable. Those who had a problem with my presence on campus most often didn't even look my way, and they certainly never said anything to my face. I think basketball insulated me from any open prejudice. As an athlete, I was widely accepted, even popular.

Not long after I arrived at Carroll that year, sororities and fraternities began gearing up to take in new members, and I was among the young men invited to attend the rush for Beta Pi Epsilon, then widely known as the local "jock fraternity." The fraternity seemed a natural fit for me since many of my teammates were members already or were planning to pledge. I joined the "Elegant Eight" pledge line and became the first Black member of Beta. I'll say this about pledging: Hazing was in full force. We were subjected to the kinds of crazy stunts that now get fraternities kicked off college campuses—cruel mind games, regular paddling with thick wooden paddles, and we were blindfolded and abandoned in the middle of nowhere during a Wisconsin winter. That forced us to rely on each other to make our way back to campus. Pledging was brutal, but I never felt singled out for ridicule or poor treatment because of my race. Big brothers issued out equal opportunity punishment, which helped me forge an even tighter bond with my line brothers. The next year, I moved into the frat house, located on the edge of campus, and later would serve as pledge warden, the one responsible for making sure my frat brothers didn't go overboard and seriously hurt one of the pledges.

In my sophomore year, my schoolmates also voted me Commissioner of School Spirit. I think this happened because I'd stepped up on a whim during my freshman year and led fellow students in cheers at the university's annual football bonfire. As part of my scholarship, I was assigned in my junior year to oversee an old Victorian house that the university had converted into campus boarding for male students. The university owned several of these houses, and about twenty students resided in each. I shared a suite and supervisory duties with Doug Irwin, another junior who had just transferred to Carroll on a basket-ball scholarship. Doug, whose Presbyterian parents thought their son could use the religious education the college offered, had come from a junior college in east central Missouri. He had played football, basket-ball, and run track there. I didn't know it then, but when Doug drove to Carroll for a meeting about the terms of his scholarship, the dean informed him that the only available room was with the university's sole Black student. The dean seemed surprised when Doug shrugged and responded, without hesitation, "fine with me."

From the beginning, I suspected that my new roommate had been around Black people before. He had a level of comfort with me that just couldn't be faked. First thing, he knew what I was talking about when I occasionally slipped into my slang around the house. I'd even-tually learn during our many late-night conversations that Doug was part Native American and that he had been raised to respect all peo-ple. One of his closest friends in high school was Black, and they were teammates in several sports. The two of them had been stars on their basketball and track teams. In Ptosi, Missouri, Doug's hometown, elementary school students of all races went to school together, but when they reached junior high school, Blacks and whites went their separate ways. The Black students were bused forty miles away to a segregated school in Hillsboro. But in 1955, Doug's high school began admitting Black students to comply with the U.S. Supreme court rul-ing outlawing segregated schools. Doug was reunited with his Black elementary school playmates, and he was thrilled that many of them helped vastly improve the school's sports teams. When one of Doug's Black friends was killed in a car accident in their senior year, Doug's father, a Washington County deputy sheriff, took a bold step to assist the deceased Black student's visiting relatives, who had come to town for the funeral. The family members had been turned away from the closest hotel, which did not rent rooms to Black people. But Doug's father intervened, demanding that the hotel owner allow the family to stay there. During the funeral at a Black Baptist church, Doug and two other white teenagers were among the six pallbearers carrying their friend's coffin.

It seemed designed by fate that the two of us wound up as room-mates. Doug and I had a couple of classes together and sometimes

pulled all-nighters studying for biology tests. We grew close and began
calling each other "Rooms," our nickname for one another to this day.
Like me, Doug had been an all-around high school athlete. He could
jump higher than any white ballplayer I'd ever seen, and he could really scrap on the basketball court. He was a fearless rebounder. Unlike
most college students of our era, he had a car, a 1956 Chevy. It had a
stick shift, which I didn't know how to drive, and so Doug sometimes
played chauffeur and drove me home to Milwaukee when I needed a
haircut and had no bus fare. My mother and grandmother both dot-
ed on him when he came to visit. My grandmother had relocated to
Milwaukee from Shreveport while I was away at Carroll after she got
sick and was too old and frail to live alone. During the trips home,
I took Doug with me to Lapham Park to play basketball. He wasn't
the least bit intimidated and held his own against the neighborhood
ballers, which was no small feat. Lapham Park was one of two courts
in the city where the real ballers went to play. Some of the ones who
played there and at Franklin Square were good enough to make it in
the NBA, but they never got the opportunities that I did to go to college. I often thought about them and how fortunate I was while I was
at Carroll, which motivated me even more to succeed.

Doug later became a Beta, as were four of the starting five on the
basketball team. Since most of my fellow basketball players were also
frat brothers, we were together all the time. Once, after a game in
southern Illinois, a small group of my teammates went to a bar near
the town of Moline. When the rest of us joined them there, I immediately felt the energy in the room change. The room grew silent and
still. White men glared at me over their bottles of Miller beer. One of
the waiters then approached our group and issued a warning to my
teammates: "If I were you, I'd get him out of here." We all rose together
and walked out. In another town, a waiter once tried to direct us to a
separate room inside a restaurant, clearly because of me, but our coach
signaled us all to leave. We would eat nowhere as a team where I wasn't
welcome. I always appreciated my friends' loyalty, and I can honestly
say that I don't recall a single racial incident among my frat brothers,
basketball teammates, or on the wider Carroll campus, which is really
pretty astonishing when you consider the times. Occasionally, I heard
racist taunts from the stands when we played games out of town, but I
just ignored them and tried to let my performance on the court speak
for me. I loved basketball, and I think it showed. I started in every

single game for all four years in college and was named "Most Valuable Player" for three of those years. I was the leading rebounder for two years, leading scorer for three years, and a team captain in my senior year. I also was named to the All-State Wisconsin Colleges team and was an honorable mention selection for the Little All-American team in my last year at Carroll. I even managed to set records in rebounding, and two of them, the leading career rebounder and number of rebounds in one season, still stand. Eventually, both Doug and I would be named to the college's Athletic Hall of Fame.

Off the court, my friends also did what they could to help me fit in. After basketball games on campus, we all headed to the student union and gathered in booths and around tables. The students cheered and applauded us athletes, and a jukebox played the most popular hits of the day—Elvis, Chubby Checker, the Everly Brothers (rarely any of the R&B artists emerging from the new Motown studio in Detroit). When spontaneous dancing broke out, some of the girls always made sure I had a dance partner. Judy Blom, a fellow sociology major who later became Doug's girlfriend and wife, often joined me doing the twist. Two other friends and dance partners—Kathy Meccia from Chicago and Barbara DePeaux from Green Bay—loved doing the bop with me. My friends also rallied around me and helped to elect me as their student body president in my senior year.

I made lifelong friends at Carroll, created some beautiful memories, and got a great education. That's why people are surprised when I say this: I would never ask another young person to go through what I went through.

I didn't doubt that my friends' affection for me was real; my feelings for them certainly were. But I always felt a bit like an outsider. I could have fun with my white friends, but we all knew there was an invisible line I couldn't cross. I could dance with the white girls at school, but it was unacceptable to date them, even in the Midwest, nearly 800 miles from the Mississippi town where Emmett Till had been murdered for allegedly just flirting with one. Likewise, when my fraternity brothers crept to the female dormitories for panty raids, I listened and laughed with them about their drunken exploits, but I didn't dare join in. When my friends traveled to Florida for Spring break, I was left behind. When they got back, I was there to listen to their tales of wild partying with wild girls. To get any action myself, I had to make my way to Milwaukee, which wasn't very often. I didn't even come in contact with any Black women when the basketball team traveled out of town because the schools we played were usually all white. By my senior year, another Black student, Irie Grant, a star player also from North Division, had joined me on the basketball team at Carroll, and once during an out-of-town game we got unusually lucky. We were preparing for a game at Illinois Wesleyan when we looked into the bleachers during the warm-up and spotted two Black women in the crowd. This had never happened before, and I was so excited that I couldn't wait until the end of the game. It wasn't difficult to figure out how to hook up with the women afterward, and Irie hit the jackpot. He eventually ended up marrying Georgia, the lady he'd met that night.

Some part of me surely resented that my frat brothers and teammates got to have typical college boy-girl experiences that were closed to me, but the issue wasn't that I yearned to date white girls or participate in a bunch of wild partying. Quite frankly, some of my white friends were doing things I'd never even heard of, like drinking so much that they thought snakes were crawling all over them. They would be hollering for help and clawing at themselves, battling the imagined reptiles. That kind of stuff scared the hell out of me. For me, the issue boiled down to this: I was their "brother," but the realities of race in America sometimes stood in the way of us having shared experiences.

It seemed that it surprised some of my white peers that I could speak articulately and think, write, and perform well off the basketball court; to understand how this was possible, they needed to separate me from my Black brethren into some special category. A few of my white friends often told me, "Howie, when we see you, we don't see a Black person." I knew they meant it as a compliment, but that comment always baffled me. I wondered: what *did* they see? Perhaps my schoolmates intended to say that they saw me as just another human being. But even so, I *am* a Black man, all six feet four inches of me. And in this country, that means something—that I am a descendant of slaves, a survivor of government-sanctioned oppression, and part of a proud people who'd somehow managed to shape a soulful way of being from hundreds of years of pain. Was it necessary to negate my blackness and all that comes with it to find me acceptable?

The most hurtful thing of all, though, was that I was also beginning to feel like an outsider among my own people too. When I made it home to Milwaukee for a weekend, holidays, or summer vacation, I went to parties and found that my Black friends were singing songs, doing dances, and using expressions that I knew nothing about. I was relegated to the sidelines. I began to feel that I was straddling two very different worlds, and I didn't quite fit in either. The college years were supposed to be that important time of personal maturity when students living away from their parents for the first time gained confidence in their own ability to navigate the world alone. Instead, I felt I was losing any confidence I had and losing a part of me. At times, the loneliness was excruciating. I occasionally pulled away from everybody, grew silent, and just sat alone in my room with a pain that no one else understood. I wondered: What in the hell was I doing there? Who had I become? During those times, Doug tried to pull me out of what seemed to him just moodiness. He tried to get me to go shoot some hoops or hang out in the student union, but he backed off when it was clear that I didn't want to be around anyone, including him. I didn't want to talk. I didn't want to laugh. I didn't want to pretend everything was cool. There was no way I could make him or any of my white classmates understand how it felt to be in my skin. I'd heard about Autherine Lucy, the Black woman who in 1956 had integrated the University of Alabama, faced a hateful mob, and ended up being suspended after just three days when the university claimed it could not guarantee her protection. I couldn't even imagine what she had gone through in such a hostile environment when the atmosphere at Carroll was the opposite, and I still felt so tortured.

As graduation from Carroll neared, I decided to pursue a master's degree. I was awarded a Whitney Young scholarship from the Urban League to cover some of my graduate school expenses. Mr. Scott had talked to me often about the responsibility to use my education and talents for the good of the community, and I figured the field of social work would enable me to do that. But the two more traditional forms of the field, case work and group work, didn't appeal to me at all. I viewed those areas as helping people manage oppression, and I wanted no part of that. I wanted to help end oppression. A new area of social work had emerged and seemed a perfect description of what I envisioned: community organizing. One of the schools I was considering, Western Reserve University (now Case Western Reserve) in Cleveland, offered a graduate degree in that field. When I traveled to Cleveland to be interviewed as an applicant for the school, I rode in an airplane for the first time. I liked the program, and the city met my other criteria: it had a large, vibrant Black community. I wanted to be around Black people again. So, Western Reserve was my choice.

The day before my graduation from Carroll in May 1962, I joined some of the guys for one last game of pickup basketball in the gym where we had practiced and played the past four years. But when I jumped up to grab the ball in a move I had done a million times, I felt an excruciating pain in my back like nothing I'd ever felt before. I crumpled to the ground, writhing in pain. I was taken to a doctor, who said I'd suffered a wrenched back. All I was able to think about was how I would be able to walk across the stage to receive my degree. My grandmother and mother were coming, and I could only imagine the pride they felt. I was the first in our entire family ever to graduate from college. The only way I wouldn't walk across that stage, I told myself, was if I were unconscious. So, the doctor ended up taping my body from the waist almost to my neck to restrict my movement and lessen the pain. I could barely move. On the day of the ceremony, two of my classmates sat next to me with smelling salts, in case I passed out. But when my name was called, I stood and made my way across the stage. I'd finished this part of my journey, and the satisfaction of knowing that dulled the physical pain for a moment. Nothing could compare, though, to the exhilaration I knew that my grandmother and mother were feeling, and allowing them that moment meant more to me than anything else.

The pain subsided, and, a week later, I returned to Milwaukee to begin a summer job inside Schlitz brewery, where I spent a good portion of the day lifting barrels. There were hardly any Black people working in the breweries at the time, but a well-known local business consultant named Ben Barkin, who had taken interest in me, had helped me get the job to save money for graduate school. While my back pain eased for awhile, I'm pretty sure I made my condition worse. My back troubles would return many years later, leaving me at times debilitated, and I eventually would undergo a serious surgery to try to correct the problem.

In the fall of 1962, I moved to Cleveland for graduate school. I knew no one there and felt a little lost until I met a woman named Jean Harris, who was in one of my classes. She was a few years older and very outgoing and friendly. She struck up a conversation one day in class and invited me to a party. She also introduced me to her older sister and the two of them embraced me as their little brother. It must

have been obvious to them that I was a bit of a square because they
guided me socially through the next year. They introduced me to their
circle of friends, taught me the latest dances, and helped me hook up
my wardrobe. They also gave me advice on how to approach women
and ask them out. I had zero confidence in myself as a Black man, especially when it came to dealing with women. The world those two sisters brought me into was unapologetically Black, and they helped me
reconnect to the part of me that I felt had been lost. Jean was dating
John Wooten, a lineman for the Cleveland Browns and through her
I got to know a number of the team's players, including star running
back Jim Brown and defensive back Walter Beach. Several years later
in 1967, both men were among the top Black athletes who stood with
Muhammad Ali to show their support for his refusal to be drafted
in the Army during the Vietnam War. Being around Black men and
women again and reconnecting to my culture was electrifying, and I've
always felt tremendous gratitude to those two sisters for reaching out
to me at such a crucial juncture in my life.

By then, it was the early 1960s, and if you were Black, it was impossible to ignore the civil rights battles being fought down South, largely by college students. Starting with four Black students from North
Carolina A&T in February 1960, young people had been defiantly sitting at segregated lunch counters, accepting beatings and ridicule with
quiet dignity in an effort to force restaurants and department stores
to change their racist service policies. The next year, Black and white
college students from all over the country, calling themselves Freedom
Riders, had boarded buses together—and even faced a brutal attack
and bus bombing outside Anniston, Alabama—to test a U.S. Supreme
Court decision banning segregation on interstate travel. In '62, state
troopers had tried to block James Meredith's entry to the University
of Mississippi in defiance of the U.S. Supreme Court, sparking riots.
The next year, young protesters in Birmingham, Alabama, were bitten
by police dogs and hosed with explosive fire hydrants, and the Rev.
Martin Luther King, Jr., was jailed there. Medgar Evers was murdered
in his own driveway in Mississippi, four little girls were murdered in a
church bombing in Birmingham, and President John F. Kennedy, who
had intervened on behalf of civil rights protesters a number of times,
was murdered during a motorcade in Texas. My people were suffering,
and the leaders who dared to support us were being murdered, and
my heart ached as I watched from afar. I saw young men and women

my age and younger stepping up, putting their lives and futures on the line for the pursuit of justice, and I knew I had to find my place in this struggle.

Then one day, as president of the student government association at Western Reserve in early 1964, I learned that CORE, the Congress of Racial Equality, the same group that had organized the Freedom Rides, would be recruiting on campus. Volunteers were needed to participate in a local school desegregation battle. I decided to attend. It was a choice that would change my life forever.

At Carroll with my good friend and fellow North Division basketball
teammate, David Heinbuch.

Basketball Team 1961-62 yearbook photo. Irie Grant #15. Doug Irwin #35.
(Photo courtesy Carroll University Archives.)

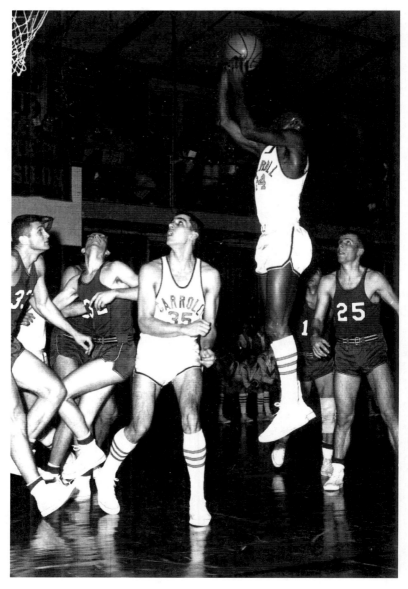

Howard going up for a shot. Doug Irwin#35.
(Photo courtesy Carroll University Archives.)

Graduating from Carroll College in 1962.

3

WE SHALL NOT BE MOVED

We shall not, we shall not be moved
We shall not, we shall not be moved
Just like a tree that's planted by the water
We shall not be moved.
—*unknown*

By February 1964, Black parents and a coalition of civil rights organizations in Cleveland had been engaged for years in a heated battle against the public school system over desegregation. The migration of Black families from the South in the 1950s had dramatically increased crowding in Black neighborhoods. To address the problem, school officials had begrudgingly begun busing Black children to white schools with low enrollment. But to minimize contact between the races, the Black students and their teachers were required to stay in their assigned classrooms all day. They were not permitted to eat in the cafeteria, visit the school nurse, or participate in any school-wide activities. The children were permitted to go to the bathroom just once a day at a designated time. Infuriated Black parents, who were part of the Hazeldell Parents Association, had joined a civil rights coalition, called the United Freedom Movement, to protest the treatment of the bused group. But months of negotiations with school administrators failed, and the coalition then reached out for volunteers to expand the protests.

When I attended a meeting and heard a representative of the Congress of Racial Equality (CORE) explain what was happening, I was outraged. I signed up for a demonstration at the school administration building on February 4, 1964. I had never protested anything, but this situation smacked of the kind of racism I'd experienced during my summers with my grandmother down South. It was just wrong.

On the day of the protest, I worked at the local welfare department as part of my social work field training and then, still dressed in my suit and tie, headed to the school board office. I was unsure what to expect. A crowd of nearly two dozen people gathered in the hallway outside the Superintendent's office on the third floor. The hours passed slowly, without any developments, and at some point it became clear to me that this would be an all-night sit-in. Our directions came from Ruth Turner, the executive secretary of the Cleveland branch of CORE, the younger, more militant civil rights group in the city. Turner was just twenty-four, one year older than I. I later read news accounts that said the older, more established NAACP had wanted to settle the issue more privately by negotiating with white school officials. That may have explained why most of the demonstrators that day were affiliated with CORE or the Hazeldell Parents Association, including two women in their fifties. The youngest among us was an eighteen-year-old stock boy for a local drug store.

The next morning, the police showed up in force and demanded that we leave. But when we didn't move, all hell broke loose. A police captain stepped into the crowd of demonstrators sitting on the floor, and his foot landed hard on a woman's thigh. He pulled her hair, and officers began dragging the protesters, one by one, down a long hallway toward the stairs. I was shocked. Everything was happening so fast. Before I knew it, an officer grabbed my suit coat, ripping it, and began dragging me across the hard floor. Instinctively, I drew into a fetal position. When we made it to the stairwell, I could see that the police officers had formed a gauntlet on both sides from the top to the bottom. One of them shoved me, and I began tumbling, head first, down three flights of stairs. Other protesters were pushed down before and after me. As we rolled down, the officers standing at the sides beat us with their batons. Each time I reached a landing between the floors and thought the ordeal was over, I was pushed again and suddenly felt my body slamming against the concrete and nightsticks cracking against my flesh. I tried as best I could to protect my head with my hands. As a woman rolled down in front of me, her head hit each concrete step with a loud thud. I will never forget that sound, or her screams. When I tried to reach out to her, an officer kicked me. Finally, we made it to the bottom of the stairwell, which was visible from the outside. Officers then lifted us gently and paraded us to paddy wagons.

I had no idea that the police had blocked the stairs and elevators, preventing a reporter for the Black newspaper, the *Call and Post*, from entering to investigate. One of the women told reporters that she pleaded with officers to take her to the hospital, but they refused. Instead, about twenty of us were arrested, transported to jail, and put into holding cells. Anger burned inside me. We had been guilty of nothing more than assembling in a public building and expressing our constitutional right to protest peacefully. Yet here we were being treated worse than criminals. I felt solidarity with my Southern brothers and sisters, whose protests often ended in this brutal way. A white jailer smirked as he walked alongside the cells and scraped his baton against the bars. He taunted: "Sing 'We Shall Overcome' now." That hymn had become the battle cry of the Southern movement, and we wouldn't respond to his mocking. We stared at him and sat defiantly, drawing strength from one another. I could feel my resolve hardening. If the police thought that dragging me, beating me, and pushing me down stairs would scare me away, they had better think again. I was twenty-three years old, angry as hell, and I was just beginning to fight.

It seemed so clear to me in that moment that this was what I was supposed to do. I didn't have children in the Cleveland school system. I wasn't even married. But this was my fight as much as it was that of the parents whose babies were being bused across the city, only to be mistreated. If the people in power were allowed to get away with this, they might try anything to keep our people down. Most of the protesters arrested that day, including me, were charged with misdemeanors and released the same day on a $200 personal bond. But two men were charged with assault and battery on a police captain, who claimed they tripped him as he walked through the group. Three others—two women and a man—were charged with obstructing an officer while making an arrest, and I would later testify on their behalf at a trial.

Like all of the leaders and mentors I admired, I believed without question at the time that integration would make things better for my people. It would give us access to the high-quality institutions, including schools, which those with power and resources had created for themselves. I didn't question the nonviolent tactics of Dr. King and the Civil Rights Movement, which had begun slowly dismantling legalized segregation throughout the South. But other, more radical voices were beginning to resonate, particularly in large urban centers like New York and Chicago. I'd heard about Malcolm X, this Muslim from Harlem, whose fiery speeches about Black people fighting back made white folks nervous. The truth is he made plenty Black folks nervous, too, including me. Folks talked about him like he was the devil incarnate, the antichrist. We didn't understand his religion, or his message, which, when filtered through the media and other naysayers, seemed hateful and dangerous. His split from the Nation of Islam in March 1964 generated lots of media speculation about the surprising rift between Malcolm and the Nation's leader, Elijah Muhammad, and about what Malcolm would do next. When I heard just a few weeks later that he would be speaking in Cleveland, I was intrigued. He was coming to town to debate journalist Louis Lomax, who had written a controversial book about the Nation of Islam, and I wanted to see for myself what was so scary about this man.

On the evening of April 3, 1964, I filed into a crowded Cory Methodist Church to hear the two men debate the future of the civil rights struggle. I found a seat in the balcony and waited eagerly, fully expecting Lomax to discredit his challenger. The speech that Malcolm gave that night would become famously known as "The Ballot or the Bullet." And from the moment he opened his mouth, I was transfixed. This man was BOLD. He took a moment to clarify that he was still a Muslim minister, but he assured the mostly Christian crowd that he was not there to try to change anybody's religion.

> *I'm not here to argue or discuss anything that we differ about, because it's time for us to submerge our differences and realize that it is best for us to first see that we have the same problem, a common problem, a problem that will make you catch hell whether you're a Baptist, or a Methodist, or a Muslim, or a nationalist. Whether you're educated or illiterate, whether you live on the boulevard or in the alley, you're going to catch hell just like I am. We're all in the same boat and we all are going to catch the same hell from the same man. He just happens to be a white man. All of us have suffered here, in this country, political oppression at the hands of the white man, economic exploitation at the hands of the white man, and social degradation at the hands of the white man...*

The mostly blue-collar crowd went wild with applause. Nothing about him seemed crazy or frightening. He explained that he wasn't anti-white but anti-exploitation, anti-degradation, anti-oppression.

And if the white man doesn't want us to be anti-him, let him stop op-
pressing and exploiting and degrading us…

There was a raw honesty and bravery about Malcolm, and the crowd seemed to sit on the edge of our seats as he talked about politics in plain, simple terms. But Malcolm warned that Black people were slowly awakening to their political power, and that a new kind of Black man was emerging, one "who just doesn't intend to turn the other cheek any longer." He called for a broadening of the movement to include Black nationalists who were not willing to compromise on their voting rights and were ready to fight back, by any means necessary. He not only made perfect sense to me, but he connected to something deep in my soul.

A few days later, I joined other CORE protesters in the ongoing school desegregation protest, this time at the construction site of a school being built on Cleveland's east side. By then, to quell the violence and the dissatisfaction among white parents, school administrators had announced that the system would build new schools to alleviate the overcrowding in Black neighborhood schools and return the bused students to schools closer to home. But Black parents and the coalition saw the plan to build the schools in solidly Black neighborhoods, instead of in areas where Blacks and whites lived in closer proximity, as a way of reinforcing segregation. We were determined not to let them get away with that ruse.

When we showed up at the site of the new school on April 7, we began fanning out across the site in hopes of stopping the construction, but the police were on high alert and blocked our access to the open field. Several of us somehow managed to break through the human barricade, rush out into the lot, and lie on the soft dirt in front of a bulldozer. One of CORE's leaders, Rev. Bruce W. Klunder, a twenty-seven-year-old white Presbyterian minister, stationed himself behind the bulldozer. We were all young, invincible, and we were going to change the world, right? The bulldozer operator suddenly gunned the engine, but he wouldn't dare move, would he? I lifted my head just as the driver backed away, and before any words could even fly out of my mouth, the bulldozer rolled over Bruce and then jolted to a halt. Suddenly everything seemed to move in slow motion. Onlookers were screaming, pushing, and shoving with police officers in the distance. I lifted myself up in a haze as the scene exploded into bottle- and brick-throwing chaos. But Bruce didn't move or say a word. He just lay there, completely still and quiet, face down in the dirt. He had to be dead. I knew it, and I was too stunned to feel anything but rage. This wasn't supposed to happen. Why didn't the driver just keep the bulldozer still? How could he just roll over another human being? The thirty-three-year-old bulldozer operator, John White, later said it was an accident and that he was trying to avoid the protesters in front of him when he backed up. He said he didn't see Bruce on the ground behind him and had no intention of crushing him to death, but that's exactly what happened. Police ultimately ruled Bruce's death an accident. All I knew was that a comrade was dead and that his death felt violent and wrong, no different than if he'd been gunned down in cold blood. Nothing made sense.

Between 1,500 and 2,000 mourners later showed up at a memorial service for Bruce, and I learned more about him—that he had come to Cleveland in 1961 as executive director of the YMCA's Student Christian Union and was ordained as a Presbyterian minister the following year. He was a founding member of Cleveland's branch of CORE, believed in social justice, and had frequently picketed for fair housing and against segregation. He left a wife and two young children, and although I had not known him personally, his death affected me deeply.

I stuck with the protests and even missed a final exam to participate in another demonstration. Fortunately, I was allowed to take a make-up test and graduated on time in May 1964. Just three days later, I walked down the aisle in a Cleveland church to marry Viola Williams, a fellow social worker from Alabama, whom I'd first noticed during my field training at the welfare department. We'd locked eyes for a long moment during a staff meeting one day and just stared at each other. She had nice eyes, and it didn't escape my attention that she was also tall and fine. But we didn't hold a conversation until we saw each other again by chance sometime later at a neighborhood convenience store. We recognized each other immediately, stopped to talk, and, as it turned out, she lived in the apartment complex next to mine. With our social work background and desire to help our people, we seemed to have much in common. We started dating and got serious pretty quickly. One day, as graduation neared, I was watching the old romantic drama "For Whom the Bell Tolls," based on the Ernest Hemingway novel, and something about it made me want to get married. Maybe

I saw myself in the idealistic young American expatriate who fell passionately in love before ultimately giving his life fighting Fascists in the Spanish Civil War. I've long since forgotten how I proposed, but Viola agreed to marry me. When I shared our plans with my mother and grandmother, both thought I was too young. They had nothing against Viola, whom they barely knew, but in their eyes I wasn't ready. I hadn't yet sown my "wild oats," they said. They were more right than I believed at the time, but I'd already made up my mind.

As part of my Whitney Young scholarship, I was obligated to work for the Urban League for at least a year after graduation. I'd heard that the Chicago chapter, headed by Edwin C. Berry, whom everybody knew as "Bill," was the largest and one of the more progressive branches and that it also had a community organizing division. I applied to work in Chicago, was accepted, and, just days after our wedding, Viola and I headed there to start our new life together. Chicago was great for a young married couple. It was an exciting city with much for a fun-loving couple to explore. I was determined to make the marriage work, to be faithful, and most of all, to be there. I didn't want to repeat the abandonment and abuse I'd seen from my father and stepfather. My job was also good for the marriage. I had set hours, and when I left the office, I left the work there—something I would learn later is much more difficult when your job becomes your passion.

My primary role with the Urban League was as an employment relations specialist, helping to integrate workforces by putting Black people in jobs that had been held exclusively by whites. Companies would call in with a job order, and it was my responsibility to find Black people to fill those jobs. This was a big deal because we were helping to open doors that had historically been closed to our people, but at the same time the job was maddening. White personnel managers would call up and in various terms order up the kind of "Negro" they wanted, from skin color to speech and attire. I remember one conversation with this white guy who told me he didn't want someone too Black but also not so light-skinned that people wouldn't know that the new hire was Black. I helped place some of the first Black flight attendants at major airlines. But I once recommended a sister to a major airline, and she was turned down simply because she had a facial mole.

I yearned to get into community organizing, which I believed would help the masses of poor Black people, but it seemed at times that the Urban League's methods were not driving change fast enough. At the first national convention I attended as part of the job, about eight or nine of us like-minded twenty-somethings—the Young Turks, we called ourselves—got together and decided we were going to shake things up somehow. We were going to change the world, right? But the word about our dissatisfaction seeped out, and before we could even come up with a plan, one of the more experienced brothers—someone older than us but younger than the old heads—was promptly sent to counsel us about how the Urban League worked. I didn't fully appreciate it then, but I learned some valuable lessons from the experience. First, before trying to change an organization, you really need to understand its role and how it works. Also, stable organizations tend to set up a system of protection from the kind of "change" my friends and I were considering. I had much respect for the Urban League, the role it had played in my life and in the broader community, but it became clear to me that it would not provide the platform for me to do the kind of community organizing I yearned to do. I focused on finishing my year in Chicago and began looking for someplace to land where I could have the kind of impact I desired.

Just as I began thinking seriously about my next move, a couple of my friends, James "Kwame" McDonald and Morris Cohen, called out of the blue with news about a potential job opportunity. They had gone to work for a new statewide antipoverty program, called the North Carolina Fund, and were aware of an opening in Durham that they believed would be a good fit for me. The Durham-based program, called Operation Breakthrough, was looking for a Black person to coordinate its antipoverty efforts in some of city's poorest Black neighborhoods, my friends told me. I'd known Kwame and looked up to him since my days in high school, when I participated in the Urban League's "Tomorrow's Scientists and Technicians Program, " which he ran. He was from Milwaukee and had studied law at the University of Wisconsin before returning home to work for the Urban League. I'd met Morris years later, while we were both graduate students at Western Reserve. The Operation Breakthrough job sounded like just what I had been seeking. I applied and was interviewed by the program's new executive director, Robert Foust, as well as two of Durham's most influential Black men, John Wheeler, president of the Black-owned Mechanics and Farmers Bank, and attorney/civil rights activist Floyd McKissick. I must have said something right because I got the job.

I was ready to go to war. We could win this war. I was sure of it. My weapons were simple but mighty: a little book sense, some big ideas, and a whole lot of hope.

Graduating from Western Reserve in Cleveland, with Morris Cohen, who later would recommenc me for a job at Operation Breakthrough in Durham.

4

AIN'T NO STOPPING US NOW

I arrived in Durham on May 5, 1965, at 2 p.m. When I clicked on the television that evening, the first face I saw was Jesse Helms, then an executive and popular commentator at a Raleigh-based station, WRAL-TV (Channel 5). This was long before his rise to the U.S. Senate, and he was delivering his nightly editorial. He had a sidekick, a white man dressed in a hunting shirt, sitting before a crackling fireplace with a rifle propped against the wall. The sidekick uttered something about "Martin Luther Coon." The words seemed to jump out of the screen at me, and I froze there for a moment, outraged. I thought: *How dare these racists go on television and demean a key leader of the Civil Rights Movement.*

That was my initial welcome to North Carolina. But I would soon learn that it was a much more complex place, particularly Durham, where I was based. While I would discover significant poverty and suffering among Black people there, I would also find an established Black middle class, bolstered by the presence of North Carolina College, one of many historically Black colleges and universities throughout the state. In 1969, four years after my arrival, North Carolina College would be renamed North Carolina Central University and become part of the University of North Carolina system. It was the bedrock of Durham's Black elite, which boasted landowners and entrepreneurs who had created their own social institutions and businesses, including North Carolina Mutual Life Insurance Company, the nation's oldest and largest Black-owned business of its type, and its sister institutions, Mutual Savings and Loan, and Mechanics and Farmers Bank. The bank was headed by one of the most powerful Black men in the United States, John Wheeler, who in 1961 had been appointed by President John F. Kennedy to his Committee on Equal Employment Opportunity. Mr. Wheeler would also establish deep connections to

Kennedy's successor, Lyndon B. Johnson. The white power structure in Durham often turned to Mr. Wheeler for advice on matters concerning the Black community, but he was equally respected by his own people. He would in time become to me a sounding board, a voice of reason, and a man whose wisdom and status I greatly appreciated. And I am absolutely certain of one thing: I wouldn't have been hired for the job that brought me to Durham without his approval.

I had come there because of the state's progressive, multiracial approach to fighting poverty. In 1963, Governor Terry Sanford had gone around the traditional channels of government and pulled together private investors to create the North Carolina Fund, an independent agency formed to battle poverty throughout the state. Sanford united white and black power brokers around the idea and raised $7.5 million to finance it. When President Johnson launched his national War on Poverty the next year, he modeled parts of it on the North Carolina Fund. The federal government then funneled millions of dollars through Johnson's Economic Opportunity Act to innovative local programs working to assist the poor. No other state was in a better position than North Carolina to claim some of those federal dollars. The organization created for that purpose in Durham was Operation Breakthrough.

I was hired to coordinate Operation Breakthrough's poverty-fighting efforts in one of three areas of the city targeted for help. Mine was Target Area A, made up of the poorest Black neighborhoods: Hayti, Pickett Street, St. Teresa, Hillside Park, Morehead, and the McDougald Terrace public housing project. Though I'd grown up in public housing and spent my earliest days in a poor southern community, I'd never seen poverty and neglect like this. Hayti, the largest neighborhood in my target area, sat in the heart of a major city, yet some areas still had dirt streets. *Dirt streets! In the middle of town.* That was incomprehensible to me. Shotgun shacks were everywhere, and some of them had no running water indoors. My heart hurt when I saw how my people were living and how they had accommodated themselves to survive under conditions that no human being should have to endure. Anger burned deep inside. But far from feeling overwhelmed, it made me even more determined to figure out how to change the conditions.

During my research for the job, I discovered a potent but then rarely-discussed line in President Johnson's Economic Opportunity Act, and it would shape my whole approach to the work. Section 202 included a mandate that antipoverty programs receiving federal funds must be "developed, conducted, and administered with the maximum feasible participation of residents of the areas and members of the groups served." The words *maximum feasible participation* stood out to me. This was significant. It said to me that poor Black people, who had long been dictated to even by well-meaning whites, should play a major role in determining what they needed and how they should get it. As I understood the law, it meant that poor people should be involved in the antipoverty programs at every level, from the governing boards to the workers. I decided then that I would work to make sure this happened. There was no blueprint for how to do it, but I knew I wouldn't be successful sitting behind a desk in an office far from the people I needed to reach. I had to embed myself in the community. People needed to see me at church, in the barber shop, the pool halls, the restaurants they frequented, and at their doors to believe in my commitment to them. I'd never bought into the school of thought that the people social workers serve are our "clients." I couldn't stand that word. Neither did I buy into the whole idea of "professional objectivity." What is that? If you're going to work with people like I wanted to work with them, you have to care deeply about those people. You have to love them. You have to feel their pain. You can't be sitting up in some office somewhere "observing." To be an organizer, fighting for people's rights, you have to be totally in the fight with them. The people I was working with in Durham were my brothers and sisters, not some "clients." I refused to put distance between me and them and to view them from a prism that automatically assumed an unequal relationship. And how could I be "professionally objective" about the systemic racism that had relegated my people to such abject poverty? I was in this fight with them with my entire heart and soul.

I found office space above Scarborough Funeral Home, which owned the two-story building that anchored a small strip of Black businesses on Pettigrew Street. Soon afterward, I hired Lottie Hayes, a devoted secretary who kept the office together administratively, scheduled my appointments, and helped me learn more about the city and its people. The *Carolina Times*, Durham's Black newspaper, was also located on Pettigrew Street. It was run by Louis E. Austin, who had been the paper's editor and publisher since 1927. He was a fierce spokesman against racial inequality and injustice, and I often stopped by his office to chat and seek advice. I also began eating lunch regularly at a restaurant owned by two sisters down the street and hanging out with the brothers in the pool hall nearby. It was difficult to get more than a handful of the brothers engaged in attending meetings and planning sessions, but it was still important to me to spend time shooting the bull with them. They taught me to play pool. One of the regulars was a guy everybody called Wise Owl. He was obviously an alcoholic, but he was also brilliant. He was one of those guys who seemed to know something about everything, and the other brothers respected him. I talked to him often, and our friendship was instrumental in helping me to earn the other brothers' trust.

On Sundays, I occasionally spoke at local churches, where I met people like Nathaniel and Louise Balentine, a young married couple in their early twenties, who would become two of the movement's most dedicated and committed warriors. They were among the few married people living in McDougald Terrace. They had heard that a young Black man from "up North" had been traveling around town, telling Black folks that they didn't have to accept how they'd been living. So, they came to Mount Zion Baptist Church on Fayetteville Street one Sunday night to hear for themselves what I had to say. My message about the need for poor people to come together and change things tapped into their own simmering anger and frustration. Later on in life when I asked Nathaniel what attracted him to the movement, he told me: "There were these fires burning inside of us with the way we were treated. And you came along and started blowing on those flames." Nathaniel and Louise joined the movement and never looked back. They were true salt-of-the-earth North Carolinians—welcoming, unpretentious, dedicated, and determined.

Those were exactly the qualities I looked for when I began putting together my staff. I wanted to hire local people who would pour their hearts and souls into the work. I found just that in Charsie Hedgepeth, who would become my field supervisor. She had grown up in Durham, attended the North Carolina College (now North Carolina Central University) and worked the previous summer for the North Carolina Fund. We made it our mission to get to know the people in the target area and what *they* saw as their most pressing issues. We got started simply by knocking on doors.

That's how I came to meet Ann Atwater, a mother living in Hayti with her two young daughters in one of the most substandard houses

I'd ever seen. Ann had grown up in a tiny North Carolina town, gotten married and moved to Durham in 1950. But when her husband became abusive and abandoned the family, she was left to take care of their children alone on a $57 monthly welfare check and the little she earned working occasionally as a domestic. I could see skepticism on her face that August afternoon when she answered the knock on her front door and found Charsie and me standing there. I explained briefly why we had come and asked Ann whether she had any issues that needed addressing. "No," she said, guardedly at first. But I just stood there, staring at the house another moment, hoping she would open up. She noticed me staring and began to talk. There was indeed a problem in her bathroom, she said, and she led us through the house to take a look. It was worse than I could have imagined. The bathtub had rotted through the floor and was practically sitting on the ground. Water sometimes shot up from the drain like Niagara Falls, she explained. Holes in the floor made it easy for rats to get inside, and cracks in the roof and walls in other parts of the house were so wide that you could see outside. When it rained, Ann and her girls rushed around the house to place buckets in strategic places to catch the gushing water. The wiring in the house was so messed up that she could turn her lights on and off by stomping her feet. Ann had discovered the faulty wiring by chance when her utilities were disconnected because she couldn't pay the bill. Though it was dangerous, the struggling mother managed to avoid paying the bill for an entire year, which seemed to her a blessing from God.

"How much do you pay to rent this place?" I asked.

The rent was $100, and she was behind that month. I proposed an idea: If Ann would attend an organizing meeting with my staff, me, and a few other tenants, I would pay her rent and go with her to talk to the landlord about making needed repairs. The plan turned out to be fortuitous. Ann attended the meeting, and I joined her in taking the $100 to the landlord. But instead of handing over the money, I told him that we would set up an escrow account and he wouldn't see a dime of it until he'd made the repairs. Ann was astonished when the landlord responded by sending a contractor to fix her bathroom floor. Though the repair was far short of all that was needed, Ann was overjoyed. It had never occurred to her that she could demand even that much. That small accomplishment helped her feel a sense of power, and she quickly spread the word to her neighbors, who began crowding future meetings to discuss their own housing concerns. Maybe there was something to this community organizing, Ann told them. Maybe if they tackled their problems together, they had more power than they realized. Slowly, the residents began to awaken to the possibilities, and it was gratifying to watch.

As I made my way through the neighborhoods, meeting people, I kept hearing about a dude named Ben Ruffin, who had grown up on the "West End," another of Durham's impoverished Black neighborhoods, made it through college, and was a youth worker for another agency. I tracked him down and persuaded him to join my team. It was one of the best decisions I ever made. Just two years younger than I, Ben was eager and idealistic, and we hit it off right away. Like Charsie, he became a key player in Operation Breakthrough's organizing success. Ben took the lead in planning my team's first big event: a communitywide cleanup. We figured the cleanup would give us a chance to have an immediate impact and enable the residents to come together to help themselves. If local officials saw that the residents had worked to address their own problems first, that could possibly help to deflate potential criticism down the road when we started making demands on the landlords and government. The prevalence of junk throughout the community—broken furniture, discarded car parts, and more—reflected the city's neglect and the people's inability to handle the problem on their own. Few residents owned trucks or could afford to rent one to cart away the garbage. Ben helped arrange for the city to loan Operation Breakthrough some garbage trucks, and on the Saturday of the event, our staff members and volunteers rode up and down the streets on the West End, loading and hauling the junk away. At the end of a long, rewarding day, several women brought food, and we all gathered to celebrate the event's success. The residents felt tremendous pride that their neighborhoods were clean and that they had done it themselves. The cleanup also offered tangible proof that Operation Breakthrough was beginning to mobilize people, which is the first step to change.

One of my main goals was to identify and train leaders within the communities. It made sense to me to begin by setting up small groups, called neighborhood councils, throughout the target area. Each group would be responsible for electing officers and meeting regularly to define their issues and decide how to address them. In McDougald Terrace, the tenants, mostly single women with children, agreed during a meeting that their most immediate need was a daycare center for their preschool children. Childcare would make it easier for the mothers to look for jobs. The residents requested a meeting with Housing Authority representatives, who refused even to discuss the issue. The tenants decided to keep pushing through their neighborhood council. We gave serious thought to what we should call the organization and eventually decided on the McDougald Terrace Mothers Club. Who would be against an organization with that name?

The women elected one of their most vocal members, Joyce Thorpe, a young mother of three, as president. Joyce had grown up middle-class as the daughter of a carpenter and school teacher in a tobacco town just north of Durham. But her marriage fell apart, and life changed dramatically. Joyce was pregnant with her third child when she had to drop out of college, leave a house with a yard, and move into McDougald Terrace. It was a common pattern among the poor women I encountered. They were left vulnerable by the whims of men who decided with impunity to just walk away from their responsibilities. The circumstances of the women's lives at times made me think of my mother. Who knows if she had endured the abuse from my stepfather to avoid this very situation.

On August 11, 1965, the day after Joyce was elected president of the Mothers Club, she received an eviction notice from the Housing Authority. Her lease would be terminated by the end of the month, the notice said, and there was no further explanation. Joan Alston, my staff organizer for McDougald Terrace, called to deliver the news, and I was furious. The agency was clearly trying to quash the group and intimidate the other mothers. No way could we allow them to do that. I called the Department of U.S. Housing and Urban Development's offices in Washington and Atlanta but got no help. Our only option seemed to be to take this issue to the people. My team at Operation Breakthrough began planning a protest outside the Durham Housing Authority, but the agency's intimidation tactics already were working. Just a few tenants, including my faithful friends, Nathaniel and Louise, agreed to participate. So, we came up with Plan B and recruited students from North Carolina College to increase our numbers. As always, we held a meeting before the protest to plan our strategy. We agreed that only McDougald Terrace residents would talk to the media, leaving viewers to assume that the other protesters were also residents. The next day, the Durham newspapers reported that sixty tenants had participated in the protest.

We had succeeded in drawing attention to the case, but the Housing Authority didn't back away from the eviction. Joyce tried to fight it in a local court, but her appeal of the eviction was denied. Then, on September 20, a sheriff's deputy showed up at her home with an eviction notice. Joyce panicked, locked the door, and yelled to the deputy: "Step through that door and I'll blow your brains out!" She didn't have a gun, but the officer relented and called for backup. Again, Joyce called Joan and me, and we contacted attorney Floyd McKissick, who began working on obtaining an emergency court order to prevent the eviction. For the next few hours Joyce did her best to stall, keeping up the ruckus with the police until McKissick arrived with the order from the North Carolina Supreme Court. Then, to the officers and bystanders who had gathered outside her doors, Joyce declared: "The show is over!"

Joyce was allowed to stay in her apartment while her case bounced back and forth for years between the state court and the U.S. Supreme Court. Finally, the high court settled the matter on January 13, 1969, with a ruling in Joyce's favor. The case set a landmark precedent that protected the due process rights of public housing tenants across the country. That is directly because of Joyce and was a proud product of our work.

By the fall of 1965, my organizers had helped to establish five neighborhood councils, and it didn't take long for the residents to decide housing was the number one issue that needed to be addressed. It was important that my team and I understood what we were fighting. So, we spent time studying how the city's building inspections process worked, who made the decisions, what the tenants' responsibilities and rights were, what wasn't working, and where the pressure points were. The last thing we wanted was to get caught on a technicality and have our grievances ignored because we didn't follow protocol. Once we understood the process, we began organizing residents to show up at barely-publicized hearings and meetings. The residents also began speaking their minds on issues that had been acted upon before without their input.

For the first year or so, I stayed mostly in the background, helping to provide residents the tools, strategies, and motivation they needed to address their problems. I believed strongly in developing leadership among the people so that they would be the ones speaking out at public events, standing before the media, and defining their own issues. While I often spoke out to rally the crowd and help drive home our message, our strategy was never built around a single person. My team and I held pre-meetings before any picket, sit-in, or other demonstration, so that everyone involved could work out the details—who would speak, what they would say, and even where they would sit or stand. Then, after the event, we met again to discuss what went right, what went wrong, and what we could do better the next time. Some of those who would become our most articulate leaders had never even spoken in public before a group and worried at first about using improper grammar and possibly making a fool of themselves. But I constantly reassured them. It didn't matter that some of them were not fully educated. They had all they needed: lots of common sense, courage, and natural ability. "Don't worry how it sounds," I told them. "Just say it like *you* say it."

As 1965 wound to a close, some members of the Operation Breakthrough board were uncomfortable with the way the neighborhood councils were challenging the status quo, and they began complaining that the program was changing its focus. I have no doubt that when I got there some of those same board members assumed I'd fit right into their notions of what the program ought to be. Here was this young Black man with a master's degree in social work. Surely he'd be a master at helping those poor Black people get healthcare and welfare services. But I had no intention—ever!—of just helping people learn how to manage oppression. This was a poor people's revolution, and we were just getting started. Poor Black people were rising together at last, challenging the institutions and individuals that had inflicted or perpetuated their suffering. Even Operation Breakthrough's own board of directors would not escape our scrutiny.

It was shocking to me to discover during my research that among the agency's board members was real estate developer Abe Greenberg. I'd heard his name again and again from residents who lived in the dilapidated housing that he owned and rented, houses that had no bathrooms or hot water, large holes in the walls and ceilings, rotting porches, roaches, rats, and even snakes. This man was the biggest slumlord in town, and he was sitting on the board of the chief local antipoverty agency. So, I began to question publicly: "How is it that if you are fighting a war, you have the enemy sitting on the board, helping to plan strategy? I mean, explain that to me!" Such duplicity became more obvious than ever in the fall of 1965, when Greenberg hiked the rents on about forty shabby units he owned in a poor neighborhood known as Edgemont and refused to make repairs. Edgemont had been a poor white community until the late 1950s, when city officials began tearing down old, blighted properties in poor Black neighborhoods with the promise of rebuilding new and better housing. The promised "urban renewal" was never fully realized, and, as white residents began moving to other parts of the city, Black men and women moved into places like Edgemont, where they had never been before. The demand for affordable housing became even more critical in 1965, when the city cleared out a large swath of Hayti to begin constructing a new expressway. By raising the rents, Greenberg immediately began profiting from the high demand and limited supply of affordable housing. My staff joined residents at city council meetings, where they demanded that officials enforce its housing codes and force Greenberg to comply. But even after city housing inspectors cited him on numerous violations, Greenberg still refused to make the repairs, and city officials backed off, claiming they had no enforcement options.

The controversy was just beginning to pick up steam in January 1966, when Robert Foust, executive director of Operation Breakthrough, ignored some board members' concerns about me and promoted me to Director of Community Development for Target Areas A, B, and C. The new assignment put me in charge of all of the communities covered by Operation Breakthrough, including the more rural and white areas. It also signified the good working relationship I had with Bob, who seemed on the surface the polar opposite of me. He was a gentle, soft-spoken white man with a deep southern drawl. He had a degree in social work, and my guess is he probably thought Breakthrough would be just another social work agency that would give him a chance to do some good in the city. I'm positive he had no idea he would have to encounter the kind of controversy that ensued because of my approach to this battle against poverty. But I came to respect him for his willingness to stand behind me and our work, even when it was very difficult for him to do so. I believe the respect was mutual because I never lied to him. From the start I made him a promise that I always kept: no surprises. I knew he would have to answer to the white power structure for whatever my staff and I did, and I needed him in our corner. So, I never left him out in the cold. I informed him beforehand about everything we were planning to do. There were times that I was spare on the details so he could have plausible denial when folks came to him to complain. But I always at least gave him a heads-up and explained *why* we were taking the chosen steps. Most of my interactions with him had to do with how he should respond to the board members and politicians who were pressuring him to rein me in. It was such a conversation in early 1966 that led to the creation of the United Organizations for Community Improvement (UOCI), an independent confederation of the seventeen or so neighborhood councils that my staff and I by then had helped to create. The group would elect its own officers, seek its own financing, and operate as a separate entity from Operation Breakthrough. It also would free the neighborhood councils to take an even more militant stance, while giving Bob an out. He would be able to tell critics that UOCI was stirring up the trouble, not Breakthrough.

At the first meeting of the new organization in May 1966, residents elected domestic worker Rubye Gattis as president. The group turned its attention almost immediately to the Edgemont housing crisis. Poor white residents refused to participate in an interracial group, but a fired-up group of mostly Black women decided in bold fashion to confront Greenberg head-on. Beginning June 16, dozens of residents showed up daily outside Greenberg's offices in downtown Durham and marched for hours with picket signs that addressed him directly: "Greenberg, Fix Our Houses," "Our Roof Leaks, Does Yours?" "High Rent for Your Fire Traps," and "We Don't Have a Bathtub. Do You?" He didn't respond, didn't even bother to try meeting with us. The next week, we escalated the protest, moving the picket line to the street in front of his home with signs that read: "Your Neighbor Is a Slumlord," and "Mrs. Greenberg, My Children Sleep With Rats."

Greenberg eventually resigned from Operation Breakthrough's board, but he never made substantial improvements to his neglected properties. And city officials just threw up their hands, saying there was nothing they could do. That's what was maddening to me—the people in power were indignant with *us* about the nature of our protests. How dare we go to this businessman's offices and home with such signs? Yet none of them said a word or showed an ounce of concern for the people who were living in the hell holes that had helped to make Greenberg a wealthy man. Instead, the critics blamed the poor for their condition, and the news organizations were eager to blast the unsympathetic comments: If the houses were so bad, why didn't the families just move out, clean up after themselves, or set a few mouse traps?

The critics refused to see that poverty had stripped poor people of options. Because most of the poor men and women were undereducated, they held low-paying or no jobs, and because they had little money, they could afford only the most basic housing. But I refused to accept that they had to live with the rats and crumbling structures in unsafe, unsanitary conditions as just the price of being poor. We had to show the powers that be that poor people had a voice, too, and that their voice mattered. My team at Operation Breakthrough and the staff of UOCI, which worked closely together on most issues, began registering people to vote in large numbers. All of a sudden, poor Black people began showing up at once-exclusive white precinct meetings and participating as never before in the electoral process. That level of participation posed a particular threat in areas where Black residents outnumbered whites but had never elected Black representatives. Opportunistic white politicians took note and jumped on the criticism bandwagon, complaining that Operation Breakthrough was misusing federal funds by transporting residents to the demonstrations and meetings in the program's vehicles and by holding registration drives. Federal investigators were drawn in and spent time scouring the program's books, but they found no evidence of wrongdoing. Hoping to quell the criticism, the board still banned the use of Operation Breakthrough's funds or vehicles for protests. The pressure of it all overwhelmed Bob, who resigned as executive director on June 25, 1966.

For me, the work was exciting. This was exactly the kind of community organizing I had been longing to do, but the work consumed me. It became the center of my existence. I was away from home night and day. Viola, my wife, had found a job, but we were in a new city with no family, and she was often alone. Even when I was home, my mind was often occupied, always thinking about the next demonstration or how to handle a certain problem. The pressure was constant. It just didn't go away. I mean, I was in my twenties, in charge of a program, trying to define the work, while a staff and a community looked to me for answers. You can't get people all roused up and then tell them, "Well, I don't know what to do!" I always tried to have an answer, to anticipate the issues and problems as much as I could and offer a range of possible solutions. I knew the critics were watching, too, and that Operation Breakthrough was under a microscope. I wanted to do things right, both administratively and strategically.

My absence definitely put a strain on my marriage. Still, Viola was as supportive as she could be. On March 29, 1966 she gave birth to our first child, a beautiful daughter, Kelli Pilar, whose middle name was taken from the strong female character in *For Whom the Bell Tolls*, the movie that had inspired me to marry her mother. I wanted her to have a name that signified strength. For a short while, everything stopped. I was there when Viola's water broke, at the hospital for the birth, and when I saw my daughter for the first time—what a phenomenal feeling. I mean, how could you not love a child? I jumped right into fatherhood, and I loved it. I really wanted to be a good father. When Kelli was old enough, I took her out with me in the neighborhoods and to the office. My team and I would be sitting around a table, planning an event, and Kelli would be sitting on my lap or crawling all over the floor. Still, I was away from my family a good bit. If I have any regrets in life, they are the lost moments with my children. But the truth is, I didn't know another way to be, another way to do the work that I was doing, except to be all in.

While I was experiencing the happiest time in my life at home, work became increasingly more difficult. Bob's departure did not end the criticism of Operation Breakthrough or of me. In fact, calls for my ouster grew even more strident a month after his resignation, when I spoke at the People's Conference on Poverty in Woodland, North Carolina. The conference in July 1966 had been organized by Black activists in the Choanoke region, four counties that were mostly rural, predominantly Black and poor. Poor residents of the area were ready to form their own organization after two years of conflict with the Choanoke Area Development Association (CADA). CADA was the community action program financed in part by the North Carolina Fund to fight poverty in the region. The residents, inspired by the grassroots activism in Durham, complained that CADA's leaders were out of touch and resistant to challenging the racist practices that had fostered oppression and poverty. There was no better example of the organization's paternalistic style than when CADA's program director, Fred Cooper, addressed the crowd at the poverty conference. He gleefully announced that the federal Office of Economic Opportunity had granted CADA a half-million dollars to open centers for social services throughout the region. But instead of the enthusiastic response the director expected, activists in the crowd began questioning him about why he had not involved poor people in the process of developing a plan. The director dodged the questions and responded: "I think I just gave you some good news about the multi-purpose centers being funded. I think we should make some noise over this fact…"

He instructed the crowd of about a thousand Black people to yell when he threw his handkerchief in the air and to stop when he caught it. I was stunned when the audience followed suit. They yelled loudly every time he pitched the handkerchief in the air and stopped suddenly when he grabbed it. After a couple rounds of this madness, he faked throwing up the handkerchief, and the crowd yelled anyway. He then had the nerve—whether he was being playful or not—to admonish them for not following directions. I was livid. It was my turn to speak next. I stepped to the microphone, looked out at the array of Black faces in the crowd and told them that I'd just witnessed the most outrageous thing I'd ever seen in my life:

"I'm sitting here in a meeting in the year 1966 and see a white man take a handkerchief and throw it up in the air and tell us to yell…and what I don't understand about it is the fact that you yelled when he threw it up…I think it's time…that we had a little soul talk."

I told the crowd that white folks had been controlling Black lives, for too long, and I talked about the unevenness of white and Black power in America. "Let me show you an example," I told the crowd. "If I got a baseball bat, and you got one of them little skinny sticks, I'm gon' beat you to death…The referee can say 'Go,' but if I got a baseball bat, and you got a little stick, I'm gon' beat you to death. And that's what our society is all about. We got to get a baseball bat in our hands to fight the baseball bat in their hands."

I'd intended the stick reference as a metaphor, but the critics skewed my words to claim that I was advocating violence. They also pounced on my use of a new term that was beginning to circulate among young Black activists: "Black Power." To many white residents and politicians, I sounded scary and threatening, and they demanded that I be fired. But the new director of Operation Breakthrough, William "Bill" Pursell, refused. He had gotten to know me during the years we worked together under his predecessor, and he knew that their claims were off base.

As the word about my so-called radical brand of organizing spread, representatives of a Chicago-based agency called in early 1967 and made me an intriguing offer to head community organizing efforts on the city's west side. I told them I would think about it, and I did. I considered whether it would be better for my family. A move to Chicago would have put us much closer to my family in Milwaukee. But I'd started something in North Carolina, and I didn't want to leave my work unfinished. The news about the job offer spread to George Esser, executive director of the North Carolina Fund, who moved quickly to try to keep me in the state. He asked me to join him at the Fund as his Director of Community Development, which would give me a chance to do statewide the kind of organizing that I had begun in Durham. By then, I'd come to trust George as someone I could engage in discussions about strategy and get great advice. He was a strong intellectual who had graduated from Harvard Law School and spent years as an urban issues and government affairs specialist at the University of North Carolina's Institute of Government. Beyond his academic credentials, though, he was just a fine human being who didn't back down when it became clear that confronting the underlying issues of poverty would make those in power uncomfortable. He was a white southerner who had been raised in Virginia, but many white North Carolinians accused him of "destroying the Southern way of life" from the start of the Fund, when he put together an interracial staff that included well-educated Black men in top-tier positions. They were men like William Darity, the Fund's director of program development, who had just become the first Black student to earn a doctorate degree from the University of North Carolina in Chapel Hill, and later Nathan Garrett, the director of finances and one of few Black certified public accountants in the country. The white staff members included many compassionate souls, like Billy E. Barnes, the public relations specialist who often traveled with me and other Black employees throughout North Carolina to document our work in photographs and videos. George never wavered when white North Carolinians complained about Black and white field workers and volunteers traveling and eating together and sometimes sharing housing. I accepted his job offer and in February 1967 went to work for the North Carolina Fund.

Soon, I was traveling across the state, trying to build on the momentum the poor residents had started in Durham and the Choanoke region after the poverty conference. Poor people in both areas had formed their own organizations—Durham's United Organizations for Community Improvement (UOCI) and the People's Program on Poverty (PPOP) in the Choanoke—to address their issues in their own protest-oriented, confrontational style. When the groups received direct grants from the North Carolina Fund , it signaled a growing recognition within the agency that change at times had to be messy.

One of my first initiatives with the Fund was to recruit college students and recent graduates and to train them to work as interns in community organizing. I spent seven days with them at a retreat site in Bricks, North Carolina, where other Fund staff members and I taught them the nuts and bolts of our work. We then dispatched them to communities throughout the state. They were talented young people like Thelma Jean Miller, who had grown up on a farm, owned by her family since 1906, in a small community in the northeastern part of the state. Her parents, both full-time farmers, had scraped and struggled to put her through college, and they were not thrilled when she accepted the internship paying $10 a day. But Thelma saw an opportunity to make a difference in her home state. I assigned her and five other students to the Rocky Mount area, and they immediately began knocking on doors and getting to know the residents. The interns were greeted with the same initial fear and skepticism that my team and I had faced in the early days in Durham. But Thelma and her peers kept going back, and by the end of the summer they had organized six neighborhood councils. When the internship ended, I hired Thelma as a full-time organizer, helping the new councils take their concerns about inadequate or nonexistent public services to the appropriate authorities. She was tough in an era when Southern white men were unaccustomed to seeing strong Black women in leadership roles. Once, T.J, as we affectionately called her, was even escorted out of a city council meeting by the police when she refused to address a belligerent and racist white official as "sir." But the protests, sit-ins, and other demonstrations that she helped to organize got results. Streets were paved, houses were repaired, street lights were installed, and in a few cases, businesses hired their first Black employees in skilled and professional jobs.

Organizers assigned to work in other parts of the state, including Raleigh, Greensboro, Wilson, and Goldsboro, reported similar successes. It made me proud to see poor Black people standing up for themselves, demanding better, and the people in Durham continued

to lead the way. When the city tried to push through an urban renewal plan that would have displaced hundreds of poor Black families,
the United Organizations for Community Improvement packed a
city council meeting on July 17, 1967, with residents to protest. Near
the end of the meeting, I stepped to the microphone and issued this
warning: "You all better wake up to what's happening, and you better
listen, because these are the voices of the people, and they're the people
that you have forgotten, they're the people that you have pushed across
those railroad tracks, they're the people that you have moved out of
urban renewal areas… 'Cause they're tired, and they're frustrated, and
people who get tired and frustrated do things they wouldn't ordinarily
do."

Even as I spoke those words, the ashes were still smoldering in
Newark, New Jersey, where Black rage had erupted into six days of
riots that left 26 people dead, hundreds injured, and millions of dollars in property destroyed. The morning after the Durham council
meeting the local newspaper trumpeted this headline: "ANOTHER
NEWARK THREATENED HERE."

It wasn't an idle threat. I could sense the frustration of people building. They had finally realized that they didn't have to live like they were
living, but now they were tired of being ignored, of being told 'no,' of
waiting and waiting for change. The challenge for me and for UOCI's
leaders—Ben Ruffin, who had been hired as the group's executive director, and Rubye Gattis, who remained president—was to figure out
how to contain that anger, while providing some way for our people to
express themselves.

On July 19, UOCI assembled more than two hundred people at St.
Joseph's African Methodist Episcopal Church in Hayti for a march
downtown to city hall. Ben and I walked alongside as marshals to
maintain the peace. The marchers were mostly restrained and dig-
nified, but on the way home, a few group members began throwing
rocks, which broke a few windows and slightly injured a police officer.
Even the media reported the incident as a minor skirmish. But the
next day, when the mayor of Durham heard that residents were again
meeting at St. Joseph's, he contacted the governor, who called out the
National Guard. Before we knew it, more than 350 soldiers and police officers, dressed in full riot gear, were converging on downtown.
We had gathered at the church to strategize and hadn't even planned
to march that day, but it seemed to us the authorities were trying to

intimidate us, and that wasn't happening. We amassed an even bigger crowd this time, more than 300 people, and marched single file downtown. Again, the march was peaceful, even as we met with crowds of jeering white men along the way. Media reports mentioned that again a few rogue members began throwing rocks and turning over trash cans on the way home. Both incidents were minor, but they gave fodder to influential critics, like new Republican Congressman James C. Gardner. He had blown into office on a wave of discontent among white North Carolinians who saw the Civil Rights Movement and antipoverty programs as threatening and wasteful. Gardner had begun attacking President Johnson's War on Poverty, the North Carolina Fund, and Operation Breakthrough even before he took office. And in the weeks before the marches in Durham, he'd used his platform on the House floor to complain that the North Carolina Fund and Operation Breakthrough were using government funds to build a "political machine." He accused us of using poor people to influence elections. Then, on July 25, just five days after the second march, Gardner held a news conference and reiterated those accusations. He described my speeches about "Black Power" as inflammatory and called for my firing. He also challenged the North Carolina Fund's tax-free status, pushed for Esser to be suspended, and asked that federal funds to Operation Breakthrough be eliminated.

I'd never even met the man, and so I tried not to give his attacks any of my attention or energy. But it meant a lot to me that Esser fired back immediately, saying the accusations were "untrue, demagogic, and grossly distorted." He set the record straight, explaining that UOCI leaders and I had worked hard to make sure that the demonstrations did not turn violent. I was also heartened by the support that came from the community. Respected Black business owners and professionals wrote letters to Sargent Shriver, head of the Office of Economic Opportunity, in my defense. I was particularly surprised when Watts Hill, Jr., a wealthy white business and civic leader, wrote a letter to Shriver in my defense, and it ran in the local newspaper. In his letter, Hill said I was "the single person most responsible for there not being riots in Durham."

Still, the political fight that Gardner had picked dragged on. Though the federal Equal Opportunity Act survived the initial attacks and was reauthorized by the end of the year, Republicans managed to tack on restrictions banning "clients" served by an organization

from involvement in setting policy. It was a major blow. I'd built my
entire strategy around the "maximum feasible participation" of the
poor, getting them involved at every level. The new limits would have
set back much of our progress. All of us at the North Carolina Fund
were concerned. The mood of the country had changed. Republican
politicians such as Gardner were gaining ground, capitalizing on the
dissatisfaction of Southern whites angry with the Democratic Party's
support of civil rights and antipoverty legislation. In October 1967,
George Esser and the board of the North Carolina Fund came up with
a well-thought-out plan: They created a new independent organization, called the Foundation for Community Development, to work directly with the neighborhood councils and community programs that
had been established. Among the objectives of the new agency was "to
sponsor further experimentation in the concept of maximum feasible
participation by the poor in programs and processes affecting their
welfare."

Esser and the board also came to the stunning conclusion that the
Fund had served its purpose and would not seek to renew its financing
when the five-year period laid out in its initial incorporation expired
in 1968. It was a brave decision by Esser and the board to go out on
their own terms. The Foundation for Community Development was
the first of three spinoff programs created by the Fund to receive its
entire remaining assets.

Nathan Garrett, the Fund's brilliant controller, was named executive
director of the new Foundation. The agency's rules required that at
least fifty-one percent of its board of directors had to be made up of
representatives of the poor. Thirteen of the initial fifteen members met
that criteria, including UOCI's Rubye Gattis and Alice Balance, one
of the founding members of PPOP. The Foundation began operations
in December 1967 with an initial grant of $262,838 from the North
Carolina Fund and thirteen staff members, mostly from the Fund's
community development department, including me. I was named director of community development training for the new agency.

This was clearly the beginning of a new era. For the first time, poor
Black people and their leaders had real power and the resources to
fight the War on Poverty their way.

Sitting on the steps with a child soon after I arrived in Durham to work
as a community organizer for Operation Breakthrough.
(Photo Courtesy of Billy E. Barnes.)

The brothers, including Ben Ruffin (on the truck to the right) and me
(to the left) during the first community-wide cleanup in Durham.
(Photo Courtesy of Billy E. Barnes.)

With Ann Atwater, who was a single mother living in a substandard
house in a Black community, called Hayti,
in Durham when we first met in 1965.

5

BLACK AND PROUD

By the time I moved over to the Foundation for Community Development, I was one of the most hated Black men in North Carolina in certain circles of white people with power. To them, I was an "outside agitator," stirring up discontent everywhere I went. But as Frederick Douglass once said: "Power concedes nothing without a demand. It never did, and it never will."

It was clear that white people in power in North Carolina weren't giving up anything willingly, and my new boss, Nathan Garrett, fully embraced the notion that confrontation was a necessary part of our strategy for change. Though I knew Nathan, this would be my first time working directly with him. We were both Black men, but I think it surprised many people that we got along so well. Our styles were very different. Nathan had a calm, laid-back demeanor with an analytical, unemotional approach to his work. But he communicated clearly what he needed from his staff to be successful and then let us do our jobs. He didn't try to be what he wasn't, or micromanage us, and he didn't try to act like he knew everything. He shared what he knew and kept an open mind when I went to him with something new. Most importantly, though, I believed that we were both committed to the cause and working toward the same goal. I knew that I needed him and that our program would not exist without the confidence that our backers had in his level-headedness. And so, I promised him, as I'd promised my previous bosses: no surprises. I always let Nathan in on what I was planning, no matter how crazy or controversial. He never told me I couldn't do something or tried to talk me out of it. Instead, he sometimes offered me an alternative way of looking at things, which occasionally prompted me to rethink my strategy. But we appreciated and respected one another's roles: He raised the money, kept our supporters happy and the program afloat, while I raised hell. Over time I would discover just how tough Nathan was, and the brother always had my back.

I trained our field staff to use the same approach to community organizing that I had first tested in Durham. Our workers spent time getting to know the neighborhood residents and their issues and then invited them to community meetings. The residents then decided whether to form an organization that would represent their interests. The organizations could apply for an individual grant from the Foundation to pay for a staff person whom we would train to develop strategy, organize events, and keep the group on track. The Foundation conducted workshops to teach the chosen community leaders and interested citizens the basics of how local government works and how to follow the proper channels to negotiate for improved services. But our staff also instructed them on the ins and outs of various types of protest demonstrations that could be used if their negotiations failed.

Ten community-wide organizations eventually were formed in that way, including the original two groups that had been established under the North Carolina Fund—United Organizations for Community Improvement (UOCI), headed by my friend, Ben Ruffin, and the People's Program on Poverty (PPOP) in the Choanoke region. Ben helped twenty-two other neighborhoods hold cleanup campaigns similar to the first one we had sponsored in the Durham community where he was raised. Through the Foundation, UOCI also started a food cooperative, helped tenants fight unfair housing evictions, and held a selective buying campaign that resulted in nearly a million dollars in lost revenue to the boycotted stores. The campaign was successful in pushing some of those businesses to hire Black employees for the first time. Likewise, the Fayetteville Area Poor People's Organization helped to bring water service to an impoverished neighborhood that had been trying to get it for seven years. The Greensboro Association of Poor People assisted tenants in filing lawsuits against slumlords and conducted a rent strike that forced a change of superintendents and improved services in a housing complex of 177 units. The organization also registered so many Black voters that Greensboro had the highest percentage of eligible Black voters in the state. In Hertford County, PPOP's voter registration drives helped to give Black voters the power to defeat a $2.5 million hospital bond issue, which showed their discontent with officials who had rejected requests to make the hospital more accessible to the poor. The Foundation also provided funds to a group of poor white craftsmen, who were able to incorporate and sell their wares in tourist areas of the state and in New York.

The improvements that we began to see took time, and I was pleased with how the residents and the Foundation's staff stuck to our mission, even as local white officials grew increasingly more uncomfortable with our push for change. In October 1969, two years after the Foundation's incorporation, an independent evaluation that had been commissioned by the North Carolina Fund found that the Foundation's work was essential. By then, the Foundation had trained more than two hundred fifty neighborhood workers, two hundred forty "indigenous" leaders from all over the state, and three hundred students and volunteers.

"There is no ongoing viable alternative to FCD in the state of North Carolina," the report said. "FCD is one of the new things that must be done while society readjusts to a whole series of new and unfamiliar but just demands. Old institutions and the people who run them will not and perhaps cannot shift fast enough on their own. FCD serves as the vital link between the desperate needs of powerless people and sources of some relief."

The team of five evaluators included civil rights activist John Lewis, long before his ascent to the U.S. House of Representatives. The team found that one of the most significant contributions of the Foundation was "the upsurge in pride among many Blacks in the state and a determination to do something about their own problems through confronting the institutions that are supposed to service them and demanding and getting action." But while the report credited my community organizing efforts as part of the reason for the Foundation's success, it also cited my association with the agency as a factor in its negative image among whites and many middle-class Blacks. This impression, no doubt, was colored by the white media's portrayal of me as a "dangerous extremist," the report said. That wasn't at all how I saw myself. But if fighting to help poor people find their voice, if demanding that their voices be heard was extreme, then I guess I was. I didn't much care what people called me or thought of me. I was singularly focused on making life better for the masses of my people who happened to be poor. And I was crazy enough to believe that if we fought hard enough, we could do just that.

To me, it would have made little sense to fight against poverty without fighting against the racism and economic oppression that caused and perpetuated it. That's why I found myself drawn to the larger battles against injustice. I had been at the Foundation just two months when a violent episode, which came to be known as the Orangeburg Massacre, erupted next door in South Carolina and escalated racial tensions throughout the entire region. I happened to be meeting in Durham with activists from North Carolina, South Carolina, and Virginia on February 8, 1968, when I got word that police had fired into a group of protesters at the historically Black South Carolina State College in Orangeburg and killed three students. The news was horrifying and heartbreaking. Students killed on their own campus by the police for protesting? The military and police shootings of Vietnam War protesters at Kent State and Jackson State universities were still two years away, and so this kind of thing was unfathomable. All I could feel was rage, and the more I learned about the incident over time, the angrier I got.

The protests had started two days earlier when a small group of Black college students were turned away from a whites-only bowling alley near campus. Students who gathered at the scene to protest the incident clashed violently with state troopers, and the tensions just escalated over the next couple of days as the demonstrations continued. When state troopers fired into a crowd of protesters on campus on February 8, two South Carolina State College students and a high school student fell dead, and twenty-eight others were injured. Many of them had been shot in their backs as they ran away; some were even struck in the soles of their feet. The troopers declared they had been fired upon by the students and were acting in self-defense—claims that have been largely disproven. But authorities needed a scapegoat and found one when they noticed Cleve Sellers, a South Carolina native who was the national advocacy director for the Student Nonviolent Coordinating Committee (SNCC), in the crowd. They arrested him on charges of inciting the violence. Like all of us who had been advocating Black power, Cleve had been on the radar of white officials in the region. Although he maintained—and later investigations determined—that he had nothing to do with organizing the protests, he was arrested on a bunch of trumped-up charges. Most of them were thrown out, but Cleve was convicted on the single remaining charge, rioting. He ultimately served over seven months in prison, which was a grave injustice. Cleve and I later became friends, and even now, I get angry when I recall that nearly a year of his life was snatched away. And for what? Because he was a Black militant who dared to fight for his people? Not even the full pardon that the state granted him twenty-five years later could ever give him back one moment of that time. It was clear the authorities were trying to silence Cleve and I believed it was just a matter of time before they tried to do the same to me.

On the day of the Orangeburg massacre, the other activists and I, who were meeting in Durham, felt a strong need to do something to memorialize the dead students and protest police brutality. We immediately turned our attention to planning simultaneous marches that would take place in various cities throughout our three states. On February 15, I led a protest in Durham that drew a crowd of at least two hundred people, who marched together downtown and gathered in a Main Street park known as Five Points, where five major streets intersect. You could just feel the collective hurt as we huddled together in the freezing weather. Someone strung a homemade burlap figure on a pole with the South Carolina governor's name across it and set it on fire. We had also carried makeshift coffins to the scene, and a blaze was set inside those, too. The Fire Department arrived to put out the blaze, but we had locked hands around the scene. I read in later news accounts that firefighters said they were unable to get through the crowd and returned to the truck for a larger hose that would reach the blaze from where they stood. All I knew at the time was that they turned those huge hoses on us, and it was thirty-two degrees outside. The crowd of mostly college students scattered, running toward Main Street, headed home. As we ran, one of the protesters grabbed my cane, which I usually carried during marches to ward off the Klan members' dogs. Full of frustration, he began slamming the stick into store windows. Glass crashed to the ground all around us. Suddenly, the cops grabbed him, handcuffed him, and began beating him. I saw the arresting officer constantly jabbing the student in his stomach with a nightstick, and I moved toward them, yelling for the officer to stop. When the officer raised his stick again, I reached out and grabbed it to stop the beating. Suddenly, officers converged on me, handcuffed my hands behind my back, and slammed me facedown against a cop car. Then, they began beating my legs and lower body with their nightsticks. I was charged with assaulting a police officer and resisting arrest. At the police station officers threw me in an elevator, dropped a telephone book on my stomach, and began slamming their clubs down hard on top of the book, presumably to avoid leaving any signs of the beating. They then locked me in a cell with a Black man who had stabbed his wife fifty times. Maybe they figured this dude was crazy and would do something to harm me. Instead, I actually knew him. The woman he'd killed had worked for me, and once the officers left us alone, he started trying to explain what had happened. I was trying not to hear it, but I was able to calm him somewhat.

When a local newspaper called my boss for a comment about my arrest, Nathan turned the focus on how the authorities had acted that day and defended me: "The incident which arose as a direct result of what appears to be the ill-advised hosing of these students, cata-pulted him into a somewhat different role—that of an adult citizen concerned for the safety of college students. I am convinced that Mr. Fuller broke no moral laws with his conduct, and it is doubtful that he broke any man-made laws."

I had anticipated the march would be somewhat controversial. Two days beforehand, I'd told my social work students at the University of North Carolina at Chapel Hill that I was resigning my teaching posi-tion at the university. I'd been recruited there during the fall of 1967 by my friend and former North Carolina Fund co-worker, Morris Cohen, to teach a course in community organizing. The students and faculty seemed to like me, but my hiring became highly politicized when the state's governor called a press conference to denounce it. I figured my role in the march would draw more unwarranted attention to my job at UNC, and I didn't want to cause any trouble for my friend. The day after telling my students, I sent a letter of resignation. In spite of the controversy, I was hired a short time later by James E. Cheek, the pres-ident of Shaw University, an historically Black institution in Raleigh, to teach a similar course. The same year, Dr. Cheek went on to become president of Howard University.

During a trial two weeks after my arrest, the officer testified that my elbow struck him in the face when I grabbed his stick, but the assault charge was thrown out. I was, however, convicted of resisting arrest and sentenced to four months in jail. Three student protesters from North Carolina College also were convicted on various charges related to the incident and sentenced to four to ten months in jail. My case was appealed, and I never served time on the charge. But I don't re-call specifically how the case was resolved, and Durham court officials have been unable to locate my old files. A search of newspaper archives also turned up nothing.

I remember vividly, though, the telephone conversation I had with my mother and grandmother after the arrest. Both were disappointed and hurt. They had sacrificed tremendously to help me through college and raise me "right." And to them, that did not include going to jail. I tried my best to explain to them the difference between going to jail for committing a crime and being arrested for taking a moral stand. I'm sure it took some real soul-searching on their parts, but it would not be my last arrest. They came to understand, and they were as supportive as a mother and grandmother could be.

The year 1968 continued to be a brutal, bloody one throughout the country. Just two months after the Orangeburg massacre, Dr. Martin Luther King, Jr., was assassinated on the balcony of a Memphis hotel. King was beginning to talk more about the link between racism and poverty and had announced his Poor People's Campaign. He had gone to Memphis to support striking sanitation workers. On April 4, 1968, the day that King was killed, Congressman Adam Clayton Powell, Jr., the once-powerful figure whose influence had helped to pass important social measures, was in Durham to speak at Duke University. Powell had just returned from a yearlong self-imposed exile to the Bimini islands, where he'd fled after his expulsion from Congress on corruption charges. But Powell was so drunk that his aide ended up delivering the speech. The news about Dr. King's assassination broke in the middle of the speech. We were all stunned and hurt. I soon got word that enraged students had begun gathering a few miles away in an auditorium at North Carolina College and were planning to march downtown. With the Orangeburg massacre fresh in my mind, I worried that some of these young people, so full of pain and rage, would go out there and end up dead. And for what? How would that honor Dr. King? I rushed to the university, walked onstage and just started talking to the students. I told them that, no, we were not going downtown that night. We would act the way Dr. King would want us to act and pull together for a massive, respectful march the next day. A voice from the audience yelled, "Uncle Tom!" But my argument prevailed, and the students calmed down and dispersed.

The rest of the night I stayed up with a group of armed brothers, guarding Powell, who was convinced that Dr. King's death was part of a conspiracy targeting all Black leaders. The next day, hundreds of us met at St. Joseph's church, marched downtown to city hall in a solemn single-file line that stretched for blocks, and held an emotional rally at city hall. Afterward, as we walked back to the Black community, I gazed up toward the sky and was stunned to see a bunch of white men with rifles on the roof of a bank building. I had no idea who they were. Were they Klan snipers? With police on every block, I pointed out the gunmen to an officer, who told me they were fellow lawmen. I can't say I was relieved because it still wasn't clear to me what they might do. Fortunately, the march remained peaceful, and I was surprised when Mayor Wensell Grabarek, who had been among my critics, spoke at the rally and credited me with preventing a riot in Durham. But rioting erupted in many major cities across the country, including Washington, DC, Baltimore, Louisville, and Chicago. In those cities alone, at least thirty people died and millions of dollars in property were destroyed.

The nation was still mourning the loss of Dr. King two months later when U.S. Senator Robert F. Kennedy, the younger brother of the late president, was gunned down in a California hotel on June 5, 1968. The younger Kennedy, who had made social justice and poverty issues the focal point of his campaign, was the leading Democratic presidential candidate.

Sometime later that year, I read the groundbreaking book, *Black Rage*, and it spoke to me in a deep way. The authors, renowned Black psychiatrists William H. Grier and Price M. Cobbs, used patients they had counseled throughout the 1960s to help make the case that this country's history of racism had left all Black people, regardless of their education level or social status, in a constant—and often unknowing—state of rage. How we survive over the long haul depends largely on how we are able to negotiate that rage over time, the book explained.

While the nation was in tumult, so was my personal life. I stayed on the go, traveling around the state, moving in and out of hotels, working long, odd hours. I found that when you're always in the spotlight with lots of people depending on you, looking up to you, telling you how great you are, you have to be extra careful not to let that stuff go to your head. I think I managed that part pretty well. The other part, though, was more difficult. The temptation of beautiful women was constant, and sometimes the strength and discipline it took to avoid giving in to those feelings was more than I had. On April 16, 1968, a woman with

whom I had been intimately involved gave birth to a baby boy, and
she sent me pictures introducing the infant as my son, Darwin Mills.
Torn about how to handle the news, I kept the photos in my office
drawer for a while and didn't realize that they had disappeared. When
I returned home one day, Viola handed me the pictures and an anonymous note that she said she had received in the mail. I never learned
who sent the packet, but my wife was, of course, devastated, angry, and
full of questions. There was plenty of resentment on all sides, and I felt
horrible for the pain I'd caused. I eventually agreed to a loose financial
arrangement, but instead of working through the mess I'd created to
do what was best for the child, I made a selfish, irresponsible choice: I
walked away, and, for the first twenty-five years of my son's life, I was
absent, just as my own father had been. No explanation could ever
justify why or how I was able to do that. I will forever regret the way I
responded, the lost days with my son, and the pain my absence caused
him. I am grateful though that unlike me Darwin wanted to know his
father. And as a young man, he eventually would come looking for me.

Thanks to Viola's incredible capacity to forgive, my marriage survived. But my work didn't let up. By then, the threats to my life had
become regular. I often received telephone calls and letters warning
that I would be killed if I participated in a certain event or showed
up in a community. A Black police officer in Durham once told me
that his white colleagues had a pool on my life; whoever killed me got
the winning jackpot. Given the racial atmosphere in Durham, I didn't
doubt it one bit. I spent a lot of time traveling the back roads of North
Carolina, often late at night with friends and colleagues, and I needed
to be able to protect myself. I had no philosophical opposition to guns
or to using them, if necessary. So, my traveling companions and I all
bought rifles and carried them with us wherever we went.

One day, when I left my work vehicle at a gas station to be serviced,
I forgot to unload the trunk. When the mechanic popped it open and
noticed the guns, he called police. Since the vehicle was registered to
the Foundation, the police notified Nathan, who issued a press release
on June 21, 1969, when the press got wind of it. "Howard Fuller has
likely the most dangerous job in North Carolina," Nathan said in the
release. "He receives threats to his own safety and to his family's safety... I [told him and his coworker] that if they felt that they needed
this protection, certainly with memories of Martin King and Robert
Kennedy and Medgar Evers and Malcolm X and John Kennedy fresh

on my mind, I could not prevent them from taking legal steps to arm themselves against the possibility of crank threats becoming real dangers."

Nothing ever came of the incident because the guns had been obtained properly, but it provided juicy fodder for the critics, who were convinced that I was planning an armed revolution. I was indeed part of a revolution, but not the Nat Turner-style rebellion that most white folks feared. Those of us who were committed to the Black Power movement had determined that we would no longer turn the other cheek and be spat on, stomped, and killed without fighting back. We'd grown tired of begging white folks for a seat at their table when they clearly didn't want us there. I'd become convinced that it was time for us as a people to create our own institutions, where our culture and history could be taught and valued. Such an opportunity would come far sooner than I ever expected.

During the summer of 1968, Chuck Hopkins, a Black student leader at Duke University, worked under me as an intern at the Foundation. Chuck, who was president of a Black students' group called the Afro-American Society, trained in community organizing and spent time working in poor neighborhoods in Raleigh. Chuck was an intelligent guy with a good command of history, and he was an articulate spokesman for the students. So, I wasn't surprised when he returned to campus for the fall semester and began pushing the administration to address some simmering racial issues. One of the students who stepped up to assist was Bertie Howard, who also was very smart, energetic, and full of ideas. In October, the Afro-American Society, led by Chuck, presented President Douglas M. Knight with a list demanding that the university: 1) publicly support a selective buying campaign in downtown Durham aimed at obtaining reforms in housing, welfare, legal protection, and recreation, 2) contract a significant portion of Duke's business to Black-owned companies, 3) hire a Black recruiter to attract more Black students, 4) hire a Black faculty advisor for Black students and, 5) establish a meaningful Black Studies program.

The university agreed to make a few changes, such as hiring a Black barber and no longer playing "Dixie" at its events, and a month later a committee was appointed to research a curriculum for a Black studies program. But the Afro-American Society believed the administration was moving too slowly. After celebrating "Black Is Beautiful Week" with celebrity guests that included activists Dick Gregory and

Fannie Lou Hamer in February 1969, the Black students were ready
to make a move. On February 12, they marched with Dick Gregory to
the home of President Knight, who invited them inside for a discussion. The conversation lasted two hours without significant progress.
Knight left the next day for a business trip to New York. What the
students did next caught even me by surprise.

I was speaking at a late-morning convocation at Bennett College
in Greensboro when I got word that about sixty Black students had
taken over the Allen building, where Duke's administrative offices
and student records were housed. The students had put everyone else
out, barricaded themselves inside, and were threatening to burn records if police were called to the scene. I was immediately concerned
for their safety and canceled my plans to travel to Atlanta for another
speaking engagement. Instead, I headed back to Durham and straight
to Duke. The news of the takeover had spread quickly because the
students had confided their plans in advance to a few trusted white
reporters for the main campus newspaper, the *Duke Chronicle*, which
led its front page with the story. The young journalists also released
a prepared statement from their Black colleagues to the national media on the morning of the takeover. "We seized the building because
we have been negotiating with the Duke administration and faculty
concerning different issues that affect Black students for two-and-a-
half years," the statement said. "We have no meaningful results. We
have exhausted all the so-called proper channels." The students listed
thirteen demands, which included several new ones added to the list
that had been presented to Knight in October. They included: the reinstatement of Black students who had failed the previous semester;
an increase in the Black student population to twenty-nine percent by
1973; an end to police harassment of Black students; an end to the
grading system for Black students; earmarked fees for a Negro student
union; and self-determination of working conditions by the university's non-academic workers.

By the time I arrived on campus, the Black students had strung a
large, handwritten sign from a window, renaming the Allen building
the Malcolm X building. I walked around to the side of the building, climbed through a first-floor office window, and the students let
me into the main hallway where they were gathered. They were calm,
pretty well organized, and determined. There were meetings throughout that long afternoon, and at other times we sat around talking for

hours. Knight, who had cut short his business trip and returned to campus, refused to negotiate. He also threatened to suspend the Black students and have them charged with trespassing if they did not vacate the building. The faculty was split. While most of them either supported Knight's hard-nosed stance or remained quiet, a sizeable and vocal contingent of them backed the Black students. In fact, about twenty faculty members walked out of an emergency meeting called by Knight that evening when he declined to say whether he had called in the police. Unbeknownst to me at the time, the faculty members rushed to the Allen building, and formed a human barrier at the door.

Meanwhile, as darkness approached, I knew it was just a matter of time before the police came, and I worried that the situation quickly could turn deadly. The resolve of some of the students appeared to be weakening. A few of them grew quiet and somber, and one said to me: "My parents did not send me to Duke to go to jail." I understood their conflicted feelings and wanted to help them leave the building with a feeling of triumph, even though their demands had not been met. Ultimately, we decided to exit through a rear door with our fists raised high. The students had spent ten hours inside. Few people saw us leave, including the police. Unaware that we were already gone, police later stormed the building and found it empty. Some bystanders in the crowd of about 1,000 mostly white students, faculty, and onlookers shouted and hurled objects as police officers tried to disperse the crowd. The police responded with tear gas. The yard erupted into chaos, and twenty-five people, including some of the police officers, were injured.

The police overreaction backfired, generating outrage among some white students and faculty who had been just casual observers. Tensions continued to escalate and on February 15, I joined an estimated 1,000 Black and white students and supporters in marching to Knight's home. He was expecting us, addressed the crowd outside briefly, and then met with a large group that included five Black student representatives, several administrators, members of a faculty task force, and me. The task force, which had been meeting practically round-the-clock since the takeover, recommended establishing the Black studies program and implementing some of the other demands. The negotiations were tense as we worked out the details. Knight struck me as a decent guy who was genuinely trying to figure out the right thing to do under tremendous pressure. He was in a tough

position, though I didn't care much about that then. I was on one side
hollering at him, while powerful alumni, the university's board, and
even the governor were on the other end, pressing him not to negotiate. His entire campus was in turmoil. He easily could have said, "To
hell with y'all" and found tremendous support from a southern white
community that largely wanted all of the 1960s protests and protesters to go away. But he didn't. He stayed at the table, he listened, and
he was reasonable. When we finally emerged from the meeting three
hours later, we had worked out a tentative agreement to make Duke
the first university in the South to offer a Black Studies Department.

The next day, Knight and I were supposed to stand together at a
press conference announcing the agreement, but life took a sudden,
unexpected turn for me. Viola, who was pregnant with our second
child, went into premature labor. I rushed her to Lincoln Hospital,
which served Durham's Black population, and she gave birth the same
day, February 16, 1969, to our son, Malcolm Marcus Lamar (whose
name reflects those of my two heroes, Malcolm X and Marcus Garvey,
and my middle name). As soon as he was born, the nurses whisked
him away and began preparing him to be placed in an incubator.
The first time I saw him was through the window of the Neonatal
Intensive Care Unit. His mother and I couldn't even hold him. I had
never seen a baby so small. Tiny wires protruded from all over his little
body, and he looked so fragile. Something obviously was wrong. I just
stood there staring at my son, wondering whether he would survive,
and the hurt and fear were like nothing I'd ever felt. Our doctor, who
was Black, confirmed our suspicions that Malcolm's premature birth
had caused serious complications. He was diagnosed with hyaline
membrane disease, a respiratory condition that occurs in newborns,
particularly those who are premature. The condition, now called respiratory distress syndrome, is caused when a newborn's lungs aren't fully
developed. It is the leading cause of death in preterm infants. In 1963,
just six years earlier, the infant son of President and Mrs. Kennedy
had died of the same condition two days after his premature birth.
Our doctor tried to prepare us for the real possibility that our son
might not survive. But there was hope, he said. We were near a hospital that had the best facilities and expertise in the southeastern region
to treat babies with the condition: Duke University. I was speechless.
I had spent the week protesting institutional racism at the one place
I now needed to save my son's life. Viola and I agreed for the baby to

be transferred to Duke. As my wife recuperated at Lincoln, I mostly stayed at Duke with the baby and watched as the medical team took care of him. They gave our son the highest level of medical care, which ultimately saved his life. Such are the contradictions of institutional racism—that even in an environment where individuals are capable of seeing the humanity of others and treating them without regard to race, there may be policies and practices at the institutional level that make it difficult for members of a minority group to thrive in that organization. During the month while my son was hospitalized, I sometimes left him to help the students negotiate the terms of the agreement for the Black Studies program at Duke. I was on campus so much that a newspaper article noted—facetiously, I think—that I must have been sleeping on the grounds of the university at night. Actually, I was! I slept in the hallway outside the neonatal intensive care unit, where baby Malcolm was kept.

Within a month of the agreement, talks broke down between the Black students and a faculty committee appointed to help plan the new Black Studies program. Knight had promised that the students would play a major role in developing the curriculum. The students assumed that meant they would be involved with creating a curriculum from scratch, but they were stunned when the committee showed up at a meeting with a fully outlined plan. The students had no interest in just being a rubber stamp. The relationship between the two sides dissolved even further when they could not reach a consensus on the amount of student representation on a committee that would supervise hiring and implementation of the Black Studies program. Meanwhile, during my regular interactions with the students, someone threw out an idea: What if we started our own university, an institution that we controlled and operated for our community? We could teach what we wanted, hire who we wanted, and become an invaluable resource in the community. And just like that, the seed was planted. The more I thought about it, the more sense it made, and I promised the students I would explore the possibilities. I turned to Nathan, my boss at the Foundation, who thought the concept was significant enough that I could spend time on the job developing it. The Foundation's board awarded a $14,300 grant toward the effort.

Still, the controversy with Congressman Gardner wasn't going away. He wrote a letter to Sargent Shriver, then head of the federal Office of Economic Opportunity, calling for my suspension, as well as a suspension of federal funds to the Foundation. When Nathan refused, federal officials stepped up the pressure. Word trickled down that, unless the Foundation got rid of me, it would not receive a grant that had been requested to start a promising economic development project, called United Durham, Inc. I didn't want to see such a worthwhile community project get caught up in politics, and so I resigned. I knew I was leaving my position at the Foundation in capable hands because Nathan chose my good friend and colleague, Jim Lee, to replace me. Jim had worked directly under me at the Foundation, and I'd found him to be a deep thinker who was committed to the organization's vision and mission. By early March 1969, I was working full-time on establishing Malcolm X Liberation University.

Black students continued trying to work out their issues with Duke, but when a final attempt to resolve the matter failed on March 10, about forty of the Black students pledged to withdraw from the university.

"We will put an end to the constant destruction of our minds and humanity," Chuck, the student leader, said to the crowd that rallied outside a campus auditorium in support of the Black students. He then announced that the students were working to establish their own school, which would become known as Malcolm X Liberation University. The name at once invoked the memory of the man whose message of self-love and awareness had changed my life, and it harkened back to the homemade sign the students had made during their takeover of the Allen building. But mostly, it encapsulated the hope that this place would be different, that it would be an institution where higher learning was relevant to the lives of Black people.

That night, there was a long torchlight procession from the university to Five Points Park in downtown Durham. Black students led the way, followed by supportive white students and faculty. I led hundreds of community members in a separate procession and met the student group at the Five Points intersection. From there, we all marched together to St. Joseph's A.M.E. Church for a rally. The procession was intended to be symbolic: The Black students were in essence returning home to their community with the support of their white peers from Duke. It was an historic moment. Then, the hard work of building an institution began.

With Black and white students from Duke University and community
supporters in a symbolic march to Five Points Park in Durham.

6

REVOLUTION

Everything about Malcolm X Liberation University was defiant, even my new title: H.N.I.C., Head Nigger In Charge. The phrase was a kind of inside joke among Black folks. So, those of us who came together for a three-day retreat in May 1969 to formally organize the university figured such designation for me would be appropriately irreverent. It was our way of validating our vernacular and saying we didn't really give a damn what anybody else thought of us.

"I don't care what they write about me," I told a crowd gathered for a community meeting in Durham later that summer. "I don't care what cartoons they draw. I don't care if they think I'm violent. I don't care if they know that I own a rifle. The only thing I care about is you."

By the time I delivered that speech, I was on the road regularly, trying to make the case for an independent Black university that would be controlled totally by us. I was also trying to generate much-needed moral and financial support, and my title at times made that difficult. Within a few months, my title evolved to Mwalimu, which means "teacher" in Swahili. It was more reflective of the university's serious mission and the deep connection we felt to Africa. We weren't just Black revolutionaries. We saw ourselves as Pan-Africanists, part of a global community of people of African descent around the world who also were fighting for their liberation from white oppressors. And the university's mission, as described in our organizing documents, was to produce "scholars and workers totally committed to the liberation of all African people throughout the Diaspora."

I had sought guidance and feedback from every segment of the community on how to structure the new university. My advisors included community leaders and residents, as well as intellectuals and academic scholars from all over the country. Many of us came together on May 2,

1969, for a three-day work retreat in Bricks, North Carolina. Among the participants was Cleve Sellers, who had become an instructor at Cornell University after his wrongful arrest in the Orangeburg massacre. Cleve was well connected, had good ideas, and knew a lot about how to create organizations. Despite all that he had been through, he was level-headed and had a calming influence on me. If he told me he was going to do something, I knew I could rely on him to do just that. He was very organized and extremely helpful throughout the process.

Cleve also had invited a super smart sister named Faye Edwards, who was the student activities coordinator at Cornell. They both came to the retreat on the heels of a highly-publicized campus uprising by Black students on the campus of Cornell. The Black students had taken over the Willard Straight Hall student union to protest the university's unfair discipline of three fellow Black students, an anonymous cross-burning incident on campus, and the administration's slow progress in developing a Black Studies program. When the Black students emerged from the building after a compromise thirty-six hours later, many of them were carrying rifles, and one of their spokesmen, Eric Evans, wore a bandolier full of bullets strapped across his chest. The students had smuggled guns into the building to protect themselves after a group of white fraternity brothers stormed the hall in an unsuccessful attempt to evict the protesters. The image of Eric with that band of bullets across his chest and his head and rifle held high shocked the nation, and an Associated Press photo of the moment won journalism's highest honor, the Pulitzer Prize. But the event left the campus deeply divided over how the Black students should be disciplined. Faye had worked closely with the Black students and was sympathetic to them. She would come to play a key role in developing MXLU and eventually left her job at Cornell and moved from Ithaca, New York, to Durham to immerse herself in our mission. Faye, who later married fellow Milwaukeean and journalist friend Milton Coleman, worked tirelessly to ensure that our grand ideas for MXLU became a reality.

Faye and Cleve were among the eleven people elected during the retreat to serve on an interim operating committee that would be responsible for developing policy and procedures, overseeing the curriculum development, and recruiting and screening the first faculty members and students. A few college students were also elected to the committee, including Duke University student Bertie Howard and a brother named Nelson Johnson, vice president of the student body at North Carolina Agricultural and Technical State University in Greensboro. Nelson had led some massive student protests on the North Carolina A&T campus and really impressed me with his relentless pursuit of social justice. Duke student leader Chuck Hopkins was named to a smaller task force with Bertie and Faye to take care of whatever administrative duties were needed to get the university up and running.

There was no playbook for what we were trying to do: create from scratch a revolutionary Black university with a Pan-African mission. It was an unbelievably difficult but exciting task. Our ideas began to take shape during the retreat as we laid out the official five goals and objectives for the university:

1) To respond to the needs of the Black community and provide an ideological and practical methodology for meeting the physical, social, psychological, economical, and cultural needs of Black people.

2) To analyze existing political systems and institutions of colonizing societies, and how they relate to and influence Black people.

3) To develop a total understanding of the relationship between Black people in this country and the whole Pan-African liberation struggle and to establish a Black Revolutionary ideology and positive self-awareness for Black people.

4) To be a real alternative for those seeking liberation from the misconception of an institutionalized racist education.

5) To seek accreditation from the Black community.

Those of us planning MXLU were determined to set it apart from the traditional historically Black colleges and universities, which seemed to us at the time just carbon copies of their white counterparts. So, in addition to my nontraditional title, we agreed to call our faculty and staff "resource people," and to admit anyone who accepted our goals and objectives. We agreed that the university's operational structure would include a head governing body, called the "Council of Elders." In addition to me, other top staff members included: Jim Lee, my colleague at the Foundation for Community Development, as Director of Operations; Faye as Curriculum Developer; and a hard-working brother named Frank Williams as Field Representative.

The plans called for attracting a minimum of one hundred students from a variety of sources: withdrawals from white colleges, students dismissed from Black colleges because of their politics, grassroots leaders, embassies, returning veterans, and more. We wouldn't be asking for diplomas or transcripts, which was bound to draw potential students with a range of academic and maturity levels. The only requirement was that they take a full load of courses and attend every class. Tuition was set at a minimum of $300 (more for those who could pay more), and we hoped to be able to offer financial assistance. The big question was money. Would we be able to raise enough to carry out our ambitious agenda?

The retreat participants made clear that my primary role was to continue traveling the country, telling the story of Malcolm X Liberation University, and, of course, raising money. I tried to do just that. Often, as I spoke about how white people had mistreated my people in this country, my words reflected my rage and frustration. But even then, I never believed that *all* white people are racist. I knew better. Some of the people I trusted and respected most in the world were white. People like Doug Irwin, "Rooms," my college roommate, and his wife, Judy, who never turned their backs on me or stopped worrying about me, even when they didn't completely understand my anger or my work.

One time when I made a trip home to Milwaukee to raise money for the university, Doug and Judy came to hear me speak. As I stood in the pulpit in my dashiki and 'fro, I looked and sounded radically different than the clean-cut guy from my Carroll days. I talked passionately about how white folks had wronged my people historically and how Malcolm X Liberation University would help to create a new reality for us. All the while, my two white friends sat in the front row. One thing I've never done is temper my message when white people are in the room. The way I see it, if you're not racist, I'm not talking about you. Doug and Judy knew that. After my speech, Doug joined me at my mother's house, where we reminisced, as always, and my grandmother fed us pie and ice cream. Soon, I was on the road again, making the case for MXLU.

We projected an initial operating budget of $378,375, most of which ($163,000) would be used to hire the twelve resource people at a yearly salary of $10,000 each, three cooks for a total of $23,000, a custodian, and part-time business manager. But, according to a financial report dated July 17, 1969, we had only $850 in the bank, which had come primarily from individual and private donations. The financial report noted, though, that we were expecting some large grants from religious organizations.

Later that month, the national Episcopal Church came through, offering us a lifeline with an emergency award of $15,000. It was the first of a two-part grant totaling $45,000, awarded by the church's General Convention Special Program, which had been established to address poverty and racial injustice. The program's director, Leon Modeste, was responsible for administering $9 million earmarked for that purpose. I will be forever grateful to Leon and two of his staff members— civil rights activist Viola Plummer, who became a lifelong friend and trusted fellow warrior, and Herb Callender, former chairman of the Bronx chapter of the Congress of Racial Equality. They courageously shepherded the grants through the church's process. It took courage, because anything with my name attached to it became controversial. The approval process included a review by the Episcopal Diocese of North Carolina, which found our proposal within the parameters of the program and signed off on it. I was also summoned to New York to testify and answer questions before a committee appointed by the national Episcopal Church's presiding bishop. The grants were approved, and we received the remaining $30,000. But that was hardly the end of the story.

When Bishop Thomas A. Fraser, who headed the North Carolina Diocese, made an announcement about the grants on October 13, 1969, many of his local congregants went berserk. They complained bitterly on the pages of the local newspaper, questioning whether the university would teach violence and why the Episcopal Church would support a non-Christian entity. Members threatened to withhold financial contributions from the church and apparently did so in staggering numbers. Donations to the Episcopal Church dropped so severely from North Carolina and other Southern dioceses that some of the church's social programs were cut or scaled back, and new rules were implemented to restrict how future church funds could be distributed.

It's a shame that the fear of MXLU was that pervasive, but I didn't spend much time back then thinking about the disruption inside the Episcopal Church. I'd come to accept controversy as a way of life for me because of the work I was doing. Therefore, I couldn't allow myself to be sidetracked by feelings of hurt or disappointment based on the reaction I received from other folks. I was singularly focused on getting the university open, and the only way I knew to do that was to look constantly ahead to the next day, the next dollar. But the pressure was so great that I couldn't even look too far into the future. As far as I was concerned, the next day *was* the future.

While we worked on opening full-scale, MXLU had begun offering weekend and after-school classes at a local theater beginning in March and continuing throughout the summer, and many Duke and North Carolina College students and members of the community participated. The classes included the study of Malcolm X, African history, community organizing, and Swahili language.

In September 1969, just one month before the university's scheduled opening, we finally found a building to house our operations. It was an abandoned warehouse in the heart of Hayti at 426-428 East Pettigrew Street, located in the same block as my old office at Operation Breakthrough. The beauty of it was that the community really rallied around us to rehab that old place into a comfortable, functional school building. Brothers I'd met in the pool hall and others they knew used their skills in carpentry, plumbing, and construction to create classrooms, administrative offices, a library, and even science labs. We built a huge library with books that had been "liberated" from some of the finest universities in the country. For months, we received the book donations anonymously through the mail. We painted the exterior of the building in the colors of the Pan-African flag, red, black, and green. Instead of dormitories, we leased five houses, which we furnished to accommodate fifteen students each. The students would have to take care of their own housekeeping. Since we had no cafeteria, we arranged for two neighborhood restaurants to prepare the students' meals (though, in keeping with the times, the female students initially were required to do the bulk of the cooking).

Not all Black folks were supportive of the university; nor did I expect them to be. Black people's opinions have always varied as much as the hues of our skin, and never was that more apparent than in the 1960s and '70s movements for change. Given the way Dr. King is revered today, you would think that every Black person under the sun supported him. These days, you never hear about the Black folks who met him at the airport in Mobile, Alabama, and told him to go home because their white folks were treating them just fine. And when he opposed the Vietnam War and announced his Poor People's Campaign, the critics' voices became even more strident. Likewise, from the moment

Willie Ricks and Stokely Carmichael (later known as Kwame Toure) started talking about Black Power, Black folks were first to condemn them. You don't start a movement for change by trying to figure out how people are going to *feel* about it. You make a decision to fight because you believe that what you're fighting for is right, and you are willing to take the weight that comes with that decision. So, I eventually learned not to let criticism of me or my work bother me. In some cases, I'd hold civil conversations behind closed doors with some of the same people who had just blasted me in public the day before. We all had our roles to play. I understood that. But I'm willing to bet the public criticism of me and MXLU was tempered because of the working relationships I tried to maintain with my people, whether or not they outwardly supported me. There were times, though, when I felt it necessary to strike back.

Two weeks before MXLU was scheduled to open, Kelley M. Alexander, president of the North Carolina chapter of the NAACP, stood before a captive audience at the organization's state convention in Durham and attacked the university during his keynote address. He hadn't even bothered to talk to us about what we were trying to do, yet he stood there and claimed that the proponents of separatism were just afraid of being unable to compete in an integrated society. Segregation, he said, always hurt Black people, as if anything all Black was automatically all bad. "I'm not going to debate on whether you should go to a Malcolm X University or to any other kind of university," he said. "But I'm saying to you that if you're going to be a bookkeeper or an accountant, you had better go where you can learn to be a bookkeeper or an accountant. I want you to know that when you get out in this world, they're not going to ask you if you can speak Swahili or not."

The white press, of course, ate that stuff up. The next night, a group of about twenty of us from the university disrupted the NAACP's Freedom Tribute banquet when we showed up wearing our Malcolm X sweatshirts. We didn't cause a big ruckus. We just stood there silently, proudly, to make a point: We didn't give a damn what he or anyone else thought of us. And then, we left.

Finally, on October 25, 1969, about 3,000 people—students, staff, and supporters of Malcolm X Liberation University—gathered outside our Pettigrew Street headquarters to celebrate the grand opening. We had accomplished what we'd set out to do, and the moment felt victorious. What made the day even more special was that our keynote speaker was Betty Shabazz, the widow of the university's namesake. Malcolm had inspired the man I'd become, and having his wife there was about as close as I could get to feeling his presence. Her message was right on point as she talked about the importance of Black unity and our people coming together to build a Black nation. At one point during the ceremony, a train sitting on the railroad tracks behind our building began sounding a loud bell, disrupting our service. When the bell sounded repeatedly, a small group rushed to the tracks to try to get the conductor's attention, but to no avail. I will never forget the image of my friend and former colleague, Kwame McDonald, climbing atop that train and grabbing part of the bell to stop the clanging. Some members of the crowd, suspicious that the bell incident was an intentional disruption of our celebration, began pitching rocks at the train. When the noise finally stopped, we resumed the program and enjoyed a memorable, meaningful day.

Classes began on Monday, October 27, with fifty-one students from seventeen states and varying backgrounds. It had become clear early in the process that we wouldn't be able to rely heavily on the students who had pledged to withdraw from Duke for our enrollment. Though forty-eight of the students who participated in the takeover were found guilty of violating Duke's policy restricting pickets, they were placed on probation, instead of being expelled. Of the forty-two Duke University students who said they would withdraw from Duke, only fourteen actually did. None that I can recall enrolled at MXLU. Most of them, including Chuck Hopkins, returned to Duke. Bertie did not officially withdraw from Duke but quit attending classes. She did not officially enroll at MXLU either, but she attended classes and played a number of roles to help in the development of the university.

Nevertheless, our student body was an interesting mix of college and high school students of all ages, most of whom had been engaged in the liberation struggle in some way. At least five Black students and one Puerto Rican who had been involved in the 1969 protest at Cornell, including leaders Eric Evans and Edward Whitfield, withdrew and came to Malcolm X as "resource people." Another group came from an Arkansas high school from which they had been expelled after walking out to protest discrimination. Three or four students had come from Wisconsin State University–Oshkosh (now the University of Wisconsin Oshkosh), and one even hailed from Nigeria.

The ages of our students ranged from fifteen- and sixteen-year-old high school dropouts to a woman named Queenie, who was retired.

Like our students, the resource people came with a range of experience and academic credentials. Some had PhDs, and others barely had a high school education, but all were skilled in ways that we considered important to our students. They included some part-timers, such as scholar Leon Moore, a phenomenal expert on independent African civilization and the founder of the famed Chad School, a private school in inner-city Newark with a Black-centered curriculum that helped its mostly poor student body outperform their public school peers academically. He'd travel to the university each week from New Jersey, leaving on Sunday and staying through Tuesday.

At MXLU, the curriculum strongly reflected our goal: to train students who would be willing to go to Africa and help those nations obtain their independence and rebuild. Our program was divided into two parts. The plans called for students first to spend ten months learning about Nation Building through an historical-cultural study of African people, covering the following subjects: Independent African Civilization, Slavery, Neo-Colonialism, Colonialism, and the Independent African World. Students also would study an African language (Swahili, Hausa, or Yoruba) and take courses in physical development. Then, students and staff would travel to Africa for two months to get a close-up, real-life view of what they had learned. When they returned to the states, the students would move into Areas of Concentration, which would include technical training in the twelve jobs that we believed were most needed to sustain a Black nation: food scientists, tailors, architects, engineers, medics, cadre leaders, communications technicians, physical developers, teachers, Black expressionists, administrators, and linguists. The technical training would last up to ten months, followed by internships in the Black community where students would get to use those skills. While we carried out many of those plans, some proved to be too ambitious for our budget.

During the first year, we opened a daycare center, named the Betty Shabazz Early Education Center in honor of Malcolm X's widow. Located in the basement of my old office at Operation Breakthrough, the center had seventeen students, ages three to five, including my daughter, Kelli. It was run by a full-time director and staff member, and a cadre of part-time workers and volunteers, including my wife, Viola.

Most of us at MXLU felt like we were part of something with a purpose greater than each of us individually. We tried to create a truly democratic atmosphere, where the opinions of students and resource people were equally valued, and the rules of behavior were clearly spelled out in a multi-page document. The guidelines prohibited anything that would shed a bad light on the university, such as engaging in unprovoked violence, drinking, doing drugs, or stealing from other African people. Engaging in intimate relationships with white people also was prohibited. When one of the rules was broken, we'd sometimes have nightmarishly long meetings to discuss and resolve the incident. Once, somebody took another person's food out of the refrigerator without asking, and there we were, sitting around for hours, trying to hash it out. But the appointed twelve-member Indaba Council, selected randomly on a rotating basis every term, had the last say on disciplinary matters. And their deliberations and decisions were kept confidential.

Even though trying to keep the university afloat was itself more than a full-time job, I still felt compelled to stay involved in community issues, particularly if poor Black people needed help. When cafeteria workers at the University of North Carolina went on strike in November 1969 to demand better pay and working conditions, it was the perfect opportunity to provide our students the kind of real-world education that I believed was important. A group of us traveled to Chapel Hill to join the two hundred fifty or so striking workers on campus, and within fifteen minutes of my arrival, I was under arrest. Campus police had been waiting for me, and as soon as I walked up, a group of my students who had gotten there a bit earlier surrounded me in a kind of protective posture with bricks in their hands. An officer approached and ordered the students to put down the bricks. Harsh words were exchanged, but the students complied. The same officer ordered us off campus, but we couldn't leave immediately because we were waiting for our buses. Carloads of officers rushed to the scene and began making arrests. Two of my students, ages eighteen and nineteen, and I were charged with rioting, disorderly conduct, and failure to disperse. The officers also put us under a temporary restraining order, banning us from the campus—and essentially all of Chapel Hill, since the university took up most of the town. During a trial three months later, a judge dismissed the charges.

A short time later, I would be charged and acquitted once more after showing up to support four Black students who attempted to take over Belmont Abbey College, located just outside Charlotte. I'd been invited to speak at the school for a Black History program when a small group of students told me afterward that they were planning to take over a building. Concerned for their safety, I returned the next day to check on them and was charged with trespassing. The authorities also dug up an old state law and charged me with cursing on a public highway. Both charges were ridiculous. Where I stood on campus was yards from a public highway, but the authorities produced some white witnesses who said they were standing on the highway and heard me curse. A judge threw out that charge right away, and I was found innocent of the other when the priests testified that I had been invited to the campus.

Meanwhile, trying to keep the doors of MXLU open continued to be a struggle. The lack of money was a constant issue. In addition to the $45,000 from the Episcopal Church and $14,300 from the Foundation for Community Development, small individual and group donations trickled in from my speaking engagements. But they were not nearly enough to sustain the university even through the next year. In April 1970, we received our second-largest grant, $35,000 from Cummins Engine Foundation. The money had some strings attached, basically forbidding any of the funds from being used to influence the legislative process, register voters, or pay for administrative travel. But that wasn't a problem because I had greatly cut back on voter registration and other political activities after leaving the Foundation for Community Development.

Unfortunately, we at the university never raised anywhere near the kind of money we had projected in our budget, which meant things were often in flux. We had to cut salaries, reduce the number of paid staff, and reduce other expenditures. We also were never able to carry out some of the more costly aspects of our planned curriculum, like sending the students to Africa. We simply made do the best we could.

By the spring of 1970, enrollment at the university had dropped to twenty students. Some of them had been expelled for disciplinary reasons, and others just couldn't cope with the academic demands, or they lacked overall maturity. But the academic programs were functioning fairly well, given our budgetary restrictions. As with any new institution, we experienced growing pains, which was my main reason for trying to control the access of the media to our school. I just didn't trust the mainstream white press to report on us fairly, though we did at various intervals allow reporters to visit and conduct interviews. One of the areas that was a perennial problem was recruiting enough resource people to cover our course offerings. Therefore, we had to adjust our curriculum for the following year to reflect not just our budget but also our staff capabilities. To address that issue, we decided to use third-year students as instructors, and some of the core first-year courses changed.

On May 1, 1970, our Council of Elders met to continue planning our future, and among the items on our agenda was the possibility of relocating the university to Greensboro. We'd known from the beginning, when the university set up shop in the Pettigrew Street warehouse, that our time there was just temporary. The city had long been planning to cut through that area with a new expressway and tear down everything in its path. While the timing of those plans still seemed uncertain, our building in Durham seemed too small for our expansion plans the following year. Plus, it would have been impossible to find an existing building that was spacious enough in Durham's Black community.

Other factors also hastened our plans to move: Greensboro seemed to offer a more favorable political climate and a strong base of support, vocally, financially, and behind the scenes. We had received a warm welcome during an exploratory trip earlier that year. The move also would put us closer to North Carolina A&T and the technical assistance it could provide. Also, there was a feeling among some at the university that my strong ties to Durham and the university's resulting involvement in so many local issues pulled us away from our primary mission: training students to help rebuild an independent Africa. Through Cleve, I'd met some of the country's leading Black Power advocates, including Stokely Carmichael and Willie Ricks, who were steering the movement increasingly toward a Pan-African agenda. A move to Greensboro seemed to offer a chance to further those goals and give us adequate space to expand our course offerings.

The initial site that we considered leasing needed extensive renovation, and it was tied up in a separate court battle over ownership. But there were two more remote sites that seemed promising: King's Mountain, fifty-two acres of land with three or four buildings, located near Charlotte, and the Palmer Memorial Institute, a Black college preparatory school with a rich history dating back to 1902. The school, which was bankrupt and deeply in debt, sat on about three hundred acres just outside Greensboro in a town called Sedalia. With existing classroom space and dormitories and acres of farmland, the property had boundless potential. We would be able to move our farming cooperative on site, as well as housing for the students. I even envisioned a conference center that could draw all types of Black organizations and also produce revenue. An official at the school had indicated to me that the university likely would be able to work out an arrangement to lease or buy the property. But not everyone on the Council of Elders supported the move. Nathan Garrett, my old supervisor and friend, warned that a move so soon could signal instability and make it even more difficult to secure much-needed additional financing. He also advised that the university was not in a solid enough financial position to consider either of the larger properties. We agreed to table the matter for further evaluation.

I also sought the Council's support for a month-long trip to two West African countries, Guinea and Gambia. I had hoped to forge a connection between the countries and the university, gain a deeper understanding of Pan-Africanism and pave the way for future student visits there. But when the trip didn't work out, movement contacts suggested I visit Guyana, a Caribbean country with people of African descent who had just won their independence from the United Kingdom in 1966. The trip, set to begin July 26, 1970, would be my first time traveling outside of the United States. Stokely promised to arrange some contacts, but they never materialized. Nevertheless, I managed to make some connections on my own and spent much of my trip with Eusi Kwayana (formerly Sydney King), a revolutionary and intellectual who was revered among the country's poor. I had deep respect for him and spent many hours learning from him about Guyana's rich struggle for independence and the people's efforts to rebuild as a free nation. The whole mission of Pan-Africanism was no longer an abstraction. I'd never even heard of Guyana before planning the trip, but there I was, among people who looked like me, trying to develop a life for themselves in the dense, untouched forests known as the bush. I spent about a week with them there, chopping trees and clearing out what would become a new village. It was an enlightening trip.

At some point, the university's Council of Elders reconsidered the move to Greensboro and decided to pursue it. Soon after I returned from Guyana in August 1970, the Elders held a press conference in Greensboro to confirm that MXLU would be moving there and that classes would begin in about two months. I was very hopeful when a group of local ministers and other community leaders showed up at the press conference to support us and welcome us to town.

Viola and I then packed our belongings and headed with Kelli and Malcolm to make a new home in Greensboro. The move went smoothly for both my family and the university.

On October 5, 1970, MXLU opened in a building at 708 Asheboro Street with sixty students, ranging in ages from sixteen to twenty-two. In addition to their regular studies, our students created and operated a farm just outside the city, where we raised chickens and tended a small vegetable garden. It was great exposure to farming for the students, who also set up a darkroom and print shop. We produced all of our booklets, brochures, leaflets, posters, and other promotional materials in-house. Everyone had to learn a skill, including the resource people. I learned how to do some plumbing, specifically how to replace toilets.

The surrounding community was important to our mission, and we occasionally invited our neighbors onto campus for festivals or evening classes. On New Year's Eve, instead of going out to party and drink, the students and staff who remained in the area gathered at the university for a ceremony that included discussing what we would do for the community in the coming year. At the first ceremony, our Nigerian brother helped to give fellow students and resource people African names. The new names chosen for me were Owusu ,which I was told meant "one who clears the way for others," and Sadaukai, "one who gathers strength from his ancestors to lead his people." There are still people today who do not know me as Howard Fuller. To them, I remain Owusu, and the name continues to be meaningful and important to me. My wife's name was changed to Rabia; Kelli became Y'ar Armashi Mayamuna; and Malcolm was named Kwesi.

The university reopened the Betty Shabazz Early Childhood Education Center, and Rabia was selected to take over as director. The position worked out well, enabling her to be close to our children and more actively involved in the movement and my work. Our family continued to grow, and on July 24, 1971, Rabia and I were blessed with our third child, another girl. She, too, was born prematurely and had to stay in the hospital until she gained enough weight to be brought home. But she had none of the serious health issues that Malcolm had suffered. Rabia and I wanted to give the new baby an African name, and we chose Kumba (the name bestowed on the second daughter in some parts of Africa) Miata.

As usual, though, work continued to pull me in many different directions. The Council had agreed to pursue purchasing the Palmer Institute, and negotiations were heating up. We made an offer to buy the school. With no other offers forthcoming, the Palmer board agreed to the sale, but when the word leaked that MXLU would take over the space, certain people in the community revolted. The controversy caught me off guard, but I shouldn't have been surprised. The rumor mill had been churning relentlessly, spreading lies that we were planning to open an armed militia camp. A Palmer board member even resigned in protest of the sale. The board's attorney was able to nullify it, though, because the vote on the property had lacked the necessary quorum. Such reaction was disappointing, though certainly not new or surprising to me. The talks continued, and some of the university's Elders met with the Palmer board, including renowned scholar Dr. Benjamin E. Mays, who had retired as president of Morehouse College in 1967 after twenty-seven years. It was a calm, thoughtful session, but in the end the pressure from the surrounding community against selling the campus to a school so different than the one before it was just too great to overcome. By the time our Council of Elders formally withdrew our offer on September 3, I had left for another foreign trip—this time to Africa, where I was getting an entirely different kind of education.

I'd been invited to participate with a group of ministers in a conference in Dar es Salaam, Tanzania, to discuss independent education for African people. But a surprising chain of events would give me a closer-than-anticipated look inside the African independence revolution. And it would begin to change much of what I'd come to believe about the goals of Black Americans in the Pan-African movement. It would also cause me to rethink the mission of my beloved Malcolm X Liberation University.

Speaking at a college in North Carolina in the late 1960s.

Ben Ruffin leading a demonstration by United Organizations for Community Improvement (JOCI).

The MXLU building in Durham.

Speaking at the opening ceremony of MXLU.

Leon Moore, from Chad School in Newark, teaching a class at MXLU.

MXLU student learning a skill, as required by the curriculum.

One of the many talented MXLU faculty members.

With Cleve Sellers and Kwame Toure (Stokely Carmichael) during the celebration dinner for MXLU moving to Greensboro.

With Kwame Toure (Stokely Carmichael),
during the dinner to celebrate MXLU moving to Greensboro.

MXLU Building in Greensboro.

7

HANGING WITH FREEDOM
FIGHTERS

I left New York on August 18, 1971, headed for Africa. The conference that I was participating in had been called by the National Committee of Black Churchmen (NCBC) to coordinate the efforts of Black clergy in the United States and their counterparts throughout the African continent. I was traveling with a group that included Ron Daniels, a fellow Pan-Africanist, whose organization, Freedom Inc., was doing some interesting things in Youngstown, Ohio, to spur economic development among our people. He had been asked to talk about those efforts. I had been invited to discuss the building of Malcolm X Liberation University. The group included about two dozen NCBC delegates and Black staff members of various churches.

After a one-day stopover in London, we flew first to Nairobi, Kenya, where I was struck immediately by the two-faced dualities of African independence. In the city, there were plush, tall buildings (the tallest being the newly completed Hilton Hotel), complemented by a flood of other modern structures, white settlers, tourists, and even Playboy magazines. In a lot of ways, there was actually very little difference between Nairobi and the New York I had just left. The same products, the same publications, the same people, the same values. But later, when we visited the Mathari Valley, a large settlement only a few miles from the center of Nairobi, the harshest truths came forth. The grandeur and plushness that was Nairobi suddenly vanished. There were no tall buildings, towering hotels, or sun-soaking tourists. Instead, there were acres and acres of shacks made of cardboard, salvaged crate wood, and mud. These were not even the more soundly built mud homes common in Africa, where the mud is packed on log frames. Instead, these homes were made from mud packed on more mud. It rained quite frequently, and the mud huts that hadn't already collapsed were well on the road to deterioration. And everywhere I looked I saw shabbily-dressed brothers and sisters, bent over and crippled by disease, children with the bloated stomachs of malnutrition, and a people generally marked by the hard scars of survival in a condemned place.

How could this be? Kenya was hailed by many as a leader on the African continent. It was easy to see why when visiting certain parts of Nairobi, her capital city. But the Mathari Valley was an entirely different story. I'd seen places in rural North Carolina that were miserable, places like Wadesboro and Halifax counties, where Black people lived in company towns in 1965 with no running water, no bathrooms, no windows, no nothing. I had seen the wretched lot of Florida citrus workers in migrant camps and also the Black ghettos of Harlem, Brooklyn, Newark, Gary, and Chicago's West side. Yet here in the Mathari Valley were some of the worst conditions I'd ever seen. What made this even more deplorable was that this was a Black country, with a Black head of state and a Black government. What difference had the flag of independence made in the lives of the poor people of the Mathari Valley? This question would haunt me for the rest of my trip.

Tanzania was different. Its Socialist doctrine was apparent in many ways, even in its capital city, Dar es Salaam. Cities in Africa were generally the most stubborn retainers of European thoughts, ideas, and values. The minority of people in African countries live in such urban settings, and they are mostly those who have been educated and generally more acculturated. Dar was no exception, for, contrary to some notions spread about its total revolutionary nature, it, too, had some remaining vestiges of European occupation. Still, it was vastly different from Nairobi, and when you considered its contradictions, you saw them not as indicators that Tanzania was not really revolutionary, but rather that, despite everything revolutionary the government was doing, deep changes had not come overnight. Even in one of Africa's most revolutionary states, the battle was still going on for the creation of a new Africa. And perhaps what made Tanzania more hopeful was the fact that she was continuing to fight, while many others on the continent had apparently called it quits after gaining political independence from the white man.

It had never been my intention while traveling in Africa to assume a tourist mentality. Instead, I had planned to gather as much firsthand information as I could about the struggle on the continent. Of particular interest to me was the situation among various liberation groups in Southern Africa. In just about every contested zone on the continent, there were at least two or more organizations vying for support in the struggle to overthrow white, settler, minority rule. Which ones to recognize, based on objective decisions and firsthand information, was a fundamental question for all Pan-Africanists. Thus, I was a most attentive listener during the conference presentations by at least six liberation group representatives. In search of even more information, I arranged to visit each group's Dar es Salaam office.

At the headquarters for the Mozambique Liberation Front (known as FRELIMO, the acronym for its Portuguese name), I met Joaquim Chissano, the brother in charge. Neither of us could have known back then that fifteen years later he would become the second president of independent Mozambique. All we knew for sure that day in 1971 was that our people were determined to be free from colonial rule and were putting their lives on the line every day for the cause. I told him about Malcolm X Liberation University and the Student Organization for Black Unity (SOBU), a group of Black college students with a Pan-Africanist philosophy. I also told him about potential support from the Interreligious Foundation for Community Organization (IFCO), which I served as a board member. The organization, made up of representatives from various religious denominations, had created a fund to support the liberation movements in southern Africa. My conversation with Chissano focused on how groups such as IFCO could aid in the progress of the liberation movement in Mozambique and other parts of Southern Africa. We agreed that one of the prerequisites was accurate knowledge of the organizations and their programs. He advised me that I could get the most reliable information from visiting various centers of operation, such as his organization's hospital and school at Tunduru in southern Tanzania, near the Mozambique border. If I was interested, he said, there was an opportunity for me to go inside liberated Mozambique.

I learned later that for the past two years a documentary of the Mozambique liberation group had been in the works by two brothers from the United States: Robert Van Lierop, a New York attorney who had abandoned his regular practice in search of ways to aid the liberation movements, and Bob Fletcher, a former member of the Student Nonviolent Coordinating Committee (SNCC), who now did freelance photography. They were to be assisted in the project by an Algerian photojournalist. Visiting the liberated areas of a contested country is usually a privilege, not open to just anyone, but more often than not reserved for members of the international press or representatives of organizations that have contributed significantly to the freedom struggle. Those of us in the United States had generally done little to assist, thus, not surprisingly, few of us had gone in. So, when Chissano informed me that the photojournalist was sick and offered me the opportunity to go in his place, I readily understood the good fortune of being in the right place at the right time. I accepted the invitation without hesitation. He told me little about the journey, other than that it would last about sixteen days, and I was instructed to be discreet with even the little I did know. I didn't tell Rabia because I didn't want to cause any additional worry. Plus, I figured I would be gone just two weeks, back in Tanzania in time to travel home with my group. My wife would be the first to hear all I'd learned when I got home. I may have told my plans to my friend Ron, the brother from Ohio who had traveled as part of our group from the States to Africa, and if so, I'm sure I swore him to secrecy. Then, I set about obtaining the essentials on a list I had been given. I was able to buy, borrow, or get as gifts many of the essential items, including some canned foods, a sleeping bag, a knapsack, blankets, and malaria and water purification pills. One of the items on the list, a pair of safari shoes in my size—I wore a 13—proved impossible to find. So, my buckle-across-the-top dress shoes would have to do. Finally, I stuffed a few notepads and pens in my knapsack to keep a diary and chronicle my journey. Little did I know that I was in for a grueling march of close to four hundred miles.

On the morning of August 27, one of the men from FRELIMO picked me up at the Luther Hotel, where I had been staying. We proceeded directly to the airport and soon left for Songea, a town in southwestern Tanzania. Robert and Bob, the attorney and freelance photographer working on the documentary, were on the flight with me, and we began to discuss the journey that lay before us. I explained that I'd discovered something wrong with one of the two cameras I was carrying. I'd never been a photographer by profession nor even as a hobby, but at MXLU we believed in everyone learning a technical skill. Realizing the value of a visual account of my overseas travels, I'd learned how to use a camera before my first trip to Guyana in the summer of 1970. Both cameras were loaded, one with film for color slides and prints for the school, the other for black and white photos for *The African World*, the newspaper of the Student Organization for Black Unity. I hoped the camera problem was minor.

My camera wasn't my only concern, though. In many ways, I was not really prepared for this trip, either physically or mentally. But I had convinced myself that it was just too important to pass up. It would be invaluable not just in terms of my own learning, but also because of what it would help me explain to others upon my return to the states. As I thought of the great physical demands of the trip, I hoped I would be able to endure the challenge.

About two hours after our departure from Dar, we arrived at the Songea airport. Songea is a restricted area, and so our disembarking from the plane with such a load of photographic equipment was a natural cause for curiosity. We had been told that someone from FRELIMO would meet us at the airfield, but nothing of the sort took place. Instead, Tanzanian police came over to question us, something that was really a cause for concern, especially since we had followed the directives given us in Dar and left our passports behind. Our worries increased when police officers, having helped us unpack our gear, promptly escorted us to their office.

Things took a turn for the better, however, when the inspector at the office welcomed us, and immediately notified FRELIMO of our arrival. We then learned what the problem had been: The telegram informing FRELIMO that we were on the way had arrived a day late. They were expecting us the next day. We left the airport in a Volkswagen bus, followed closely behind by a land rover loaded with our equipment. We drove straight to the FRELIMO compound, where we were greeted by three of the freedom fighters, including Cornelio, who would be our interpreter and constant companion, and the other two guys who would accompany us as far as the border.

The stone house where we were to stay had a long hallway and several rooms, ours being about ten feet on either side, with two beds, a chair, a table, one window, and an empty light socket overhead. FRELIMO rented this house from the Tanzanian government and used it as a resting place for all personnel who passed through the area. We turned on the radio that sat atop a table and picked up some African music coming from Kenya. The voice on the radio spoke in Swahili. From time to time, explained Cornelio, we could expect to hear Voice of America (VOA). Sure enough, we soon heard some Glen Miller-style music, followed by a VOA newscast, reporting on the upcoming elections in South Vietnam, the possibilities for the reunification of Korea, the trial of Captain Ernest Medina (a U.S. Army captain charged with war crimes in the My Lai Massacre during Vietnam), and Senator Edward Kennedy talking about the refugee problem in India and Pakistan. There was nothing on the news about the struggle of Black people in the States.

Cornelio, our interpreter, came across as very knowledgeable. He was about twenty-five years old, usually in good humor, laughing and joking, and he was keenly interested in U.S. news. He already had some awareness of the plight of our people there. His knowledge was sharpened during our first discussion when Robert summed up the condition of Black people in Mississippi as being identical to that of Black people in Mozambique. Cornelio picked up the analogy right away. He asked about prominent Black people in the states—Sonny Liston, Muhammad Ali, and Angela Davis. He surprised me when he initiated conversation about something that had just become known in the states, Daniel Ellsberg and the Pentagon Papers. We also discussed African politics briefly. As a student, Cornelio had gone to secondary school in Tanzania, where he'd learned to speak English. He spoke it almost better than we, and he was also fluent in Spanish, Portuguese, Swahili, and several local Mozambican languages. He had been a soccer player for a time, before being sidelined by injury. He often passed time reading those newsstand magazines that had all the words to popular songs in them. When songs would come over the radio, he would sing along and could recognize the voice and style of various performers, such as James Brown, Otis Redding, Percy Sledge, and others. Thus, his knowledge of English created for him an entertaining pastime and was one of the reasons he knew so much about the conditions of Black people in America. Cornelio had been with FRELIMO six years, and his dedication and commitment were unquestionable. He was very modest about himself, though, when explaining that his regular job was to work in whatever capacity he was most needed. If that meant translation, then he would translate; work in the fields, he worked in the fields; go to the front, he was off to the front. Truly a revolutionary brother.

Shortly after 4 p.m. that day, we had tea, followed by a meal of fish curry (fish, onions, and tomato sauce) over rice, along with lime juice to drink. This was my introduction to the food of Mozambique, something that was to be one of at least a dozen things that would make the most lasting impressions during the visit. The guerrillas, we learned, operated on the policy of eating when you could and when you had food because there might be times when you either would not be able to eat, or there would be no food. And so, at 7:45 p.m., we had another meal, this time corned beef, onions, and tomatoes.

Another of the things that made an initial impression was the hospitality extended to us by the freedom fighters, who were unusually generous, especially given the strain and scarcity that characterize the conditions of war. They welcomed us as their comrades yet treated us as their guests. During the first day with the guerrillas, I got my introduction to some of the living conditions we would have to deal with. In this instance, the bathroom was a hole in a brick floor outside and a faucet near the hole. As we prepared to go to bed that evening, we were told that tomorrow we would begin a 110-mile trip to the border. That was about all we were told, much in the same concise style in which I had been first informed of my trip into Mozambique. It was just my first day with FRELIMO, and already, I wrote in my diary, some things were provoking deep thoughts within me:

> I have already tried to analyze my feelings at this point. It is very difficult. I keep thinking of people in the States and elsewhere who keep referring to the liberation struggles as jive. Yet, here I am on the verge of going into an area where brothers and sisters are waging armed struggle—armed struggle as opposed to verbal struggle. We aren't even in Mozambique, yet the atmosphere of these brothers tells you something important is happening. When you compare that attitude with some of the jive, self-proclaimed "revolutionaries" in Dar and the U.S., it really has an impact.

> I haven't really thought about the possibility of an attack while we are in there, but it is quite possible. Mentally, I am prepared for that (we will see when I get there). This is what we keep talking about. All of a sudden it is no longer talk, but it is reality. I am about to jump over maps, pamphlets, books, lectures, etc. and about to physically be a part of the armed African liberation struggle. It's really deep, and I imagine it will be deeper when we actually set foot in Mozambique.

We arose the next morning around 7 a.m. Despite the fact that Robert and I had talked well into the night, I'd had a good night's sleep. There was news on the radio in English coming from Ethiopia.

After washing up, we had a breakfast of tea and wafers with plum jam and gathered our things together in preparation for the trip to the border. It was a grueling ride in the land rover over a winding, bumpy dirt road. From time to time we passed through small villages or alongside thatch-roof houses made of mud packed on wooden frames. Men and women would be all about working, many of the women with children on their backs or sides. Most of the people were busy working the land, though some of the women were breast feeding small children. I occasionally drifted off to sleep, but whenever we would hit a large bump, my head would crack up against the car, which woke me right on up. After about five-and-a-half hours, we arrived at the camp, a very impressive setting with about fifteen huts in a circular arrangement and a meeting hut in the center. Most served as living quarters, though there were also a couple of large ones for storage purposes. This camp was a staging area, we discovered, and was always manned by a small detachment of troops. Most of those who were there at the time were part of the column that would move out with us. They had been awaiting our arrival for two weeks, the delay having been caused by the late arrival of a shipment of film ordered by Robert and Bob.

Upon arrival, we were warmly greeted by Armando Guebuza, national political commissar for FRELIMO. He had been with Robert and Bob in New York, where he had spent a lot of time in the Black community, and spoke English very well. His command over this camp was obvious from the respect accorded him by others. We were led to our housing, which this time consisted of a two-room hut with a slanted, thatched roof. The hut had two doors and two windows. Each of the rooms was about six feet by ten feet, with single beds on either side. The beds were fashioned from straw set atop wooden pegs stuck in the ground, with other pegs across the top. A single piece of wood nailed to a lone log sticking in the ground provided us with a table. The two men from FRELIMO who ordinarily slept here had given up their space to us.

Shortly after unpacking our gear and taking a quick shower, using a bucket of warm water and a cup, we were invited over to meet with Guebuza and some of the army officers. We were introduced as people from the United States who were supporting the struggle of the Mozambican people against imperialism. As the officers stood in formation, Guebuza, who spoke in Portuguese that was translated for us by Cornelio, emphasized the key role the United States was playing in supporting their "enemy," Portugal. Many of the bombs falling on the people of Mozambique, he pointed out, were manufactured in the United States. Afterward, we were given a detailed explanation of what we would be doing, and each of the officers welcomed us as brothers and comrades.

Guebuza then began to give us an introductory explanation of FRELIMO's analysis of their situation. This was important. I wanted to know just how the Freedom Fighters viewed their struggle: Who was the enemy? What were they fighting for? What were they trying to build? One of the things the guerrilla movements were all too often criticized for was their acceptance of aid from non-African sources. One group of critics dismissed them for accepting assistance from the socialist bloc, while another denounced them for taking help from other European peoples. The first group of critics claimed the guerrillas were merely pawns of the Marxist-Leninists, while the second group saw the freedom fighters as "jive" because they didn't take a hard line of opposition against all whites. Was there any basis in fact for such claims?

FRELIMO had been involved in an armed struggle, and one of the fundamental challenges they had to face was constantly obtaining essential equipment for the continuation of that struggle, foremost among which were arms, ammunition, and humanitarian assistance, Guebuza told us. They had received assistance primarily from China, the Soviet Union, Bulgaria, and Yugoslavia; humanitarian assistance had come from people in Holland and Italy (people, as opposed to governments). The principal assistance from African countries had consistently come from Tanzania and Zambia. Although the guerrillas recognized the common bonds between Africans all over the world, they also placed great stress on the concept of comradeship, or practical mutual assistance. This they accepted from anyone who offered it. Those people were considered comrades.

FRELIMO had been struggling against a system—imperialism—and was not engaged in a racial battle, Guebuza explained. One of the reasons they had emphasized the struggle beyond race was because for some time there had been many Black people in the movement who rallied to the cause seeking only to replace the white man in the same oppressive system. However, it had soon been recognized that liberation would come not by exchanging white faces for Black ones, but rather by replacing the entire Portuguese system with another that eliminated the exploitation of man by man. This meant the crushing of the entire lifestyle and imperialistic structure that had been created by Portuguese capitalism. Guebuza's analysis was brief and introductory, yet it made a lot of sense to me. It certainly seemed from what little I had seen that the Mozambicans were the only ones making the decisions for FRELIMO. It also did not seem as though the country would fall under the control of some external power, other than the people whose daily actions were driving the revolutionary struggle, once it was liberated. So, I came to the conclusion that, until those of us in the United States began to come to Africa to see for ourselves or began to give some kind of assistance, we didn't really even have a right to speak, much less question the ideology of the African people.

The next morning, we got up around 6:20 a.m. and had breakfast, and, at about 8 a.m., Robert, Bob, Cornelio, and I left with Guebuza and four others on what was billed as a "short walk." It turned out to be a ten-mile hike at a pace of about four miles an hour. We followed a trail, climbing a high mountain that rewarded us with a view of the area for some twenty miles around. But on the way back to camp, we crisscrossed through the bush. For most of the way, there was tall grass all around us, but, as we passed through some areas, we noted that the grass had been burned away. That had been a traditional method of clearing the land, but FRELIMO was trying to abolish the practice in Mozambique because it eliminated the cover of the bush and was destructive to the land in the long run. During the walk, there was a great deal of discussion, fortunately in English. Time and again, Guebuza made the point that the struggle was against imperialism, worldwide imperialism. Anyone struggling against imperialism was a friend, he said. I had personally conceived of our struggle in the United States as being against white people, who represented and controlled the forces of imperialism. But there was also no doubt in my analysis that Black people who represented the forces of imperialism had to be fought against, as well. When we returned to the base, I found out that I was a little sore, but not really in too bad shape. The main thing was the shoes; they were really cool for conferences or walking down the concrete steps of the city, but just not cut out for tramping great distances in the African bush. This little jaunt was a good appetizer for the upcoming trek to the border. It helped me both physically and mentally. While we were resting, we were brought tea, and I was reaching the point where I really enjoyed it. It was always very, very hot, and

it usually took some time before I could drink it. The comrades of
FRELIMO, on the other hand, drank it right away. Soon afterwards,
FRELIMO hospitality again exceeded our expectations when some
of the men came to take our dirty clothes to be washed. We protested
vigorously, saying we could certainly do that little bit ourselves, but
they would have nothing of it. We gave in.

Various parts of the day were spent in leisure activities, during
which we got to know the freedom fighters much better, and also each
other. Robert and I had already spent a lot of time talking about things
that had become such a part of us in the United States as to become
almost like second nature. These were things that perhaps some of
us, in our revolutionary zeal, liked to think disappeared almost automatically as soon as we entered a situation of this sort. But that was
not the case. And when you think about it, as I did that day, it came
from the fact that, in many ways, we in the United States are among
the most luxurious revolutionaries in the world. For example, it was
Sunday, but it didn't feel like a Sunday, partially because there was no
football, baseball, or basketball game to watch on television. There was
no television. Anyone who knew me well knew of my enthusiasm for
athletic competition as both a spectator and a participant. Even there
in Africa, with the most revolutionary of Africans, that enthusiasm
was still on my mind. The first night together, for instance, Robert
and I had talked about sports late into the night. Even while talking
leisurely with the guys, we got on that subject. This time, though, we
placed it in a more political perspective by pointing out the difference
between sports in a capitalist country like the United States and sports
in a revolutionary nation like China. We also made a special point to
explain how Black athletes are exploited in the world of American athletic competition. Another thing that was with me automatically was
my response to Black rhythm and blues music coming over the radio.
One evening when Freda Payne came on the radio singing "Cherish," it
really sounded good. It made me think of home and especially of my
oldest daughter, Y'ar Armashi, who loved to dance. doing her thing.
Another time we had heard that Aretha Franklin would be on the radio at 8:45 p.m., and we played around with the dial for half an hour,
only to go to bed disappointed that we couldn't get to hear Soul Sister
Supreme. Cultural conditioning, I admitted, was often more subtle
and deeply felt than we realized. And although I would have liked to
think that things were otherwise with me, reality was a different thing.

One day, as I watched the soldiers clean their weapons, the sight made me feel proud to see our people at that level of struggle. Another time, the camp fell in for a weapons drill, and I kept my eyes focused on one of the sisters standing at attention in traditional African dress with an AK-47 automatic rifle draped over her shoulder. Though I'd seen photos like that many times before, I was so impressed to witness it in the flesh. I wrote in my diary:

> The talk about bombs, helicopters, seeing soldiers, seeing guns, etc., all seems so strange. I am still mentally conditioned to all of that being something you talk about, not see and be a part of. I guess the feeling will come across strong when we get to Mozambique. I feel the sense of danger, yet, not really. The real point is that we are here—I am here. We have talked and talked of the struggle. Now I am here in the midst of it. No speeches, no rallies, no newspaper articles, no press conferences, but armed struggle against the enemy. It is frightening, yet in another way it has a certain freedom or special feeling to it. It is difficult to describe.

On Monday, August 30, we were up at 5:15 a.m. and soon ready to head out for Mozambique. As I thought about the potential danger, I told myself that I was prepared and ready to give whatever this significant undertaking demanded of me. I thought about how things were going at MXLU and about my family: Rabia and the children, Y'ar Armashi, Kwesi, and Kumba Miata. Kumba had been born less than a month before I left. Her naming ceremony had been my last night in Greensboro. By the time I got home, I thought, she would probably be a lot bigger, and I looked forward to seeing her.

As our group prepared to move out, each of the freedom fighters was issued ammunition. We were informed that Robert, Bob, and I would not carry any weapons—the potential political implications were just too great. FRELIMO was concerned that if we happened to be caught with weapons, the Portuguese would spread propaganda that Black mercenaries were being brought from the United States to fight in the revolution. So, a bodyguard was assigned to us at all times. We also would not have to carry our packs—our comrades would do this for us. However, in Robert's case, this meant he still would be loaded down with a heavy vest, since he was shooting still photos and sound film. I was left only with a canteen and a radio, in addition to my camera. That was tough enough for me. It was on this march that I saw why the women of FRELIMO were considered full comrades, no ifs, ands, or buts about it. Maria, for example: twenty years old, five feet two inches tall, and just one hundred pounds. In addition to the rifle draped over her shoulder, she carried a knapsack on her back and another load of over fifty pounds on her head. She seldom used her hands to steady the load, and at one point even broke into a brisk trot. Another female freedom fighter who was part of our group was just sixteen years old. She was not the youngest on the march, for there was also a young guy, no older than fourteen, who carried a heavy pack on his head all the way. I had marched a short, but rough, nine miles through the interior of Guyana the year before, and now this stint on the way to Mozambique. It was one mind-blowing kind of thing: overwhelming, hard, beautiful, humbling, and it was just the beginning.

After four hours in the hot sun, through the bush, through elephant grass, we finally made it to a camp not far from the border. Then came something I had to see and witness to believe: After such a journey through the forest with almost a hundred pounds on each of their backs, heads, and shoulders, the freedom fighters lined up in formation and went through military drills. They sang party songs and enthusiastically shouted chants, exemplary of a commitment, dedication, and a will to win that probably made them unbeatable. After a hot water and soap shower, I was all set to bed down for the night when I spotted four rats in my room. Me and rats have a thing, a real deep thing. I managed to switch beds with Cornelio only to learn that although his bed wasn't the meeting place for the rats, it was in the heart of their main thoroughfare. So, I spent the night feeling rats run over and around me. So what, I thought. For many African people all over the world, sleeping with rats was a common experience. It wasn't exactly new to me either. In Guyana, a few rats had invited themselves into the interior of my sleeping bag. But still, that didn't mean I dug it. And neither did Bob. We decided to spend the next night outside the hut and let the rats have the room.

The next day, we mostly rested. Then, full of anticipation, we started up again. Nearly seven years after the first group of freedom fighters began the revolution, three of us—Robert, Bob. and I—became perhaps the first Africans born in America to cross over and set foot into liberated Mozambique. Robert and Bob had filmed the entire crossing, and I shot several rolls of still photos. The freedom fighters sang revolutionary songs, shouted chants, and raised their weapons high above their heads to the accompanying cries of "Viva, FRELIMO!"

One of the most striking things, apparent from just looking at them lined up on the shore, was their strong bond of unity, which made them an army. Most armies were uniform in appearance, dress, weapons, and the like. But the freedom fighters were a whole nother thing. They were all clad in mostly brown, or green, or both, or neither. There was every conceivable combination of clothes: brown pants, green pants, blue jeans, and dress gabardines; tennis shoes (of many colors), para-combat boots, desert boots, sandals; jungle hats, snap-billed caps, berets, and bare heads. Weapons varied from rocket launchers to AK-47s to bolt-action, single shots and automatic pistols. In fact, to take a good long look, it was impossible to find among the numerous soldiers there on the shore a single pair outfitted exactly the same from hat to shoe, gun included. And, of course, since FRELIMO had no helicopters, trucks, or Jeeps to deliver supplies, everything essential was carried along with us on backs, on heads, in hands and in any other way. There were large, thin-lipped cooking pots filled with other essentials precariously and intricately stacked on the heads of men and women. Other head packs were simple cardboard boxes, grease-stained and soiled, bound with twine. To speak of the loads on the backs as knapsacks is almost misleading. They were simply loads—there must have been at least three dozen different combinations. Some were regular knapsacks, but most others were burlap sacks tied on with rope, string, rags, or twine. To hold the shoulder straps together over the long march, the freedom fighters tied them with rope, string, or even a handkerchief across their chest. And some of them carried a few personal items, seemingly just thrown on at the last minute—a toothbrush in a shirt pocket or maybe a vacuum-type bottle strapped around the waist as a canteen. Most of these fighters were young, averaging about twenty years old. Their faces were those of African warriors, similar to those of Africans their age in America, Canada, the Caribbean, South America, Europe, or other parts of the world. But by their actions, by their commitment, by their decision to take their freedom, they had escaped the namelessness of history and instead thrown themselves into a vanguard position; they were revolutionaries, African revolutionaries.

It was an amazing thing to witness. And soon, I would experience firsthand the full spectrum of what revolution really meant.

8

INSIDE THE WAR ZONE

Our first days of trekking through the African bush were tough as hell—hours and hours of marching under the blazing sun and food that took some serious getting-used-to: lizard meat, dried gazelle, and lots of ugali, a porridge-like dish that I never learned to tolerate. But our real journey began on September 1, 1971, when we crossed the blue-green waters of the Ruvuma River into Mozambique. Our African brothers had warned us: We were entering a war zone. Anything could happen.

For me, things did not start well. On September 4, after having experienced dizziness, weakness, and general lethargy for a couple days, my body gave out. I wrote in my journal:

> We walked for two hours, most of which was straight up the highest mountain I have ever seen. Sometime after we reached the plateau, I passed out. They tell me I was out about fifteen minutes. They brought me to with smelling salts. After I regained my senses, we rested about a half hour and then we moved on...

Our next stop was a camp that served as an orphanage and nursery for small children whose parents were taking part in the war or had been killed. It was named "Infantario Josina Moises Machel," after a young FRELIMO freedom fighter who had pushed for women's rights and had died in April 1971 at age twenty-five of what was believed to have been cancer or leukemia. She was the first wife of an important FRELIMO leader, Samora Machel, who would go on to become the first president of independent Mozambique. Samora Machel ultimately would die in a mysterious aircraft crash in 1986, and his second wife and widow, Graça, would go on twelve years later to marry the iconic leader of South Africa, Nelson Mandela. The two were still married when Mandela died in 2013.

The orphanage camp was necessary because the militants needed to know that if something happened to them, their children would be nurtured. FRELIMO saw the camps as important in the transformation and development of the new society, but the nursery lacked fruits, milk, and protein foods that children needed—canned fruit would be important. We spent the day there, and I got to see how the children's center was operated and how we at MXLU could possibly help. They needed food, clothing, and educational materials. They could also use medical personnel, I noted. I figured our bio-medics crew would be great there, but I didn't think FRELIMO would go for that. It occurred to me that it was Labor Day in the United States. I knew many Black folks would be picnicking and drinking all day. Also, it was the day that everybody was to be back at MXLU, and I hoped everything was cool. I wondered where the school was located—in Greensboro or the campus in Sedalia that we had been negotiating to buy when I left. If Greensboro, I knew we'd have less school and more money; if Sedalia, less money and more school.

The next day, we went for a little stroll and saw where the Portuguese had set up an ambush not far from the camp. We saw their camp sites, littered with cans and boxes that had kept their food. I could just visualize the "m.f.'s" lying there, waiting for our people. The stroll lasted a couple of hours, and I rested for the remainder of the day. Though difficult for me personally, this experience was strengthening my spirited resolve to struggle harder. I saw very clearly the contradictions of my own life within our "movement" in the United States. I also saw that leadership by mouth only had no place in a revolution, or, for that matter, in a school like MXLU. Leadership comes from what you do—by example. Revolution also was no place for ego trips, pouting arguments that have no constructive base, etc. I just hoped when I got back I could somehow turn the experience into a positive force for the university and my people. But I was starting to worry a little about the amount of time I would have to stay in there. I came with the understanding that the journey would last fifteen days, sixteen at maximum. Now, that was beginning to seem less likely.

We continued walking, which was a real killer on my feet, especially with my shoes. I'd noticed that the soles were coming apart and that holes had developed in the bottoms of both of them. That was a bad sign because there were no shoes anywhere nearby to fit me. Walking up and down a rocky mountain trail for two hours straight in dress shoes—let me clue you in on what it was like: It was torture. But it was still a good experience. For one, my bodyguard was a really beautiful dude, attentive, generous, knowledgeable. Also, we got to meet some civilians, most of whom were armed and prepared to fight. It was amazing to me the amount of heart that our people there had. One of the things that came through was that these men and women were not just fighting a war, but they were building a new society, a society that would abolish not only imperialist, colonialist structures, but also traditional African structures that restricted freedom of the people. This had to be understood, or the whole point of FRELIMO would have been missed. It supported the point that we in the states could not simply talk of returning to Africa and old African traditions. We had to realize that setting up organizations based on old tribal customs was not really a step forward; rather it was a step backward. Forward people in Africa were looking ahead. Backward Africans in the United States were looking behind. It was clear we had much to learn about Africa, and Africa could learn some things from us.

On September 6, we made it to the next camp, which operated as a hospital and school. There were lots of folks there, including many civilians from surrounding villages. I passed out again, so I rested a bit. Those who prepared for us even made my bed long enough that I could stretch my legs fully for the first time since I'd left the United States. We hadn't eaten all day, and so I was overjoyed when it came time for dinner: rice, chicken, and tea. It was very good, and I ate every bit. This camp was larger than any we had seen, which was reflected in the mess hall where we ate. It seated twenty-two people, and we even had a table cloth. I was able to visit a real toilet for the first time in six days, and let me tell you, after squatting in the bush for so long, that was a real luxury.

The next day, it was again cold, cold. All of my stereotyped attitudes about the weather of Africa had been destroyed. Since Commissar Guebuza was there with guests, a decision was made to have a ceremony. It began around 8 a.m. with the entire group of soldiers marching around the camp singing, and, in step, presenting themselves before Guebuza. They were joined by schoolchildren. Then everybody, including local villagers, formed at the center of the camp and heard speeches and singing. When I was introduced, Guebuza remarked that I was very tall, and so everybody laughed. Then one of the elders came over and shook my hand because he, too, was tall, about six feet one inch. Obviously, most of the people there were short. The villagers presented Guebuza and us gifts: bananas, sweet potatoes, flour, cassava, and a chicken. The spokesman for the village then explained how they had fought Portuguese and promised to continue to fight. He ended by what had become a familiar refrain: Viva FRELIMO!

I slept much of the next day, as I still was not feeling well. The medical officer came to see me and told me he thought the problem was a lack of food and the marching. He gave me some vitamin pills (made in Italy) that I was to take three times a day. Robert then confirmed my fear that I would not be getting out of there anytime soon, which left me feeling a bit depressed. The problem was that no one who could speak English was free to return with me, and the truck that was to transport me back into Tanzania wouldn't check the border for me for another three weeks. There was nothing I could do.

I had a fair night of sleep, despite the rain. And breakfast was really tasty—antelope meat, which tasted and looked like cubed steak, sweet potatoes, and tea. I visited with a man I'd met in the village that was about a fifteen-minute walk from the camp. His name was Mpanda (one who can make things), and he lived with his eldest brother, his brother's family, and his sons-in-law—about seventy-five people in all. Mpanda had three wives, five daughters, a son who was a FRELIMO soldier, eight granddaughters, four grandsons, two great-grandsons and one great-granddaughter. His brother had four wives, five sons— two of whom were soldiers for FRELIMO—five daughters, two grandsons, and five granddaughters. It was a memorable experience to visit with them, talk to them (with Cornelio interpreting), and take pictures. They presented me with gifts: a basket of rice and two beautifully handmade pieces of pottery. I told Mpanda these would be gifts for my wife and that we would name our next son after him in appreciation of his kindness. He would return almost daily during our stay, and he often came bearing gifts. I was impressed by how the people lived completely off the land. It was a meager existence, yet they gave generously and even apologized for not being able to do more. The family ties were strong, but, unfortunately, the women were really exploited—something that FRELIMO was pushing to change. During one day of rest, I sat atop a hill and spent the entire day observing how a true African village operated. The women seemed to do all of the hard work, fetching the water and wood, cooking, working the fields, and having babies. In past generations, the men were out hunting, but that tradition had faded, and the men mostly sat around while the women worked. Nevertheless, I was impressed with the strength and wisdom of Mpanda and his brother, and visiting them gave me some

practical observations of African life outside of the European-style cities. It was a whole different existence, and the visit was the highlight
of an enlightening trip.

The next day, September 11, things would change dramatically. It
started out as usual, around 6:15 a.m., with wafers, bananas, and tea
for breakfast. I was planning to visit more of the village or to read,
something I had done quite a bit throughout the trip. But I was
straightening my hut and counting my exposed film when we heard
those damn helicopters. It didn't take long for me to realize what was
going on: The freedom fighters were under attack by the Portuguese
army. Suddenly, I was in the middle of a real war. This was no discussion about armed struggle. It was actually happening. The helicopters
seemed right overhead:

> They were coming directly at the base. So, Cornelio immediately told
> us to get the hell out of there. I grabbed the film and stuffed it in my
> pockets. We headed into the bush. The helicopters were making passes
> dropping grenades and firing machine guns. We hid in the bush and
> moved after each pass. Fortunately, I stayed with Cornelio and Robert.
> Bob got separated from us. We ended up in a banana plantation. There
> we hid inside the banana trees. Cornelio was quite worried about the
> spot because he felt there were too many clearings for the copters to land.
> These copters had the capacity to carry twelve men if the men were fully
> equipped, but the copters were known to have carried as many as twen-
> ty-five less-equipped men. Right near us were only three or four AK47s.
> A helicopter came directly over us and we thought it was going to land. I
> am wishing I had a piece or something. A lot of things went through my
> mind, mainly Rabia and the children. But surprisingly I was calm in-
> side, ready for whatever was going to go down. Cornelio had cocked his
> piece and was ready to deal. Fortunately, the helicopters went on past.
>
> We then went deeper into the bush until we reached the forest. There
> we stopped and were joined by about fifteen to twenty other comrades,
> half of whom were women. In our group was Comrade Joker; he took
> charge. We lay in the forest and watched the planes make bombing runs
> near the base. I took a couple of snapshots, but I don't know how they
> will turn out. We then regrouped and headed towards the mountains, in
> the deep, deep bush. The bombing runs ended after about an hour and
> a half. The problem then and now are the infantrymen that the helicop-
> ters landed. Their strategy is to swoop in on a given area, drop bombs,
> machine-gun the area, and while you are pinned down to drop troops
> to set up ambushes. So at any "m.f." minute, we could be ambushed. So

I am sitting on a mountain in Mozambique hoping I can make it back to tell my story.

We walked about two hours away from the base and away from the zone the comrades thought the troops were concentrating (on). It was, and is, a hell of a feeling. I don't know where I am and whether I'll be alive an hour from now. Yet, I believe that I am pursuing the correct path for my children and my children's children. I continue to be impressed with the heart of the people of FRELIMO. There was no panic—people gathered stuff and faded into the "bush." Once in the "bush," Cornelio was giving us clear directions all the time. Let me tell you, man, I am thankful as hell for the "bush" and those banana trees and trees period. I learned how to move low and fast in the "bush." How to camouflage myself deeply into banana trees. I am really thinking a lot about Rabia and the children and hoping I will get a chance to express my love and appreciation for them.

Later the same day, Bob caught up with us, just in time for lunch: sardines, banana crème cookies, cassava (a kind of porridge that I had not been able to tolerate before), and orange fizz. The cassava, incidentally, never tasted so good. Under the circumstances, the entire day was all sort of unbelievable. Maria had produced all of this in the middle of a war zone. We heard some firing quite a ways away; our fighters in another part of the bush must have been fighting the troops that landed. The day really brought home the situation our people were in—there was really nothing folks could do when the planes came, but melt into the bush until the enemy left, then regroup and fight. Around 4 p.m., word came that Guebuza had been located, and we were instructed to go to him. We left the hill and walked back toward the base, which took about an hour. It was great to rejoin our leader and the rest of the group, but a half-hour after we got to there, we heard the roar of an approaching plane. We were under attack again. We immediately dropped to the ground and began crawling low and fast toward the banana plantation. All of a sudden, bombs began exploding around us. There was no time to think or fear. My athletic career had taught me how to stay calm in dire situations to achieve a goal. In this case, the goal was staying alive. It seemed to take forever to reach those banana trees. Once there, we stood, hugging the trees to avoid detection. All the while, the lone bomber hovered low, dropping a total of six bombs near the base. As if the bombs were not enough, the enemy fighters inside the plane strafed the entire area with machine gun fire. Then, just as suddenly as it had begun, things grew silent, eerily silent. It was over.

Darkness descended about 6:00 p.m., and believe it or not, we were served a supper of rice and beans. I have no idea how the meal was cooked because fires weren't allowed that first day. We were unsure whether the Portuguese troops had completely left the area, and we didn't want to send an unintended signal. As we prepared to bed down for the night, I realized that I'd left my knapsack somewhere in the bush. So, I was left with nothing but the clothes on my back, which luckily included a sweater. Someone loaned me a blanket and tent cover to spread over the straw on the ground. Around 4:30 a.m., it started to rain heavily, and so I put my blanket on the ground and used the tent to cover myself. The rain stopped just before 6:00 a.m., and moments later we were awakened by gunfire. We fled back to the hill where we had spent the previous day. Guebeza told us that the gunfire was a FRELIMO ambush and that many such ambushes had been set up throughout the bush. About an hour after we had been on the hill, the rain started again—a hard, driving rain. All we could do was stand under a tree while it poured. Some of the brothers put together a makeshift tent, and we gathered under it. For hours, we just sat on the hill in that torrential downpour. The rain finally stopped about 12:30 p.m. We walked down the other side of the mountain, where, unlike the day before, the fighters were allowed to build a fire. We were able to warm up and dry off. My friend, Mpanda, also visited. He was really a fantastic old man. He said he had fled his house with his family, but he vowed to return. He described the Portuguese as intruders and said he was glad his son and nephews had decided to join the freedom fighters. He made a request that would stick with me long after I'd left Mozambique: He asked that, when Robert and I returned to America, we help the freedom fighters get more weapons. We readily agreed.

About 3:00 p.m., the sound of gunfire erupted again, but our leaders assured us that FRELIMO had the enemy surrounded. We stayed in place and shared another meal—juice mixed with tuna and sardines, which was surprisingly quite good. The air was cold and damp, and we had no blankets. I didn't have a jacket either, and I knew it would be a long, miserable night. So, Robert and I turned to one of our favorite pastimes to help the hours roll faster: sports. We picked our all-time favorite players for teams in basketball, baseball, and football. First, all white boys, then Black. Then, we drafted for basketball and football.

This lasted until dark, and we went to bed around 6:00 p.m. Around 3:00 a.m., I awakened to the sound of another plane, but it seemed much further away. I realized it probably a commercial flight. The next day, I wrote in my journal:

> *This is one of those days when thoughts of home are with me. It seems so far away. It is getting more and more difficult for me to transcend the boundaries that being in Mozambique presents. The boundaries of time, space and circumstances. It is somewhat depressing, but I am trying hard to overcome these periodic sets and make myself as useful as I can around here. This is difficult, believe me. I need to wash clothes and hopefully wash myself as it has been four or five days continually in the same clothes. This is my longest stretch so far without bathing or changing clothes. I hope it doesn't stretch out much longer.*

By Friday, September 17, we had been in the same area for one week. I learned the Portuguese had attacked our next stop and also, again, the camp up in the mountains, which stalled our progress. After breakfast, I was preparing for a day of reading, discussion, and writing when all of a sudden it became obvious we were getting ready to move out. Within fifteen minutes, everything was packed up and ready to go—amazing. We were returning to a base we had visited before, and we were told to move quickly, as FRELIMO was not sure whether all of the Portuguese had split. We took off, and eventually reached the site of the village near the school where we had been before. There was some evidence that mortar shells had hit, but otherwise, the place was intact. It looked like the last time we were there, a little over a week earlier. We walked around and saw a couple of areas where the bombs hit. We even saw one small bomb that didn't go off. I took a couple of pictures of our guys holding one part of it.

I heard talk the next day that the villagers were planning to return. They usually fled while under attack, and then FRELIMO checked out the areas to determine whether it was safe for them to return. At one point I noticed some civilians walking onto base with heavy loads on their backs. At first I thought they were villagers returning. It turned out they were coming from Tanzania with supplies for the army. Civilians sometimes transported supplies long distances for the freedom fighters. I had read that in *Mozambique Revolution*, but there was nothing like witnessing it with my own eyes. The civilians brought us some boiled corn, another luxury, and it tasted great. But when a plane flew overhead, once again we had to evacuate for the bush.

While I was taking a shower, I heard the faint roar of airplane engines.
I knew immediately what was happening. The comrades started scream-
ing at me to come. They need not have worried. I was already in motion.
I ran out of the shower with my pants half on and half off, undershirt
and shirt in my hand, and mad because I didn't have my sweater. Since
it was getting late, I knew soon it was going to get cooler. In any event, I
ran my fastest fifty yard dash on record to the "bush." We hid in the bush
under trees. The plane turned out to be a propaganda plane. They came
over blasting a loudspeaker in Jawa telling the people to leave this area
and go join the Portuguese at one of the Portuguese posts in this region.
They promised them a good life if they did. They went round and round
shouting this message...They bomb and strafe the people, land infantry
and send mortar shells all over the place. Then come back and tell folks
how well they will be treated if they return to their oppressors...

The announcer in the propaganda plane also warned that Portuguese
troops were amassed in the woods and that the people would be killed
if they did not leave. The plane hung around about a half-hour and
split. We then left the bush and headed back to camp. Unfortunately,
my stomach started acting up again, and I suffered another few days
of diarrhea, weakness, and general sluggishness. But on one of those
days, I sat down and tried to process in my journal some of what I was
beginning to understand:

This experience today, and all the experiences I have had, are really
difficult to explain. I mean, being here I am totally amazed at the dedi-
cation of FRELIMO people—it is just overwhelming. I am undergoing
some hardships, but mine are brief—that is to say, I will be leaving in a
manner of days, at the most weeks. Not to be compared with the life of
the everyday soldier and peasant, that is; I eat and sleep better than the
average person here because I am accepted as a guest and everything is
done to make me as comfortable as possible...These people, on the other
hand, are here for the rest of their lives. Day after day, week after week,
year after year, they live like I have been describing to you. Walking up
to eight hours without resting at a pace of five miles an hour. Carrying
knapsacks on their backs, and packs on their heads, and a rifle, all
weighing as much as seventy pounds. Carrying them the whole distance;
eating nothing but cassava for twelve to thirteen days; walking barefoot
through the bush at night for ten hours; lying in ambush for six days
with nothing but raw cassava to eat. The populace leaving their hous-
es during bombings, returning sometimes to find them burned down,
their food destroyed and then simply rebuilding until the next time...The
beauty of this is that, at a time when many of us in Africa, America,

Latin America, Caribbean, etc., are confined to reading and rhetoricizing about armed struggle as a tactic in revolution, here are Brothers and Sisters doing it. Actually fighting day in, day out, actually killing, and being killed. Actually, successfully challenging Europe, the United States, and South Africa. Fighting helicopters and bombs, troops, vicious propaganda, and unlimited resources with nothing but simple weapons (in comparison), and most important, fighting to govern themselves and develop a new life for their people...

While many of us in the states who are trying to identify ourselves as African (and correctly so) would probably think the sights are great, or maybe even in an unconscious (way) paternalistically view them as quaint or the way it should be, I really see it differently. I am, of course, in awe about seeing things I have only read about. I appreciate the strength of our people being able to survive and maintain institutions such as the family, develop division of labor, etc. Yet, I realize that much of this "quaint" atmosphere must be changed as a result of a peasant-based revolution in Africa. There must be hospitals, schools, better health conditions, better agricultural methods, better diets, etc. Some of us must begin to understand that while there are certain strengths about this "traditional African way of life," there are also many, many things that must be revolutionized if we are serious about an African existence in the modern world... Blind adherence to outmoded ways within a modern world will forever damn us to a "race of beggars." There is exploitation of women here. There is a whole labor source—men who simply sit around watching women work. (A lot of sharing and collective work, shared food, rearing children, etc.) These things must be changed if we are to seriously address ourselves to a worldwide African revolution...

Finally, on September 24, we headed out again, back-tracking toward Tanzania. We said goodbye to a number of the guerrillas who would not be proceeding with us, including our leader, Guebuza. I had been so impressed by him and his leadership; I knew I would never forget him. He would go on to become an even more important leader in FRELIMO and, in December 2004, more than thirty years after I first met him, he would be elected the third president of Mozambique.

After those of us who were headed back to Tanzania parted ways with the rest of our group, we spent several more days marching through the bush for hours at a time, stopping only for rest and meals. We battled the heat during the day and the cold at night. My damn shoes made every step for me even more difficult. By then, the soles were almost worn off. We finally made it to a base just three hours outside Tanzania on September 30, and I had a shower for the first time in about five days. After marching and sleeping in the bush for such a long time, you can imagine what it was like to get a shower and my clothes washed. The camp we were in was a production base. The main job was to grow food and transport materials. Wounded fighters came there to recuperate. A few of the men went hunting and returned with four animals that looked similar to buffalos. The hunters brought the tails tied together and showed them to me. Dinner that night was great—rice, three boiled eggs, meat, gravy, and beans. Now, when I say meat, I'm talking about chunks of fresh gazelle. Normally when we had meat, we got a couple of small pieces because it had to go around. But by then, our group was small, and the meat was plentiful. I ate far too much, but it was delicious, one of the best meals I had inside Mozambique, or for that matter, in Africa. After dinner, we sat around talking. I was told the march to the border should take three or four hours. Then, one of men casually mentioned that they sometimes ran into elephants and lions on the march—not too often, but sometimes. That, of course, gave me a little to think about overnight.

We began our march to the border at 5:35 a.m. on October 1, About two hours and forty-five minutes later, we were at the Ruvuma River. It was even more beautiful than the first time I'd seen it, and on the other side, Tanzania awaited! A man came over and picked us up in a boat, and, within ten minutes, I was out of Mozambique and in Tanzania. Thirty-one days, and then, suddenly, it was over. Incidentally, the shoes made it, too, though both soles and heels were just about off, and the leather was scraped beyond repair. But with the help of a lot of tape and a little luck, they were holding on.

The next day, a car came to transport us back to Songea. The guy who brought the car also brought my wallet and ticket to Dar. For the first time in thirty-three days, I saw pictures of my family. Believe me, they never looked so good. That night, I slept in a real bed; I'd never slept so well.

I spent my last day in Songea on October 3. It was a beautiful day, bright and sunny, and the women all wore colorful, traditional dresses. I went to five stores looking for toothpaste until I finally found one that had everything I wanted, including *Time* and *Newsweek* magazines. I bought both of them, several newspapers, cookies, and of course, the toothpaste. I craved information. All of the stores were owned by East Indians. All of the places in the market selling fruit, sugar cane, vegetable, etc., were run by Africans. I did an interview with someone from FRELIMO for a Party newspaper. He'd attended Temple University in Pennsylvania, and spoke English fairly well. He spoke no Portuguese since he'd grown up in South Africa; he used a dictionary to translate his English prose for the newspaper.

I shared my last lunch with my FRELIMO guerrillas, said my final goodbyes, and left for the airport, headed back to Dar. As soon as I got there, I called Rabia and the children. She sounded so excited and relieved to hear from me. No one knew what had happened to me and they were beginning to fear the worst, she said. It had never even occurred to me when I slipped away quietly and then missed my flight back to the United States with the ministerial group that my friends and family might think something bad had happened to me. I then felt awful for having caused such worry. This, I have learned, is one of my deepest flaws. What was best for the movement, the struggle, was most often my first thought. And as painful as it is to admit today, even the ones I loved the most then had to take a back seat in my mind.

My ankles had swollen badly, and I needed to rest in Dar a few days before heading back home, but I arranged for Rabia to meet me in New York. My friend, Viola Plummer, the Episcopal Church staffer who had helped MXLU receive the controversial grant, invited us to stay at her place. I had made it back home to my family and was just happy to be alive.

Revolution was no longer a rhetorical concept to me; it was real. I'd seen it: real lives. Real guns. Real blood. And I would be forever changed.

Marching with the FRELIMO freedom fighters in Mozambique.

Maria, one of the female guerrillas, preparing food in the bush.

Receiving gifts from the family of Mpanda,
a village leader who befriended me.

Sitting with Fernando, my bodyguard,
at the base camp in Mozambique.

9

THE BATTLE BETWEEN RACE
AND CLASS

As soon as I returned from Mozambique, I began thinking of what I could do to support the liberation struggles in Africa. It didn't take long to come up with a plan:
Organize a national demonstration that would draw
Black people from every corner of the country to the
nation's capital. My people needed to know what was happening in
Africa, that America was supporting countries fighting to maintain
the racist system that had colonized our brothers and sisters there. I'd
seen the American-made bombs used against them. A huge demonstration would draw attention to the issue, and could help bring about
a change in U.S. policies that supported the European regimes that
denied various African nations their independence.

I convened a small group of fellow Pan-Africanists to pitch the idea.
They included my friend Cleve Sellers; Ron Daniels, the Ohio-based
brother who had just traveled with the ministerial group to Africa; Joe
Waller, a Florida activist whose group published a newspaper called
The Burning Spear; and a few others I trusted. They agreed with the
concept and helped me think through the practical details. We were
aware that heads of states from thirty-one African countries had met
on May 25, 1963, to form the Organization of African Unity and that
they had proclaimed the day "African Liberation Day." I wanted to have
the march in Washington, D.C., as close as possible to the African holiday, and I figured a Saturday would make it easier for people to show
up. So, we set the date for May 27, 1972.

I began traveling throughout the country, appearing on Black radio
stations and in Black newspapers, talking about the event. I even made
trips to the Caribbean and Canada to meet with groups and generate
support. One day out of the blue I got word that a group of brothers

and sisters in New York City wanted to meet with me right away. I obliged and learned during the meeting that they had been recognizing African Liberation Day for years and considered themselves the holders of the Pan-African Movement in the United States. They had been standing up for Africa when few others in this country did, and they wanted to know who in the hell I was and what made me think I could pull off a national demonstration. The group included a venerable Harlem activist known as Queen Mother Moore, a Louisiana-born woman who had moved to New York in the 1920s to support Marcus Garvey's Black Nationalist and Pan-African agenda through his Universal Negro Improvement Association. She was about seventy-three years old when we met, and she was well-known throughout New York for fighting on behalf of poor and oppressed Black people. I now understand why she and the others in her group were so skeptical of me—they had dedicated their lives to this cause, working for decades in near obscurity, and all of a sudden some young dude seems to come out of nowhere, talking about leading a major demonstration to show support for Africa in the nation's capital. They were full of questions: Where had I been? Why didn't they know anything about me? Who was really behind this demonstration I was planning? But I was young, irreverent, and not easily dissuaded. It didn't matter that they didn't think it was the right time or that they doubted I could draw the broad spectrum of support I desired. I was confident enough to think otherwise.

They weren't the only ones who initially tried to dissuade me. I took a lot of criticism from others, too, who either didn't agree with what I was trying to do or questioned my motives. One letter even came from Stokely Carmichael (Kwame Toure), expressing concern about the timing. But none of those arguments made sense to me. When would the political climate ever be considered right to put Africa at the top of the agenda? And that's what I hoped to change. This really wasn't an ego trip for me. I wasn't trying to become some great Pan-African leader. My agenda was pure and simple: to raise awareness of the African liberation struggle and generate support for it among Black Americans. I proceeded with plans for the march.

First, we formed a national steering committee, the African Liberation Day Coordinating Committee, made up of fifty influential Black men and women who represented a broad spectrum of Black leadership. As the list of committee members grew, it occurred to me that I'd never seen such a wide range of Black leaders come together under the same banner. They included five congressmen (U.S. Representatives. John Conyers Jr., Ron Dellums, Charles C. Diggs, Jr., Walter Fauntroy, and Louis Stokes); Georgia State Representative Julian Bond; Gary Mayor Richard Hatcher; Civil Rights leader Jesse Jackson; Southern Christian Leadership Conference President Ralph Abernathy; Malcolm X's widow, Betty Shabazz; Pan-African leader Stokely Carmichael; famed poet and playright Amiri Baraka, who also was a leader in the Black Power and Pan-African struggles; Black Panther Party leader Huey Newton; former Student Nonviolent Coordinating Committee (SNCC) Chairman H. Rap Brown, who by then was serving time in Attica Prison on robbery charges; and Communist Party leader and human rights activist Angela Davis, who also was in jail fighting murder charges. Even though they were in jail, Rap and Angela were still respected among radical Black people, and it was important to me to have their support. I don't recall exactly how we reached Rap, but a movement contact arranged for me to meet with Angela's attorney, Howard Moore. I traveled to California for the meeting, and he agreed to ask her to be on the committee. She had some questions about others serving on the committee, but Howard eventually called me with her approval. At the time, there were warring factions of Black folks, and it took some cajoling to get some of them to agree to serve on the committee together, even though they never had to sit across the table from one another. In the end, though, many of them agreed that it was important to come together for the sake of Black unity. But several of the Black elected politicians that we approached seemed scared to associate with the African liberation movement, and they stayed as far away from our demonstration as possible. They didn't want to hear nothing about the African liberation leaders who were being murdered or falsely imprisoned for their activism, like Nelson Mandela, who at the time of our demonstration had been in jail nearly ten years. Mandela would serve another seventeen years in jail before he was freed, in 1990, and then elected in 1994 as the first Black president of South Africa. When Mandela traveled to the United States for the first time after his election, some of those same Black officials who refused to support our African Liberation Day celebration couldn't wait to embrace him at the airport. The sight of those hypocrites made me want to puke.

Our theme for the celebration was "Black Unity: Breaking the Chains of Oppression." A group of us set up shop on 14th and U streets, in the heart of the Black community in Washington, D.C., months beforehand and worked nearly full-time on the event. Organizers in major cities called potential supporters, handed out fliers, and arranged buses to transport participants. But no matter how hard you work on an event like this, you can never be sure exactly how things will turn out until it happens. I got a clue on the night of May 26, when buses full of Black people began rolling into the District of Columbia from all over the country. By morning, thousands of Black folks of every age, size, and hue were flowing into the downtown streets. They carried handmade signs and banners proclaiming "African Liberation Day." Groups of schoolchildren waved small red, black, and green flags. Families brought blankets, folding chairs, umbrellas, and other picnic gear. Howard University's radio station, WHUR-FM, broadcast live from the event all day. From my spot on the hill at Malcolm X Park, where we gathered to begin the march, I looked out over the streets and could hardly believe the numbers of people making their way there. Black people filled every empty space on the streets and walkways along 15th, 16th, Euclid, and W streets in Northwest D.C. The crowd stretched much farther than my eyes could see. It completely blew my mind and far exceeded even my wildest predictions. Our planners estimated the crowd at about 30,000 people, which was believed to have been the largest gathering of Black Americans in support of Africa since the Marcus Garvey movement of the 1920s. Simultaneous marches were held in San Francisco and Canada, bringing the total number of participants to an estimated 60,000. Yet, there was very little coverage in the white media. Nevertheless, I felt a strong sense of vindication. We had actually done it. We had worked like hell, brought all of these people to the nation's capital, and sent a united message to our African brothers and sisters waging war for their freedom, that their struggle was ours, too.

Just before noon, the crowd began moving out like a gigantic wave toward the Portuguese Embassy, where speakers blasted that country's white government for its tyrannical reign over African nations and their majority Black populations. We then protested in front of the Rhodesian Information Center, the South African Embassy, and the U.S. State Department for the U.S. government's tacit approval of those racist regimes. As the day wound down, the crowd made its way to the Washington Monument, which we had renamed Lumumba Square. That was our way of honoring Patrice Lumumba, the African liberation hero who had been murdered after leading his country's independence from Belgium and becoming the first democratically elected Prime Minister of the Republic of the Congo. Just three months after his election, Lumumba was forced out of office and executed by his African rivals during a political crisis backed by the Belgian government.

Finally, it was my turn to speak. As I stood there on the podium and looked into that river of Black faces. I thought of all the suffering that we had endured as a people, yet here we were. "Look around," I shouted into the microphone, wanting every member of the crowd to see the beauty that I saw and feel the exuberance of that moment. "Look around and see that in spite of all the brutalization of this beast, we still stand. Look around and see the beauty and the potential of the Black man. Look around and see that we represent the non-white world, which is the majority on this earth. Look around and see that our people are here to tell the world that everything is going to be everything one day for the Black man... But let us be clear, brothers and sisters, the road ahead will be difficult...This demonstration must be understood for what it is, one small tactic, one more thing that is going to heighten the level of our struggle."

I closed the event by leading the crowd in a chant: "We are an African people!" And I left that day feeling fulfilled. We had accomplished our primary mission of educating our people about the African liberation struggle and increasing support. As I saw it, this was just the beginning. We had to translate this outpouring of emotional support into financial support. In the months after the demonstration, those of us who had been actively involved formed the African Liberation Support Committee and held national meetings, first at Malcolm X Liberation University, and then at a conference center in Frogmore, South Carolina, to begin planning for the next year. We decided that, instead of having one big celebration in D.C., we would host multiple simultaneous celebrations in major cities throughout the country. This time, we would also focus on raising money to donate to the African liberation struggle. We formed chapters of the committee in various cities, including Houston, Kansas City, Detroit, D.C., Durham, and Greensboro. In 1973, our African Liberation Day celebrations drew an estimated 100,000 participants in thirty-one cities. We also included a call to boycott Portuguese products and Gulf Oil because of the country's continued fight to maintain control of African nations and the oil company's support of the racist governments. The demonstrations raised $50,000, and I traveled to Tanzania with two of the national committee's officers to present the money to several liberation groups. Joining me were Brenda Paris of Montreal, Canada, who spoke French and served as our interpreter in Guinea, and Gene Locke, a Houston-based brother who had replaced me as head of the committee. It was a proud moment for me. I'd kept my promise to Mpanda, the African friend who had visited frequently and lifted my spirits during those trying days with the guerrillas in Mozambique.

It would have been wonderful if the African Liberation Support Committee could have continued to build on the momentum that we had started, but by 1974, ideological differences had caused us to splinter. At the heart of the dispute was whether our struggle was purely against racism and the white oppressors or whether it was against the system of class that exploited and mistreated the poor, who overwhelmingly were Black. Those philosophical divisions had reared up even during the planning of our first 1972 demonstration, when a group of Black nationalists in Chicago initially refused to participate because some of the Black leaders were married to white women. The Black nationalists among us believed that racism was intrinsic to the nature of white people and that they were the enemy. Somehow, I managed to persuade the Chicago group to participate, but those voices became even more strident during our planning of the 1973 demonstrations. For example, some African countries had several liberation groups with differing ideologies, and the African Liberation Support Committee practically disintegrated over discussions about which groups we should support. The debate over African liberation groups in Angola turned particularly nasty. One group held a Black nationalist view and accepted support only from other Black people; the other was based in Marxism. The Marxists believed that the oppression of African people had been perpetuated by a ruling class that was economically invested in controlling poor, defenseless people. I'd learned from the leaders of FRELIMO that they and other Marxists welcomed support from anyone interested in ending tyranny, regardless of race. Personally, I had begun to lean toward Marxism. It seemed to answer some of the questions I couldn't shake from my head, like how the deplorable conditions I'd seen in the Mathari Valley slums of Kenya, just a few miles away from the celebrated city of Nairobi, could exist under the rule of Black Africans. That question had led me to books by Marx and Lenin, and I'd spent hours and hours reading and learning about their philosophies during my down time with the guerrillas in Mozambique. My studies on the subject continued long after I left Africa. While I agreed with much of the Marxist-Leninist ideology, I never completely bought into its goal of a united working class. I'd seen racism up close among poor whites in places like North Carolina. I believed then and now that race and class issues often intertwine and, because so many Black people are disproportionately poor, class struggles often appear to be purely racial when they are not.

As I expressed my views during committee meetings, some of my movement colleagues began to see me as a traitor. Hadn't I been one of the Black Power Movement's most reliable voices? These were heady times, and people clung fiercely to their beliefs. You were either with them or against them. There was no gray. When supporters of the Pan-African Movement gathered in 1974 in Washington, D.C. for an intense panel discussion, themed "The Road Forward," word got around that some dudes were going to kill me. The auditorium at Howard University was packed. At one point I looked into the audience from my seat on stage and noticed a guy walking down the aisle toward the front row with a paper bag in his hand. I just knew that was it. I was going to die right then and there. I steeled myself and just sat there, waiting for what seemed the inevitable. There was no fear or panic because I had long ago accepted that death threats and maybe even death itself came with the territory of my work. Obviously, nothing happened. But that shows how passionate people were about these arguments. Likewise, on an international flight to Dar es Salaam, Tanzania, for the Sixth Pan-African Congress (the first one on African soil) in June 1974, Black Americans on the plane argued all night long over those same issues: Black nationalism versus Marxism. The conference brought together people of African backgrounds from all over the world to discuss the continent's most serious issues, and the world watched as the Americans continued their fierce debate on the floor of the conference. Afterward, scholars analyzed those viewpoints in various published papers.

Unfortunately, a similar philosophical split over the mission of MXLU had played out and ultimately contributed to its closure a year earlier. Some faculty and students strongly believed the university should be preparing students to go to Africa to help with nation-building after the success of the liberation movements. I argued that our African brothers and sisters had told me personally during my travels there that they most wanted and needed Black Americans to work inside our own country on influencing public policy and opinion in favor of Africa. I believed that MXLU should be doing just that, equipping our students with the academic and practical skills to become effective advocates and activists for Africa *within* the United States. The rift seemed irreparable. There was also a more pressing practical concern: We were broke, and all of our sources of financing had dried up. I announced the closure of the university at a press conference on June 28, 1973. While I regretted that MXLU was unable to continue, I've always been a forward-looking person. I knew I had done all I could to help the university survive, and I believed that we had stayed true to our mission. We had created a new model for a different kind of university dedicated to meeting the needs of our community. It was time to move on. What came next, though, would lead me into one of the darkest periods of my life.

After the university closed, I decided to move back to Durham alone. My frequent travels and near total devotion to the causes I was involved in had taken a terrible toll on my marriage. Rabia and I separated. It was devastating being apart from my children, but I found a one-bedroom efficiency apartment and traveled back and forth to Greensboro to spend time with them. They also visited me in Durham. I had taken a job as a consultant for the Interreligious Foundation for Community Organization (IFCO) in 1972, and, for a while after the separation, it was my only source of income. But the job kept a roof over my head and enabled me to take care of my children, which was most important to me. I delved even more into my activism. When the kids stayed with me in Durham, I sometimes brought them along to meetings and functions.

By early 1974, different factions of Pan-Africanists were forming various groups based on their worldview. The Student Organization for Black Unity (SOBU), which was originally made up of mostly college students, had changed its name to the Youth Organization for Black Unity (YOBU). The intent was to broaden its reach and eliminate any distinctions between college students and other young people. Then, those of us who had held similar views during our work together at the university, SOBU/YOBU, and the African Liberation

Support Committee formed a national Black Marxist group, called the Revolutionary Workers League (RWL). The group was part of what was being called the New Communist Movement, as some young people who had been inspired by developments in China, Cuba and other countries fighting for liberation sought fresh ways to align ourselves with Marxist-Leninist ideology without joining the old Communist Party.

In June 1974, I went to work as the business agent for the Local 77 Union, representing maids, janitors, and cafeteria workers at Duke University. I had met many of the members, including the union's founder, Oliver Harvey, during the student protests there, and I looked forward to helping them improve their lives through the union. For that to happen, the union needed to be radicalized, and I truly believed that the Revolutionary Workers League could do just that. So, the League set out to increase its influence by recruiting union members. As part of that strategy, some of our members, including recent college graduates, sought jobs in the service industry and joined the unions. That's what brought Walter Aaron and several other Revolutionary Workers League members to Durham in late 1974. Walter had been active in SOBU and YOBU, but we didn't meet personally until he came to Durham on assignment for the League in November 1974. I offered to allow him and two female members to stay with me temporarily. We crammed into my tiny apartment for a few months until they were all able to find jobs. The four of us often met up with other League members who had come to Durham from other cities, and we'd spend hours in the evenings, sitting around my place or theirs, reading Marxist-Leninist literature and engaging in long, intellectual conversations about what it meant. Walter and some of the others also published a newsletter. We had come to the conclusion that America's capitalist system was designed to keep the poor man in his place and that this country needed a whole new structure. And we were idealistic enough to believe we could make that happen. It sounds unbelievable now that we actually thought we could topple capitalism in America. But this was the 1970s; so much around us seemed in flux. The Vietnam War had killed enough Americans—58,220, according to the government's most recent count—to rival the population of a mid-sized U.S. city, left thousands of others maimed and emotionally wounded, and exposed our military weaknesses. The Arab oil embargo, ensuing crisis, and mile-long lines at the gas pumps had exposed

our country's dependence on foreign sources for one of our most basic necessities: oil. And the resignation of President Richard Nixon in
disgrace after the Watergate scandal had exposed the brazen, corrupt
nature of our politics. All the while, unemployment was high, poverty
was widespread, and racism was rampant. America was raw. We were
just young people in the struggle for change, trying to figure out the
best way to keep struggling.

Walter and I became great friends, and to this day, we remain close.
To my kids, he was (and is today) Uncle Walter. They got to know him
when they came to visit me in Durham. I wasn't the greatest cook back
then—bacon-wrapped hot dogs and pork and beans were staples—
and Walter teased me mercilessly. I will never live down the time I
tried to make the kids some crescent rolls and didn't realize I was actually supposed to roll the dough. But we all ate them, and they tasted
fine to me, flat and all.

Walter eventually got a job as a nursing assistant at Duke University
Hospital, about the same time that Local 77 was trying to expand to
include service workers at Duke University Hospital. Walter spent
much time getting to know his co-workers, talking to them about
their lives, and trying to persuade them to join the union. He quickly
learned that our idealism wasn't transferable. He was working alongside people who were consumed by the most basic struggles: staying
alive, providing food and shelter for their families. They had no college
education to push them forward. Their low-paying jobs were their sus-
tenance, and anything that seemed remotely threatening to that didn't
stand much of a chance. Word spread that a bunch of Communists
were trying to take over the union. The specter of Communism fright-
ened folks, and hospital service workers voted down a ballot initiative
asking whether they wanted to join Local 77. I had worked so hard,
helping the union to explain the issue in the community and recruit
supporters. The loss was deeply disappointing.

Meanwhile, inside the Revolutionary Workers League, things began to take a bizarre turn. Many of the New Communist Movement
groups began to form alliances, and our leadership joined a group
called the Puerto Rican Revolutionary Workers Organization. Under
the guise of "party building," members were summoned to New York
for a forum on at least two occasions. During marathon sessions that
started in mid-afternoon and lasted until the early dawn hours of the
next day, we listened to speeches, discussed the group's mission and

goals, and participated in weird tests of our knowledge and loyalty. A group leader would pick up a book by Stalin or Lenin, read a passage, and pick out an audience member to explain what it meant. Or, the leader might ask a question, like "What is the central and only task?" If the response was deemed incorrect or inappropriate, the member was publicly ridiculed and humiliated. Members whose commitment was suspect were "purged," or expelled, from the group. Some were beaten, and to prove allegiance to the group, every person who remained in the room had to take turns hitting the alleged offender. Some members were stripped of all of their belongings, driven to a remote area in New York, and abandoned. I saw friends turn on each other—one friend participating in the humiliation and beating of his buddy to avoid being ostracized from the group. At one of the sessions that I didn't attend, Walter was even singled out and beaten. He and I had been as close as brothers, but we suddenly became distrustful of one another and estranged. We didn't know who we could trust, so we trusted no one.

At the second such meeting that I attended in late summer of 1976, I was leery from the moment I arrived at the two-day gathering in New Jersey. I sat there, paranoid much of the time that I would be singled out next. When the abuse started again, I thought to myself: "This is some insane shit! What have I gotten myself into? What have I brought my friends into? What does this have to do with revolution and changing people's lives for the better?" I don't even remember how I got through the rest of the meeting, but I left, feeling dazed and angry. I got in my car and drove nearly five hundred miles nonstop back to Durham. I thought about the people who had been singled out and hurt. I thought about the people who had become part of this group because they'd trusted me. I thought about the humiliation and beatings I'd witnessed in silence. The moment seemed surreal. How had I gotten so far off track? How had I let myself be controlled in this way? Did it matter that I had intended it all for good? I'd shattered the people's trust in me. I'd destroyed my marriage. I was living apart from my children. Everything that I'd believed and worked for over the past few years seemed in question. I felt completely broken.

Once I got to Durham, I drove straight to my apartment, packed up everything I owned, piled it into my car, and headed for the only place that felt secure in the world: back home to Milwaukee.

160 ·

Howard Fuller NO STRUGGLE, NO PROGRESS

With Amiri Baraka and Amil Cabral, the first Secretary General of the
African Party for the Independence of Guinea and the Cape Verde
Islands (PAIGC), in the months before Cabral's 1973 assassination.

With Brenda Paris and Gene Locke, fellow members of the African
Liberation Day Coordinating Committee, in Africa in 1973
to deliver fundraising donations.

At the 6th Pan-African Conference in June 1974 in Dar es Salaam, the first one on African soil.

During a plenary session at the 6th Pan-African Conference.

10

REBUILDING MYSELF

Whenen I returned to Milwaukee, I was jobless, broke, separated from my family, and totally confused about what I believed and why. I didn't even knew if I was safe. I was paranoid that my sudden departure had made me the enemy, and perhaps even a wanted man, within the Revolutionary Workers Organization. I had no idea whether some of those guys would come looking for me. Worst of all, agonizing back pain from that old college injury resurfaced and left me practically incapable of walking. The physical and mental pain fed off each other, and I was a complete wreck. But I was fortunate to have the unconditional love of my mother and grandmother, who saw my suffering and welcomed me home. They never even asked me to explain.

No matter how bad I felt, though, my love for my children pushed me out of bed each day. Suddenly, I was no longer Owusu, the revolutionary, the leader who put the movement above all else. I was just a man—a broken one at that—and a father who longed for his children. Perhaps for the first time, they alone were my priority. I felt responsible for them, and knew that somehow I had to provide for them. I didn't want them to suffer any more than they already had because I wasn't there. I needed a job—and fast. But the Milwaukee I'd left after high school had, like me, been changed. It had survived the deadly race riots of July 1967, and its once relatively compact but upwardly mobile Black community was beginning to feel the brunt of urban renewal, freeway construction, and the lack of real estate reinvestment. Manufacturing jobs, which had been the ticket to the middle class for so many Black men and women were disappearing. There were no Black colleges, as there had been in North Carolina, and there were few Black-owned businesses.

Fortunately, though, I still had friends around. They remembered me as Howard Fuller, the former basketball star and student leader, and so, as a practical matter, I began using my birth name again. One day I ran into Irie Grant, an old friend, fellow North Division graduate, phenomenal basketball player, and the other brother who had enrolled at Carroll in my junior year. He had become a general manager for the Equitable Life Insurance Company. We quickly caught up, and he offered me a job as an insurance agent, earning a small base salary plus commission. I didn't know a thing about selling insurance and had never even worked in the private sector. But I appreciated the opportunity and was determined to make it work. I learned right away that I needed to sell to customers who were likely to maintain their policies because, if they canceled within a certain time frame, I'd have to return the commission. The job was a great learning experience, but it was also very humbling. I once asked a fellow agent how to find customers, and he handed me the phone book. I was amazed to learn that there was actually a science behind selling—if you made a certain number of cold calls, a certain number of people would agree to meet you. Most would ultimately decline, but a small percentage of them would say yes. We worked the phones diligently for that small percentage of yeses. The first policy I sold was to my mother. I gradually got better at it, especially when I realized that the sales process was similar in some ways to community organizing. In both, I was trying to talk people into doing something by making clear what was in it for them. Also, I had developed good organization skills over the years, which were very helpful in my new job.

As soon as I got my first paycheck, I sent money to North Carolina for my kids and got my own place. It would take nearly a year before I was earning enough to afford a car. But within eleven months, I had risen to become one of the top sales agents in the region. That distinction brought me an invitation to celebrate my success with other top sellers at a resort in Cable, Wisconsin. I was asked to speak during the program about the techniques that had helped me make it to the top. By the time I arrived at the resort, I had decided to quit and accept a new job. So, I'd decided not to talk about how to sell a lot of insurance policies. Instead, I planned to give a speech on why American companies should stop doing business in South Africa to help bring an end to apartheid. As I spoke, some members of the audience sat there dumbfounded. Others looked appalled. When I was done, they seemed unsure whether they should even clap. There was a bit of polite applause, but it didn't matter. I'd spoken the truth. I resigned from Equitable with no regrets. I hated selling insurance, but the experience taught me the importance of distinguishing between a job and my work. Selling insurance was a job, something I had to do, like it or not, to take care of myself and my children, and I gave it my best for as long as I needed to do so. But my work centered, then and now, around those social issues that ignited my passion: advocating on behalf of the poor, building a Black-centered university, fighting for the dignity of my people, and supporting the African liberation movement. I had been fortunate that, for most of my adult life, my job had reflected my work. But when that was no longer true, I had to learn how to function. I learned to appreciate the job for what it was, to expect nothing more, and to find other opportunities to engage in the work that fulfilled my soul.

In August 1977, I got another chance to do a job that reflected my work when I landed at Marquette University. Even though Milwaukee was a large city even then, it did not have huge, major universities. The University of Wisconsin–Milwaukee, formerly the Milwaukee State Teachers College, was the largest, and it was a public commuter school. Marquette was a smaller Jesuit university within walking distance of downtown and the southern edge of Milwaukee's Black community, much as Columbia University is on the southern edge of Harlem in New York City. I owe a lifetime of gratitude to Dr. Arnold Mitchem for giving me a chance to merge my job and my work. Mitch is among the special people who intervened at a critical juncture in my life and changed its course for the better.

Mitch had founded the Educational Opportunity Program (EOP) at Marquette University. EOP was funded by Marquette and the federal government's TRIO program, the name given to three initiatives focused on improving the number of poor and minority students attending college. The TRIO program consisted of Talent Search, Upward Bound and Student Support Services. Talent Search sought to identify smart youths from low-income families and provide academic and mentoring support as early as middle school. The Upward Bound program focused on helping disadvantaged high school students make the transition to college with tutoring, financial counseling, and other support. Student Support Services recruited low-income and minority students who would not have been accepted into college ordinarily, and then provided them with additional resources. Mitch was looking for someone to head the Student Support Services program, and I heard about it from a good friend, George Lowery, who had worked years earlier as one of my interns at the North Carolina Fund. The job seemed to be just what I needed at the time, and I applied. The staff of the Educational Opportunity Program and student participants in the program interviewed me and recommended that I be hired. One of the people involved in that process was Dr. Robert Lowe, who was in charge of a program that provided writing support for the students. The two of us became very close friends and have managed to maintain our friendship in spite of fighting on different sides of the vouchers issue. Bob is one of the smartest people I know. He is a renowned scholar on the history of American Education and on Black Education and has taught me a lot.

Bob was among those who recommended that I be hired. Finally, I had a job that would enable me to do my life's work, and it came with a fixed salary and health insurance. That would come in handy over the Christmas holidays in 1978, when I finally decided to address my lingering back pain and have a spinal fusion. I spent about a week in the hospital and another six weeks flat on my back, recuperating at home. But I never fully recovered. Not a day goes by, even now, when I don't feel some back pain. Over the years I've tried everything to find relief, even visiting a traditional healer (some might say a witch doctor) during a trip to Guyana. About a decade after my surgery, though, I began going to chiropractors, whose treatments at the time were considered unconventional. Finally, I found something that helped to make the pain bearable and relieved me of the fear that I would end up seriously debilitated and, someday soon, unable to do my work.

While at Marquette, I pushed through the pain because I was back on the path of doing the kind of work that really mattered to me. Mitch was a believer in the concept espoused by renowned African American scholar W. E. B. DuBois, who wrote about developing the "talented tenth," a cadre of educated Black leaders who would return to their communities to create a better future for our people. Mitch helped generations of young people believe that it was possible to do well— have stable jobs and personal lives—and do good—work to lift our community—at the same time. His influence on me was profound. He helped me to understand the value of these kinds of programs and gave me a chance to change lives in a whole new way.

As associate director of the Educational Opportunity Program, I brought together counseling and academic support services for students who won conditional acceptance to Marquette through our program. The services included financial aid, counseling, tutoring in math and writing, and a summer program that kept them engaged in college and away from the drugs, crime, and other destructive elements that were prevalent in some of their communities. I loved meeting so many young people with untapped potential and helping them stay focused on school, despite the troubles sometimes swirling around their lives. One of them was a young man named Ricky Burt, who came to my office in the fall of 1981 to let me know he was dropping out of college. Ricky was the fifth of nine children, and, along with an older sister who was at another university at the same time, he was the first in his family to go to college. He had made top-notch grades in high school but was struggling at Marquette. He had also just fathered his second child and figured he'd be better off getting a good-paying job at one of the local plants. Milwaukee was an industrial town, and a lot of kids thought it was cool to skip college, go straight into one of the factories, and make big money right away. Ricky's mind was made up, but since I was his counselor, he figured he would let me know out of respect. He told me he planned to return to college in three or four years, but I knew right away he was making a big mistake. Most people who drop out of college never make it back. I got up out of my chair and closed my office door so I could talk to him privately, man to man. I won't say here exactly what I told him, but let's just say, I spoke in a language I knew would get his attention. I told him in no uncertain terms that he was *not* quitting. I would not allow him to quit. It would be the most foolish thing he'd ever done to walk away from a free college education. I promised him I wouldn't let him fail, that I would check on him and help him as much as I could. He had every opportunity before him, and he would be able to stay in school and take care of his children. He'd better be in class the next day, I warned. And with that, I told him to get out of my office.

I'm sure I left him stunned. I've heard him tell others over the years that no one had ever talked to him in such a way and that he could hardly believe someone seemed to want this college thing for him even more than he did. That conversation inspired Ricky to stay in school, and I tried to do exactly what I promised. He graduated with a bachelor's degree from Marquette, and today he is Bishop R. J. Burt, Sr., pastor of Greater New Birth Church, a 4,000-member congregation that is one of the largest in Milwaukee. Under Bishop Burt, the church bought a block-long old mall and transformed it into a huge sanctuary with dedicated spaces to operate all kinds of community-based programs, including counseling for married couples and people trying to buy a home for the first time, a daycare center, a car care clinic, and even a recreational center with an 18-lane bowling alley.

When I think about my work in Marquette's Educational Opportunity Program, a young woman named Gwendolyn also comes to mind. Mitch had brought her into the program before I arrived. She had been a star student and president of the student council at North Division High School in her senior year in the 1970s. Her mother was a public school teacher and her father was a factory worker, but Gwen was the eighth of nine children in her family. Without EOP, she likely would not have been able to afford to go to college. Unfortunately, in her first year at Marquette, Gwen had a baby, dropped out, and joined a commune set up like an African village in South Carolina. But by the time I arrived at Marquette, she had gotten herself together and was ready to return to college. She contacted one of my colleagues, Sande Robinson, for help to get back in the program. Sande confided in me. We both knew Mitch's stern position on students who had dropped out. He offered them all the nurturing and support they needed to succeed in college, but if they chose for whatever reasons to cut themselves off, he declared them "dead." That meant they had exhausted their chances for help from the program. Perhaps because of my own experience, though, I understood how a young, impressionable student could lose her way, and I sympathized with her. Sande and I didn't want to see a life with so much potential wasted, and so we teamed up to sneak Gwen back into the program. We actually succeeded in enrolling her without Mitch's knowledge, and she graduated in 1978 with a bachelor's degree in politics. Gwen became a well-known community activist and in 1992 was the first African-American woman elected to the Wisconsin Senate. In 2004, she became the first African-American elected to Congress from Wisconsin—Congresswoman Gwendolyn Moore. Through the EOP, I met so many students, like Ricky and Gwen, who may not have had the necessary academic background, study skills, or finances to succeed in college on their own, but they managed to do so anyway by working hard and taking advantage of the extra resources provided for them. That's why I *know* these kinds of programs work. That notion is not some kind of theory or abstraction for me. I've seen it.

While helping to save students in the program, they were, in some ways, saving me. They helped add purpose and meaning to my life at a time when I needed to feel just that. I learned that I was strong enough to endure extreme hardship and that I could make some mid-course corrections—a lesson that I often share with students. My experience also left me with a deeper understanding of cults and brainwashing and how people can get swept up in an unimaginable scenario. But it also made me super vigilant. I vowed never again to get caught up in some ideology that I didn't completely understand or fully support. I also became more appreciative of the real relationships in my life, particularly my family, whose love was always unconditional.

I sent money to take care of my kids every month, and, when the divorce was final, I never missed a child support payment. Beyond that, I wanted to make sure my children really knew me. I didn't want them to view me as just a ghost who sent a paycheck every month. I wanted them to grow up knowing they had a father who loved them and was as present as he could be in their lives. So, I did all I could to be a good dad. I talked to them regularly about school, their friends, and their social lives, and we had an agreement that they could call me "collect" whenever they wanted. Their mother helped by involving me as much as she could from a distance in major decision-making about them. Once, when she learned Malcolm had stolen something, she called me to discuss his punishment. I booked a flight to Greensboro right away, and within a few days, I was there to discipline him face-to-face. And let's just say, I had no qualms with using corporal punishment when it came to my own children. I tried to raise them like my mother and grandmother had raised me—confident that they were well-loved, but just as sure of the consequences if they stepped out of line.

Even before I could afford plane fare, though, I'd drive to Greensboro to spend time with the children, and I drove to pick them up at the beginning of every summer to spend the entire vacation with me. During those summer days with them, I got just a small taste of what it must have been like for Viola, juggling a full-time job with the responsibility of caring for three children alone every single day. I, at least, had some help from my mother and grandmother, especially when it came to doing the girls' hair. I never quite mastered that. But as the three of them grew, I tried to stay tuned to their interests and put them in various Milwaukee summer camps. I also tried to pass on my love of sports.

Kelli, the oldest, always has been the most sociable and outgoing of the three. There are no strangers to her when she enters a room. She played basketball in high school, and I got to see her play during her senior year. K.P., as I like to call her, took some time, but she hung tough and graduated from New York City College of Technology in her 30s.

Malcolm was more introverted as a child. He inherited my height but didn't play basketball in junior high or high school. I did, however, get him in a couple of summer basketball camps. He struggled academically in high school, and so, in addition to working with him at home, I enrolled him in tutoring programs. Still, Malcolm didn't like to study, and he put forth minimal effort in school. His mother and I were relentless in our encouragement, though. Finally, something in him clicked when he got to North Carolina A&T University. He seemed to realize for the first time what he needed to do to be successful and started working harder. He ultimately graduated cum laude from North Carolina A&T in industrial electronics engineering and computer technology and has since earned an M.B.A. (Master of Business Administration) degree from DeVry University's Keller Graduate School of Management. He has also received graduate certification in project management and is pursuing another master's degree in the subject. He works as the maintenance reliability engineering lead for power train operations at the Harley-Davidson Motor Company in Milwaukee. Malcolm's experience reinforced something I've always believed—we should never give up on our children. They can change if we continue to love and encourage them.

Miata, the youngest, surprised me with her athletic ability. A bit reserved in personality, she talked to me once about wanting to be a cheerleader. I tried to talk her out of it, asking why in the world she would want to cheer for the athletes when she could be one herself. She was tall and fast, and she eventually played basketball, volleyball, and track. She excelled in track, and during the summer I put her in track clubs in Madison and Milwaukee. We traveled to track meets together across Wisconsin. She even set records in her age group in Wisconsin. She also participated in regional meets in Minnesota and Illinois. I was there when her Dudley High School squad from Greensboro won the state track championship in North Carolina. I was proud of her when she got a track scholarship to Marquette and moved to Milwaukee, near me, from 1989 through 1993.

It was important to me to show up for the major events in my kids' lives, but I also tried to take some of the load off Viola when it came to handling other parental tasks, like the time Kelli realized in the months before her high school graduation that she may not have enough credits to graduate. I headed to Greensboro once again, and spent a week talking to school officials and working with her to get some papers done so that she could graduate on time. But I never viewed those actions as something worthy of applause. They were just things I should have been doing as a father. Yet, as hard as I tried, I know there was no substitute for being there all the time. Miata made that clear many years later when I asked her to grade me honestly as a father. She gave me an 85 percent. It would have been higher, she said, if I had been there. Their mother was there, and indeed, she deserves the lion's share of praise for the good people our children turned out to be.

Being back home in Milwaukee also made me more reflective about the true friends in my life. At the end of the day, what do you have in life, if not your family and friends? Maybe several months after moving home, I reached out to Walter. We had been like brothers, and at first we were just happy to be back in touch. We didn't broach the subject of what each of us had gone through in the Revolutionary Workers League. The pain was too deep. But one day, we sat down and had that tough conversation. The details of it have long since escaped me, but we both agreed that it was an insane period and that we would never again let anything like that break apart true friendship. And I haven't wasted any time since then even thinking about the organization. I also reestablished contact with the other friends I'd made during my work in North Carolina. The experiences we'd shared and the bonds we'd developed in the process—those were real and lifelong.

As the 1970s drew to a close, I got involved again in community activism. My idealism of the 1960s and early '70s had faded, and I realized that I couldn't change the world. But I also couldn't just sit back, watch racism and injustice on display, shake my head in disgust, and do nothing. That just wasn't in my makeup. So, when I got a call in the fall of 1978 about changes that the Milwaukee Board of School Directors had planned for my high school alma mater, North Division, old anger burned inside me. The school had become nearly

97 percent Black, and for years the community had lobbied for the Board of Education to replace the drab, antiquated old building. The board finally spent $20 million to open a brand new school on the same site in September 1978. Then, it approved a plan for the next year to turn North into a citywide specialty school focusing on health and science technology with open enrollment to attract white students. Neighborhood attendance zones were eliminated. That meant neighborhood Black students would have to apply to attend, and no doubt many of them would be turned away in the quest for racial balance. That's where I drew the line. I had no issue with the concept of a specialty health and science technology school, but it was so infuriating that as soon as the community got the brand-new school it had been pushing for, it was in essence being taken away. When students at North heard about the plan, they walked out, marched to the school system's administration building, and staged a demonstration. The students then reached out to alumni, who reached out to other alumni for support. Someone contacted me about plans to protest at an upcoming school board meeting. On the night of the meeting, the board room was packed. Several people, including me, signed up to speak against the board's plan. When it was my turn, I made my way to the microphone, looked around at my people jammed together in that room, fighting for a school that had meant so much to so many of us, and my words shot out like flames. I talked about the many great leaders who had come from North and mentioned by name several of the other Black schools the board had shut down. "Enough is enough," I shouted, summing up my speech.

Those three words—Enough Is Enough—became the slogan for a broad-based community group called the Coalition To Save North. I was selected as chairman, and we began holding regular meetings at the Urban League office, located across the street from the school. Though a core group of about seventy-five people made up the coalition, we drew hundreds of participants for our protests. We organized petition drives, held marches, and attended every school board meeting to let the members know we were watching. We broadcast our concerns every chance we got on Black radio, in televised interviews, and in newspapers. With support from one of my old allies, the Interreligious Foundation for Community Organization, the coalition also was able to get an attorney named Dottie Holman, who was fantastic in helping us to frame our legal argument. The board had justified its decision to change North by claiming that its academic performance was the worst in the city. North consistently ranked at the bottom when standardized test data was released. But we filed a legal petition asking the court to require the school system to release every high school's testing data, disaggregated by race. At first, the board lied, claiming the system did not have the data broken down that way. But the court sided with us and ordered the information released. The results were astonishing—the average score for Black children across the district was lower than a "C." North was not the worst in the district for Black students, after all. The school system essentially had been hiding what was happening to Black kids system-wide. Changing the racial composition of North would not address the core problem. The coalition also argued in court that the school system was unfairly putting the burden of desegregation on Black children.

The board had rarely, if ever, backed away from a decision like this, but the coalition fought diligently for more than a year. We eventually reached an out-of-court settlement that kept North a neighborhood school but created a medical specialty program within the school. In keeping with the settlement, the board voted on May 1, 1980, to reverse its decision to open enrollment at North. It was a big victory for the community. But the board, perhaps still angry about its court loss, made a final power move. After the coalition put together a small group that spent the summer working with the principal to redesign North's academic program, the board sabotaged those efforts by transferring the principal to another school and assigning a new one. Still, the coalition victory brought back many good memories of my community organizing days in North Carolina and reminded me of what can happen when people stand together to demand change and stick with it.

Later that fall, my personal life again changed dramatically. I was attending an annual financial aid conference for my job at the Abbey resort in Fontana, Wisconsin, when I met Claudetta Wright, an assistant director of financial aid at Iowa University in Iowa City. She was smart, attractive, and we hit it off right away. The next thing I knew, we were planning weekend getaways together. Over the following seven weeks, we saw each other four times and decided rather spontaneously to get married. She moved from Iowa, where she had been raised, to Milwaukee, and we had a small private ceremony at a friend's house in January 1981. She eventually landed a job in retail banking at First

Wisconsin National Bank of Milwaukee, and she got to know my children when they came to Milwaukee for the summer. But Claudetta soon would discover that marriage to me was far from the quiet, family-centered life she had envisioned.

We had been married about six months when the police killing of a twenty-two-year-old Black man named Ernest Lacy enraged the community and drew me back into the spotlight. Lacy was walking to a downtown convenience store for a snack on July 9, 1981, when he was stopped by three white police officers searching for a rape suspect. The officers wrestled Lacy to the ground, and knelt on his neck while handcuffing him face-down. The pressure cut off his air supply and left him unable to breathe. With no regard for his humanity, the officers then threw the young man in the back of a police van. As he lay dying, they answered another call. Meanwhile, someone else was identified as the rapist.

Though it took a while for all of the details to emerge, I knew in my gut Ernest Lacy had been murdered. For the previous seventeen years, the Milwaukee police department had been led by a racist tyrant named Harold Breier, whose officers were well known for their brutality toward Black men. For me, the Lacy case brought back to my memory one of the city's most notorious cases of police misconduct—the police shooting of a twenty-two-year-old Black man named Daniel Bell. I had been a senior in high school the night Bell was stopped by white police officers in 1958 because he was driving a car with a broken tail light. When he ran, an officer shot him in the back. It took twenty years before one of the officers involved admitted that his fellow officer had used racial slurs, shot Bell in cold blood, and then planted a knife on him to make the shooting look justified. The Lacy case felt like déjà vu, and there was no way in hell we as a community could sit back and let the police get away again with murder.

Within the first week, community activist Michael McGee, who among his other community activities headed an organization called Project Respect, convened a meeting in his office on 3rd Street (now Martin Luther King Drive). We discussed the case and began meeting every week to organize. We attracted broad support from African Americans, as well as sympathetic whites, including a group of nuns and Father James Groppi, a Roman Catholic priest and civil rights activist. Members of the Lacy family also joined us, and as our numbers grew, we moved our meetings to Incarnation Lutheran Church. We named ourselves the Coalition for Justice for Ernest Lacy, and Mike and I became the group's de facto leaders. He and I were an interesting pair. In some ways, we were polar opposites. Or, maybe he was more like the old me—a proudly radical, anti-establishment brother who had been fighting many years on behalf of poor and working-class Black folks and had a sizable following among them. I was working at Marquette and by then had decided on a whim to begin a PhD program because it was one of the benefits of working at the university. To people like Mike, I was part of the "system," and one day he told me so. The two of us were riding in the car together when he turned to me and said: "I really ought to hate a nigger like you." I wasn't offended, though, because I knew that was just Mike's way of expressing himself, and he and I were becoming good friends. I have a tremendous amount of respect for the brother because I know he cares deeply about Black people, as I do. Neither of us had a private agenda or any jealousy, and we actually made a verbal agreement that we weren't going to let the naysayers inside or outside of the coalition divide us. We talked practically every day about the case for a year, and when someone came to either of us with crap about the other, we told one another about it. I'm confident that our cohesiveness helped the coalition stay together for the long haul.

The fight was indeed a long haul. We held about four major marches and rallies. One rally, which started at the spot on Wisconsin Avenue where Lacy had been arrested, attracted 4,000 people, according to newspaper estimates. The next march was even larger. We also held smaller demonstrations in the community, at the District Attorney's Office and the Milwaukee Fire and Police Commission. Chief Breier usually showed up at our marches and rallies, riding alongside marchers in an unmarked police car, waving arrogantly. At one rally at the Martin Luther King Center in the Black community, Breier got of his car, surrounded by police officers, and waded into the crowd that had gathered to listen to speeches. We knew clearly what he was trying to do. "Breier's here for only one reason, to provoke the crowd," Mike warned participants. "Listen, just because he's a fool, we don't have to be no fool."

This dude was awful. Amongst the despicable things he did was, like J. Edgar Hoover, keep files on an array of people he didn't like. "Breier is not crazy," I later told the crowd. "He is a dangerous man. He knows exactly what he is doing... and we have to understand that."

The crowd never took his bait.

During this time, though, a woman who identified herself as Lucille A. Moran began trying to use my past to discredit me because of my criticism of Breier and the police department. Ms. Moran dug up a copy of a controversial 1969 document called the "Black Manifesto," which listed me as a member of its steering committee. I had been a board member of the Interreligious Foundation of Community Organizations (IFCO) during its Black National Economic Development Conference in April 1969, where the document first surfaced. James Forman, who had been one of the principal organizers of the Student Nonviolent Coordinating Committee (SNCC), walked into the last plenary session of the day with a bunch of dudes carrying guns. The guys with guns surrounded the auditorium while Forman walked to the microphone and declared that he was assuming control of the conference on behalf of the people. He then presented the "Black Manifesto," which, among other things, demanded $500 million from Christian white churches and Jewish synagogues as reparations for their roles in perpetuating slavery and other injustices against the Black community. IFCO had been created one and a half years earlier with funds donated by some of those same churches to address poverty and racial injustice. So, as a conciliatory gesture, IFCO's Executive Director Lucius Walker later that evening signed me up to serve on some kind of committee that was to take up the matter from there. That was the last I heard of the committee. Forman captured national media attention a short time later when he disrupted services at the Riverside Church in New York City with demands for reparations for Black people. But I don't recall ever attending even a single meeting or participating in any way as part of a committee connected to the Manifesto.

Nevertheless, the document listing me as a committee member was copied and, in a letter dated March 5, 1982, Ms. Moran mailed it to every elected official in the city, the Fire and Police Commission, and of course, the media. I refused to panic. My past was what it was, and, no one was going to make me apologize for it or feel ashamed. Plus, it had nothing to do with the matter at hand. I urged the coalition to stay singularly focused on demanding justice for Ernest Lacy, and that is what we did.

There were regular disappointments and delays in the case, but the coalition kept up with every development, adjusting our strategy as necessary. After three inconclusive autopsies, the coroner summoned an inquest, and a six-member jury spent nearly a month listening to testimonies from more than one hundred people, including eyewitnesses and others involved in the case. The jury, three Black members and three white ones, found that Lacy's death had been caused by the pressure on his back and neck which cut off the oxygen to his brain. The jurors recommended that the District Attorney file charges of "homicide by reckless conduct" against the arresting officers, use of excessive force against the officer that knelt on Lacy's neck, and misconduct in public office against two other officers in the police van for failing to render first aid or call for assistance. The officers were charged, which was a major victory for the coalition. But the victory was short-lived when our push for a racially balanced inquest jury was used against us. The District Attorney argued that the police officers' civil rights had been violated because race had been considered during the jury selection, and the charges against the officers were dropped. It was so disappointing, but we in the coalition were determined to keep up the pressure. We planned a sit-in at the District Attorney's Office to push for the reinstatement of charges. But we didn't want the kind of quiet, mournful sit-in of the Civil Rights Movement. Our style was more irreverent. Since we were to be there overnight, we brought hot plates, pots, and food and sat around the outer lobby of the District Attorney's Office, cooking and playing music and bid whist. We had the whole place smelling like greens and chicken. When it was time for our weekly rally at Incarnation Lutheran Church, Mike and I sent the rest of the crowd to the church, and we stayed behind, sitting on a bench in the lobby of the D.A.'s office. By then, we had been there at least two days, and we devised a plan to get arrested and generate a "Free Howard and Michael" campaign, hoping to draw more attention to the case. As expected, the sheriff's deputies showed up. We refused their order to vacate the premises, and a couple of the deputies lifted each of us up and headed toward the door. But instead of arresting us, they dumped us outside and left. There went our "Free Howard and Michael" idea. Mike and I ended up catching a cab to the church rally.

We tried every tactic we knew, including petition drives and boycotts of downtown stores and a shopping mall frequented by African Americans. Our hope was that the lost revenue would encourage business owners to wield their economic power, speak out against the injustice in the Lacy case, and speed up the legal process. In the meantime, we maintained the weekly rallies, attended every open hearing, and continued our protests to keep our people engaged. We wanted the officials involved to know that we would not be satisfied until justice was done.

Finally, in May 1983, the Milwaukee Fire and Police Commission, acting on a complaint filed by Lacy's mother, found the five police officers involved guilty of failing to render first aid to him. The commission also found that the officer who knelt on Lacy's neck used excessive force. That officer ultimately was fired, two others received a sixty-day suspension without pay, and the remaining two were suspended forty-five days without pay. This was a hard-fought victory. It was the first time that any action had been taken against the Milwaukee police department for its longtime abuse of African Americans and other minorities. For the first time, a message was sent to the Milwaukee police force that the Black community would not stand idly by and accept the killing of Black people by police. A year later, the state legislature approved a major police reform bill that gave the Fire and Police Commission more control over the police department. I'm pretty sure the measure expedited the retirement of Breier, who had been elected in 1964 and in his later years boasted that he had no plans to retire. The Lacy family also settled a civil lawsuit against the police department for a reported $1.7 million.

I'm proud of the coalition's work. Even today when there's a police violence case somewhere in this country, the Coalition for Justice for Ernest Lacy is often cited as one of the most well-organized, sustained community efforts ever against a police department. But there was little joy in any of it. A young man was killed for no reason at all. We as a community stepped up and did what we needed to do, but nothing we did could ever change that one sobering fact.

With my children, Kelli, Malcolm, and Miata, in Milwaukee
during their summer visits.

Marching in 1978 with the Coalition to Save North Division High School (my alma mater).

Marching with protesters on Wisconsin Avenue in Milwaukee to protest the death of of Ernest Lacy in police custody.

Addressing the crowd at a protest to save my high school alma mater.

With activist Michael McGee at a protest in the District Attorney's Office.

Speaking at a weekly community meeting of the Coalition for Ernest Lacy.

Speaking at an Ernest Lacy rally.

11

GETTING IN THE ROOM

It occurred to me one day that maybe I should get personally involved in electoral politics in Wisconsin. During my time in North Carolina, I had played a role in registering Black people to vote and helping to get them out to the polls. At one point, I even urged them *not* to vote as a way to send a message to the Democratic party to quit taking Black people for granted.

But my thinking about how to bring about change to benefit my people was ever evolving. For much of my adult life, I had been the ultimate outsider, always hollering at those on the inside, trying to force change. Eventually, though, I began to notice that when the change that those of us on the outside had been pushing for finally came, the people on the inside were making the decisions about how much or how little change were they willing to accept.

I started talking about the importance of "being in the room" where important decisions were being made. So, I made a decision: I needed to get in the room. Or, at the very least, I needed to be closely connected to someone in the room.

I understood that many of my friends would not understand that change in strategy. I knew to some I would be seen as "selling out." But I was convinced that it was necessary for me to assume a different role. I would never criticize those who chose to "stay on the outside," but I needed to pursue a different path. The reality is that for significant change to take place, you need to have both an inside and an outside strategy. I also knew that for those on the inside trying to make a difference, their hands were strengthened when there was outside pressure. I could not see myself ever running for public office, but I was ready to find my place behind the scene. And to me, Milwaukee was in need of some new people "in the room."

When I looked at the mayoral appointees in Milwaukee in 1982, there were no Black people in key, powerful roles. By then, Mayor Henry Maier had been in office twenty-two years. He was sixty-four years old, and it was reasonable to assume that his tenure was winding down. He might have hired one Black assistant during his time but certainly not a department head. I knew that even after he left office it still would be difficult for Black people to claim positions of authority in the city because very few of us had government experience. There had to be a way for some talented Black men and women to gain pertinent experience so that we would be ready to compete for high-ranking jobs in city government when the time came, perhaps the 1988 election.

The upcoming governor's race in 1982 seemed the perfect opportunity for me and some of my Black friends who were interested in politics to learn about campaigning and get involved on the ground floor with a promising candidate. Republican Governor Lee Dreyfus had decided unexpectedly not to run again, and without an incumbent, the Democrats saw a great opportunity to capture the seat. I identified most with Democrats at the time, and of the three men running for governor, I concluded right away that it made no sense for me to support either the leading candidate or the long shot. The top guy was an old-line politician named Martin Schreiber, who had served as a former state senator, lieutenant governor, and had been acting governor from 1977 to 1979. He already had strong backing from many of the city's Black leaders, and so I assumed my support wouldn't catch his attention in the strategic way I desired. Besides, I wanted to back a fresh candidate with new ideas. The least known of the three, James B. Wood, didn't seem to have much of a chance. That left Anthony Earl, a former state legislator who had been Secretary of the Wisconsin Department of Natural Resources. I knew nothing about the guy and had never met him, but, on a hunch, I decided to reach out to his campaign. I agreed to host a meet-and-greet event for him at my house, and that was the first time I saw him face-to-face. About twenty-five of my friends showed up. Tony was very personable, and right on the issues that were important to me. He came across as a really nice guy, and I liked him right away. At the end of the evening, I announced that I would be supporting him for governor and invited others to join me. A group of us formed an organization called the Black Political Network, and we focused our energy on Tony's campaign. We did literature drops in communities throughout Milwaukee, and one Sunday I teamed up with Ralph Hollmon, a close friend and fellow network member, and even covered an entire ward. The network also conducted voter registration drives and participated in phone banks, calling targeted voters.

Campaigning taught me so much about electoral politics. I learned that, as in sales, there's a science to campaigning and that knocking on random doors wasn't the most effective use of time. Our volunteers went through lists of registered voters, targeted those who voted consistently, and then knocked on their doors or called them to discuss our candidate. It was fortunate that I had decided to get involved during the Democratic primary election. During the primary races, Democratic and Republican voters decide separately which candidates will move on to the general election to compete against each other. The most hard-fought battles often occur early during the primaries. The backing of the Black Political Network was critical for Tony at that stage, as he worked to build more support within the Black community. And we didn't go to him with our hands out, asking to be paid for our support. Often, Black political workers sought money from candidates in exchange for their campaign work, but I always believed that's why we ended up with crumbs when it came time for the winning candidates to select appointees. Once a candidate has paid for your support, they owe you nothing. Not only did we refuse to ask Tony for money, we raised money for him. We did our homework, and we knew it would be impossible to beat Schreiber in Milwaukee because of his longtime political relationships in the community. Our goal was realistic: to increase the number of Black Democrats voting for Tony in the primary because they were willing to give someone else a chance. That would cut into Schreiber's Milwaukee Democratic base. As expected, Schreiber carried Milwaukee, but in the wards where we campaigned for Tony, the gap between the two candidates' vote totals was much smaller than in the other wards. Our support helped Tony to win a respectable number of votes among Black voters. The race was so close that we were not certain of the outcome until all of the precincts had reported. We watched and waited practically all night. Then, when the votes were counted statewide, Tony was the unlikely winner, with 45.87 percent of the vote to Schreiber's 41.97 percent. It was a thrilling victory because the most difficult race was definitely behind us. Tony went on to beat the Republican candidate with 57 percent of the vote.

In the days after the election, Tony came to my house to thank me for my support. He also asked if I would be willing to serve in his cabinet.

This was such a rare opportunity, especially for an African American. There had been only a few high-ranking Black state officials before me, including the guy I was replacing. But how many people of any race get to have close access to a governor? I agreed, and after a few discussions with me about what I wanted, he decided to name me Secretary of the Department of Employment Relations. The position would make me responsible for negotiating contracts with all state government employee unions and developing the pay plan for all non-unionized state employees, including the University of Wisconsin system and state elected officials. My department also had oversight responsibilities for the civil service system and was responsible for the implementation of affirmative action. But even before the official announcement of my appointment, the Black Manifesto documents surfaced again, and people started digging into my background. As soon I learned what was going on, I explained to Tony how my name came to be associated with the Manifesto and who I was in 1969. He never once wavered in his support of me, despite being questioned repeatedly by the media. His response was always similar to what he told a caller during a live taping on a radio show: "I want to have him in my administration. I think it's awfully important that people who are regarded as outsiders be given a chance to come into the administration."

The media also tried to make into a mini scandal the complaints of two people who claimed I broke federal law by having a federally-subsidized community group distribute Tony's campaign literature. But I explained from the beginning that I had no idea the North Division Neighborhood Residents group, which had included one of Tony's pamphlets in its newsletter mailing to members, had been a recipient of federal funds. Federal law prohibits nonprofits, which get a tax break for the status, from getting involved in partisan politics. I was not a member of the group, and its leader had assured me the mailing was proper. The issue ultimately fizzled.

On December 8, 1982, Tony called a press conference at North Division High School to announce my appointment. I had asked him to hold the event there, and about one hundred of my friends, family members, and community supporters attended. To be surrounded at that moment by many of the people who meant the most to me was really special. I thanked them all during my speech and made this promise: "The kinds of concerns you all have in this room are to be represented in whatever room I'm in."

Tony took office in January 1983, and he and I agreed that the best approach for me to get through the Senate confirmation hearing was to meet individually with every Senator. All but two of them agreed to meet with me. The two who refused had made up their minds to oppose me and didn't want to hear anything I had to say. My conversations with the others were cordial. My background did come up during the confirmation hearing, but I tried to defuse it. When asked about my affiliation with Marxism, I said something like: "I used to be a Boy Scout, too, and I'm no longer a Boy Scout." It was stupid, but that's what came out of my mouth.

My nomination was approved, and Claudetta and I moved to Madison to begin the next phase of our lives. I give Tony much credit for standing by me during this period. He put me in rooms where I never would have gained access and gave me the opportunity to see from the inside how state government really works. Of all of the people I've worked for through the years, I probably respect Tony Earl the most. He really understood state government and genuinely wanted to do the right thing for the people in the state. What a great guy, and what an unbelievably rich learning experience my time in his administration would turn out to be.

One of my first major tasks was a reorganization of my department. The changes I desired involved tampering with the Holy Grail of state government: the civil service system, the merit-based process by which employees are hired and promoted through testing. It was generally considered untouchable because any structural or procedural modifications required legislative approval and a signature by the governor. I knew the task ahead would be difficult, but it provided my first big lessons in how to get things done in public office.

From the start, the head of the Association of Career Employees (ACE), the organization that represented many of the non-union civil service employees, let me know that I would not have his support. He rejected even the idea that change was needed. Nevertheless, I turned to a key legislator and a University of Wisconsin professor who were considered the civil service experts, worked with them to draft a solid reorganization plan, and allowed them to guide me through the process. I knew it was important to give my staff an opportunity to express their concerns to me directly, and so I sat in the lunch room an entire day to meet with every employee who wanted to talk to me. Then, I began meeting privately with legislators to explain my rationale and answer their questions, even those whom I knew had not supported my appointment. The measure initially failed at the sub-committee level, but I kept pushing, making a personal appeal to every committee member. The next time around, the plan made it all the way through the legislature, and the governor signed it into law. That was a huge victory for me because it established that I could break through the good old boy network and that I wouldn't allow myself just to be pushed aside.

Among the most important aspects of my job was overseeing the state's affirmative action efforts, and I took that charge very serious-ly. I was determined to use the weight of my office to strengthen Wisconsin's efforts to correct past wrongs that had relegated Black workers, women, and other minorities to the bottom rungs of state government. As part of my department's reorganization, I elevated the old affirmative action office into a division, giving the head of that sec-tion greater authority to direct and monitor the state's efforts in this area. We required each department to submit an affirmative action plan and checked on its progress. We also studied the state's rules and formulas regarding equal employment opportunities and made some adjustments to get more people of color into the pool to be considered for top positions. Of course, there was plenty of grumbling among affirmative action opponents about my aggressive push to make the state's workforce more reflective of the racial and gender diversity of the population, but the criticism didn't bother me. I addressed it head-on during a speech to state employees who were members of the Wisconsin Association of Affirmative Action and Equal Opportunity Professionals on May 26, 1983. I told them I was concerned that affir-mative action was under attack from the top. "I submit to you that the President of the United States, Ronald Reagan, is the titular head of a neo-reactionary thrust that has as one of its primary aims the elim-ination of affirmative action in this country. I submit to you that this threat is real, and it is here right now—today."

I reiterated the purpose of affirmative action in the speech, remind-ed the crowd that affirmative action indeed was the law in Wisconsin, and responded to the various criticisms opponents generally made of such laws. I also went off-script to debunk the notion that all white folks had gotten their good government jobs through merit. I'd met enough dumb white folks in state government to know better. Some of them obviously had an inside connection—a relative, a friend. I was determined to help facilitate the promotion of more Black division heads, managers, and supervisors, and fortunately I was able to do that. With some changes that my staff implemented, we promoted the first Black warden at Waupun Correctional Institution, the state's maximum-security prison for male inmates.

As part of my strategy, I stayed in close touch with legislators, even those I knew were skeptical of me. One of the most skeptical was perhaps Representative Tommy Thompson, the ranking Republican on the Joint Committee for Employment Relations (JOCER). He had likened my appointment to oversee the state's affirmative action efforts to asking "the fox to guard the chicken coop." But I went to him right away and told him that I wanted to introduce myself, even though I knew he was going to vote "no" on all of my proposals that came before the committee. His nickname throughout the statehouse was "Dr. No." But I promised him that I was going to brief him on everything before it was taken up at the committee, so that he at least would know what he was voting against. I kept that promise, and we actually became very good friends. He went on to become the next governor, defeating Tony Earl after his first term. Tommy served an astonishing four terms, becoming the longest-serving governor in the state's history. He finally stepped down in 2001, when he was appointed by President George Bush to become Secretary of the U.S. Department of Health and Human Services.

I learned well how to play the political game. At one point several statewide elected officials mentioned that they wanted a pay raise, but, of course, none of them wanted to take the political risk of proposing it. Instead, I brought forth a proposal that included pay raises for them as part of a package that would provide salary increases for a broad range of employees. While some of the legislators made speeches about their responsibility to approve a lean budget and questioned why I would bring forth such a proposal, I remained calm and let them put on their show. It was all political theater. The measure flew through the legislature.

In this job, as with every job I've ever had, I've always tried to stay connected to the people who work for me. Since negotiating the salary and benefits of all state employees was under my purview, I visited every state institution and met with all categories of workers—prison guards at the penitentiaries, nurses and orderlies at the hospitals, social workers and caretakers at the mental institutions, professors and janitors at the universities. Those visits gave me a totally different level of respect and appreciation for the people who do these jobs. It's one thing to talk about the bureaucracy when you're outside it. But when I got to know the employees and see some of the tough, thankless work many of them were doing, it made me even more dedicated to trying to ensure that they were being treated as fairly as possible. I believe those kinds of gestures went a long way to help me win their confidence. During a serious budget crisis the first year, our department was able to negotiate a one-year pay freeze for all state employees. It was a huge accomplishment that few had imagined was possible. The agreement was that if the state were able to achieve a savings because of the benefits package that had been negotiated, we would share it with employees. As it turned out, those savings actually occurred, and Tony and I proposed a $500-per-employee reward. But when we took this proposal to the legislature, it was voted down. Employees rightfully saw the failure as a betrayal and put the blame on the administration, which may have hurt Tony politically down the road.

All the while, I continued working on my doctorate at Marquette. By the time I went to work for Tony, I had finished the coursework and needed only to complete my dissertation. I began working on it while serving on a state commission that Tony created in May 1984 to assess the quality and equity of education in twenty-two metropolitan Milwaukee public school districts. The idea for the commission had come up during a meeting I'd attended with Tony and a former legislator named Dennis Conta, who during his time in the legislature had sponsored legislation that resulted in an integration program allowing Black students to transfer to certain predominantly white schools in the suburbs. The bill also gave the MPS money for every Black child who was bused from a Black attendance area to a white one. Conta wanted to study the impact of integration on the schools. I suggested a different study that instead analyzed the academic achievement of all children in the city and suburban schools. Tony agreed, brought in state-elected Superintendent of Public Instruction Herbert Grover, and together they created a twenty-seven-member commission to conduct the study. Tony knew of my interest in education issues, and always went out of his way to involve me when the administration dealt with such matters. He named me to the commission, which was headed by George Mitchell, an independent consultant who would become a close friend and confidante over the next two decades.

Several months into my work on the commission, I also began the research for my dissertation. I decided to focus on a topic close to my heart: "The Impact of the Milwaukee Public School System's Desegregation Plan on Black Students and the Black Community (1976-1982)." Ultimately, my research provided factual data for what I had long witnessed—that Black students and the Black community had borne the heaviest burden of the city's desegregation decisions, with neighborhood school closings and busing plans that transported Black children far from their community schools. I pushed myself to finish my dissertation in just six months, and received my Ph.D., in Sociological Foundations of Education on August 14, 1985. I wasn't quite sure exactly how I wanted to use the degree, but it felt good to have achieved my goal and put the work behind me.

Two months later, the state commission released its report, and the shocking results showed that simply putting Black and white children in school together had not been the panacea for academic achievement that many had hoped. For the first time, standardized test data was broken down by race and class for every school. The study found significant disparity between the academic performance of poor and non-poor children and between minority and white children. Thousands of young people were leaving the school system without the necessary skills to function as productive members of society. The average grade-point-average in thirteen of the fifteen public high schools was less than a 2.0, or a C. The dropout rate was twice the state average, and most occurred by eleventh grade. The results were just what I'd feared: Black children in Milwaukee public schools were not learning, and if the state did not do something drastic, we were going to have a major catastrophe on our hands.

Those dismaying results were still burning in my mind when I decided in October 1986 to leave my state job and return to Milwaukee to take a position as Dean of the General Education Division at Milwaukee Area Technical College (MATC). I had done as much as I could to bring about positive change in state government, but I was ready to move back to my home city. The other thing that appealed greatly to me was that the new position would allow me to focus again solely on education. MATC traditionally attracted many young people who either had dropped out of high school or had graduated without the academic record or resources to pursue a bachelor's degree. The college offered training in technical fields such as welding, machinery, dental technology, and nursing, as well as a chance to earn an associate's degree. Those who had dropped out of high school also could earn a high school equivalency credential, or General Education Development certificate (GED). When I arrived at the college, one of the first things I noticed was that the majority of the Black students were taking classes in building "C," where the Continuing Education program and most of the remedial education courses were housed. Most of the students in the "T" building, where the technical classes were taught, were white. My goal became to get more students out of the "C" building into the "T" building.

As the state commission's study had shown, though, too many students were graduating or leaving high school without basic reading and writing skills. For many, it took years of struggle before they realized their limitations and decided to return to school with the hope of broadening the possibilities for their lives. They were often a good bit older than the average college students. Yet, when I visited the remediation classes, I saw many instructors using elementary-style workbooks to teach classrooms full of adults. I figured there had to be a better way, and so I created a Basic Skills Task Force to study the most effective methods of teaching adults. The task force made many recommendations, which we implemented to improve the way we helped adults to learn. With the cooperation of the teachers union leader, I was also able to create some positions and make staffing changes that otherwise might not have been possible without long, drawn-out, legal wrangling. The new positions enabled me to increase the number of talented Black instructors.

As the 1980s began winding down, one of my earlier political predictions was coming true: Henry Maier was finally retiring after serving as Milwaukee's mayor since 1960. My Black political friends and I had been anticipating this for years, with the hope that his 1988 retirement could be the dawning of a new era of opportunity for Black men and women in city government. It shocked me, though, that the city chose to honor Maier during its Martin Luther King, Jr., Day celebration on January 17, 1988. As far as I could see, the city had done little during Maier's nearly three decades in office to address the deteriorating quality of life for Milwaukee's poorest residents. And I'd seen zero effort on the mayor's part to change the powerlessness in the Black community. So, why was he honored?

To express my serious objection to the decision, I notified authorities that I was returning the Martin Luther King, Jr., Humanitarian
Award I had received at the same celebration the previous year. I had
been so honored and humbled when the city chose to make me the
city's first recipient of the award, which was presented to honor someone who best exemplified the spirit of Dr. King. In a statement that I
released to the media, I explained that Maier's legacy stood in direct
contrast to that of Dr. King and that honoring the mayor amounted
to "a slap in the face" of Black people. "There may very well be good
reasons for Henry Maier to be acknowledged and honored, but being
a positive force for empowerment of Black people is clearly not one of
them," my statement said.

In the mayor's race, I threw my support behind State Senator John
Norquist, who expressed a greater commitment to appointing Black
men and women to key positions in his administration. Political strat-
egists said Norquist's campaign got a huge boost when Michael McGee
and I sent out a postcard to Black Milwaukee residents to say we were
supporting John. He ultimately faced a runoff and won convincingly,
capturing the majority of the Black vote. Practically everyone credited
that for his big victory. I was ecstatic that the Black Political Network
had come to play such an important role in electoral politics, and that
the plan we had hatched six years earlier was coming to fruition. Our
plan was unexpectedly assisted by another election stunner that year,
the defeat of longtime County Executive Bill O'Donnell, who had
held the job twelve years. O'Donnell was beaten by a long-shot candidate named David F. Schulz, who had served five years earlier as
budget director for Chicago's first Black mayor, Harold Washington.
David, a Milwaukee native, held the position nearly a year before returning home to work in county government. When David was fired
by the county executive for endorsing John Norquist for mayor, David
launched a campaign to take his former boss's job and did just that.
With the election of both men, more Black men and women than ever
before were selected for leadership roles in city and county government, including several members of the Black Political Network.

In spring 1988, I was tapped by Schulz to head the county's Health
and Human Services Department. The appointment seemed to offer
another chance to have an impact on the lives of poor people and to
grow professionally, and so I accepted. But first, I had to endure another controversial confirmation hearing. The chairman of the Milwaukee

County Board of Supervisors cast the tie-breaking vote, approving me by a count of 13 to 12. The vote spoke loudly to me that there were about as many county board supervisors who were skeptical of me as there were those who supported me. I knew that, to get things done, I somehow had to figure out how to work with them all the same.

First, though, I had to get to know my department, which was huge. It was made up of the Milwaukee County Hospital, the Mental Health Complex, and the Department of Social Services, which had the old welfare department, but it also included a division that dealt with child abuse and neglect. The county's drug and alcohol abuse programs also fell under the department. With 5,400 employees and a $460 million budget, my department alone comprised more than half of the county's staff and annual expenditures. Plus, I had landlord responsibilities for more than 1,000 acres of property that housed the hospital and mental health complex and a number of other county and non-county agencies and the Children's Court. One of the first big issues I had to handle was choosing a company to replace the chiller in one of the building's air conditioning units. I didn't even know what a chiller was. But my advisors expressed great concern when Hitachi, a Japanese company, submitted the best bid. How would it look, they asked, if we chose a foreign company over a homegrown one? I don't even remember how I resolved the issue. I just recall my disbelief that overseeing the county grounds—and the politics involved—was such a big part of my responsibilities.

Of all the jobs I've had, heading the county's Health and Human Services Department was probably the most depressing. The most difficult of all was dealing with child protection. Even with my social work degrees, I never knew anything about the level of child abuse that existed in this country. In my agency alone, we investigated 10,000 cases of child abuse and neglect a year. As a Black Nationalist, I had taken the uninformed view that there were certain things that Black people just didn't do to our children. Wrong! I saw cases where people of all races did despicable things to defenseless children. In one memorable case, a dude put cigarette butts out on a baby. In another, a guy raped an infant. One time, I was shadowing a social worker, and we got a call around 3 p.m. that children were in danger in a local home. We walked into the house and found an empty pot, sizzling on the stove, about to catch fire. The mother was passed out on drugs. We found three or four kids lying in a crawl space in the attic amid all kinds of

filth. Oh my God, I'd never seen anything like that in my life. To deal
with such situations, where we had to remove children from a home
immediately, we paid citizens to keep a spare bedroom in their homes.
We would take children there temporarily until a more permanent
home could be found through the foster care system.

The process for removing kids was horrific. As we tried to take them
out, they sometimes cried and did not want to go. In some instances,
we had to call the police to deal with the reaction of the adults. Once
we got the children out of the house and into a van, the social worker
would call one of the specified homes to ask if we could bring the
kids over. Sometimes, the individuals from those houses would start
asking questions about the children—whether they were clean, if they
had lice, etc. The social worker would be responding to the questions,
sometimes, awkwardly, in the presence of the children. It outraged me
that yet another humiliation was being heaped on those children. We
were pulling them out of their homes, and now they had to listen to
a conversation about whether they had lice. Really? These kids were
coming out of a situation that no child should ever have to endure, and
someone wanted to know whether they had lice? I suppose it was a fair
question, but it still broke my heart.

Witnessing those kinds of exchanges helped me come up with the
idea for a "Safe House," a place where we could bring children, regardless of the circumstances, and someone would be there to love
and care for them, no questions asked. I was shocked that I had to
fight so hard for this proposal. It turned out that the child protection
system's policies were heavily influenced by a group of white women
who mainly lived in the suburbs. These well-meaning individuals held
sway over the county supervisors and their views about what should
or should not happen when it came to this area of the county's usual
work. Their objection to my proposal was based on their opposition
to orphanages. They felt this was a back door way to bring back the
orphanages that had been shut down years ago. In fact, the abandoned
buildings that once housed the orphanages were still standing on the
county grounds. When I began looking for a building for Safe House,
I looked in the Black community, again wrongly thinking that our
people would welcome the opportunity to have this kind of facility.
Wrong! I ran into all kinds of "not in my back yard" opposition. I refused to give up, though. Finally, I found a building in the heart of the
Black community that had been a convent, and the Catholic church

was willing to lease it to us to create Safe House. The building was just about five minutes from my own house, and it turned out to be an amazing place. I was able to convince the County Board to contract the operations of it to an organization led by three wonderful Black women who were sisters and had operated their own childcare agency and alternative school. I was so proud that they stepped up to the plate and created a warm, loving home that operated for ten years.

One of my biggest regrets as head of the department had nothing to do with the Safe House program. It was my involvement in the firing of a brother named Bill Jenkins, who was head of the county hospital and, as such, reported to me. The hospital had become a big political issue for the County Executive because of a billing problem that was getting significant news coverage. The billing issue gave the appearance that the hospital was not well run, and Dave demanded quietly that Bill Jenkins report directly to him, instead of to me. At some point, Dave decided that he wanted to fire Jenkins, but I spoke up and said that, since Jenkins technically reported to me, I should be the one to handle the matter. I did this in part because Dave was having a difficult time on a number of fronts. I did not think it was wise for him politically to get embroiled in another issue. I told him he would face a firestorm if he fired the county's rare Black department head. So, I agreed to take one for the team. I really thought I could persuade Bill to resign, but he refused. Then, I had to fire him. I actually believed that it was the County Executive's prerogative to let any of us go at any time, because Bill, like me, technically served at his pleasure.

Bill's firing became a big issue in the newspapers, which showed these two Black men fighting against each other. His family was mad at me, his church was mad at me, and I understood it. But I couldn't say anything. I couldn't say that it really wasn't me who wanted him fired. I don't think I could have stopped Dave from firing him, but in retrospect, I regretted the way I handled it and the impact it had on him. Bill was a good man, and the way he was treated nagged at me for years. Fortunately, he landed on his feet and went on to better things. But one day, still bothered by it, I picked up the telephone, called Bill, and took him out to lunch to apologize. I had never done that before, and I haven't since. I have fired a number of people in my lifetime, and in most instances, it is a very difficult thing to do. Firing Bill was the most difficult one of my career. But he was a very gracious man and accepted my apology.

The hospital eventually was sold, and is now a private teaching hospital connected to the Medical College of Wisconsin. I eventually reorganized the entire department with the help of a consultant named Susan Mitchell. She was married to my good friend George Mitchell, and, like him, would became a close friend and confidante over the next two decades. Susan was one of the smartest people I had ever met. She had a knack for making complicated issues very simple. She was also very respected by members of the county board. One of the key elements of our redesign plan was the elimination of my position. In the end, the reorganization went through, and the much slimmer department was renamed the Department of Human Services. I was proud of the job I was doing, but in so many ways the position ate away at my soul. It hurt to see so many of my people in the mental health units, juvenile detention homes, welfare department, and alcohol and drug programs. I kept at the forefront of my mind that there were real lives behind the facts and figures, and I tried to balance compassion and good business sense in my decisions. But I couldn't help wondering at times whether anything I did in that job was making things better for the masses.

By 1990, I was emotionally drained. The job was wearing me out. Plus, my second marriage had fallen apart. Claudetta and I had separated in spring 1988 and then had gotten back together, but the reconciliation did not last. I longed to get back into education. When I heard that the presidency of the Milwaukee Area Technical College had become vacant, I applied. I had served the college well as dean and was confident there was more I could accomplish in the top job. But the critics immediately got busy, complaining that I had moved around too much from job to job. While I indeed had served in many positions in a relatively short amount of time, the moves had not been lateral, and I had experienced many successes along the way. By the time I interviewed for the position, though, I was pretty sure I wasn't going to get it. Fortunately, my suspicion was right. There was something better out there for me. But even if a fortune teller had been able to peek into my future and tell me what my next job would be, I wouldn't have believed it. What came next was just that improbable, especially given that, just a few years earlier, I'd started a movement to create an independent, Black school district in Milwaukee.

12

THE PATHWAY TO
PARENT CHOICE

By the late 1980s, I was thoroughly frustrated with the poor quality of education that Black children were receiving from Milwaukee Public Schools. But my tolerance exploded in late summer 1987, when I read in the newspaper that the school system had reached a settlement in its second integration lawsuit. Here we go again, I thought.

The first suit, filed in the late 1960s, was settled out of court in 1979. But in 1984 the Milwaukee Public School Board, which oversaw the schools located solely inside the city of Milwaukee, had filed a suit against the state and twenty-four separate suburban school districts located in Milwaukee County. The lawsuit claimed that the state and suburban schools were perpetuating segregation within metropolitan Milwaukee public schools. Though minorities made up less than four percent of the suburban schools, I'd opposed the suit because I thought nothing significant would come out of it. It seemed to me we should have been concentrating our time, money and energy on improving the education of kids in the city. After three years of litigation, the suburban schools finally were agreeing to set aside more slots in their schools for children outside the district, and they planned to use a school transfer plan that was already in place as the mechanism to make it happen.

The transfer plan, known as Chapter 220, was first approved in 1975 as a result of legislation that had been proposed by Dennis Conta. Dennis initially had proposed creating a separate school district made up of schools on Milwaukee's east side, which he represented in the State Assembly, and a nearby suburban district. But instead of approving his original proposal, legislators created a compromise integration plan, enacted by Chapter 220, called Laws of 1975, to be implemented in the 1976-77 school year. The plan was aimed at creating racial balance in the schools voluntarily without costing taxpayers anything. It allowed Black students to transfer to certain mostly-white school districts in the suburbs, and the state reimbursed those schools at their per-pupil expenditure rates for each transfer student. White parents from the suburbs were also allowed to send their kids to schools in the Milwaukee public school district. The program became a popular option among Black students in Milwaukee, but very few white students participated.

Under the 1987 settlement, the practically all-white schools also were agreeing to accept the children without testing or any additional standards that were not required of residents who lived within the suburban school boundaries. In addition, the suburban schools said they would make a "good faith effort" to hire minority employees. Research in the case showed that even in the best-case scenario, the plan likely would impact no more than two percent of the Black children in public schools. But both the suburban schools and MPS would get money from the state for students who transferred to suburban schools for "integration" purposes. As I'd figured, the agreement seemed to me a waste of time.

By then, though, I'd already starting working on an alternative plan. In the years between the filing of the 1984 lawsuit and the settlement, I'd joined Dr. Michael Smith, a good friend and instructor at the Milwaukee Area Technical College, to devise a plan. We drafted a manifesto called New Directions for the Education of Black Children in the City of Milwaukee, which, among other things, called for the creation of a new pilot inner-city school district. The district would be comprised of eleven schools—my alma mater, North Division High School, and its feeder junior high and elementary schools, all of which were at least 90 percent Black. The proposed new majority-Black district would give the surrounding Black community the responsibility, as well as the power and resources, to address chronic problems in the schools: low achievement, discipline problems, high dropout rates, and low parental involvement.

We first presented the idea during a community meeting, and most of the attendees agreed that we should move forward. Among them was State Representative Polly Williams, an African American, who was willing to write a bill and introduce it to her colleagues in the State Assembly. Polly's aide, Larry Harwell, also African American, joined us in the battle. He was a master organizer who had led a struggle against the initial integration effort. His group, called "Two Way or No Way," strongly opposed that the Black community had been forced to bear the burden of integration with the massive busing of our children outside our neighborhoods and the closing of our neighborhood schools—the topic that I ultimately chose for my dissertation.

Of course, the integrationists went crazy over the manifesto's proposal. They called us separatists and accused us of trying to undo efforts to integrate schools in Milwaukee and catapult the system back to the days before the historic *Brown v. Board of Education* lawsuit that mandated the desegregation of schools nationwide. Those claims were flatly untrue. Our proposal clearly stated that any parent wishing to transfer out of the district would have the ability to do so, as would any parent who wanted to transfer to a school inside the district. That's a huge difference from the days before 1954, when school districts, particularly in the South, assigned students to schools based on their race and forbade them from attending white schools. There is no question in my mind that the *Brown* decision did much good, effectively ending legally sanctioned segregation. But my problem with the argument of the integrationists against a separate school district in Milwaukee reflected what I believe was an essential flaw in the *Brown* case: the view that an all-Black school equated to an automatically bad one. In fact, some social science research focusing on the negative pathology of the Black community is cited in the Brown case to help make the case for integration. Robert Carter, who as the general counsel for the NAACP played a major role in organizing vital social science testimony in the case, once said: "The basic postulate of our strategy and theory in *Brown* was that the elimination of enforced segregated education would necessarily result in equal education." What he and his colleagues perhaps did not consider or misjudged was the impact that would result from placing Black children in environments where their white teachers and administrators did not want them and had no respect for them or their families. It is amazing how creative educators got in categorizing kids and courses so that the most academically rigorous courses and programs were reserved for white children and, over time, the occasional Black kids of middle-and upper-class parents with political and economic resources. Children from low-income and working-class Black families rarely have been given those opportunities. The damaging results are still playing out in our schools to this day.

The argument of those of us who supported the separate school district was simply this: The old way wasn't working; at least allow Black people who had a vested interest in the success of our children to try something different. When we felt we had garnered significant support for the idea, Polly sponsored a bill creating the North Division school district. I was among the many who testified in favor of it when it went before a committee on February 10, 1988: "We have a school system that is not working. It is failing to educate children, particularly poor Black children," I said. "This is not an issue of the 'goodness' of people who are directing and working for Milwaukee Public Schools... We believe that Black people must play a central role in dealing with this problem. These are our children, and we must accept the responsibility to educate them. But with the responsibility must come power, authority, resources, and structural arrangement that creates the framework for success."

The proposal spurred a huge national debate and stunned many when it made it through the committee and passed the Wisconsin State Assembly, the lower house of the state legislature, that year. The measure ultimately died in the Senate, but it started a conversation about the kind of dramatic change needed to make our system of public education work for poor Black children.

In the months that followed, a number of neighborhood meetings were held to address the issue. Many of us in the community were searching for radical ideas that would give poor and working-class parents alternatives to public schools that were failing their children, and a proposal to support publicly-financed vouchers that allow children from low-income families to attend private schools emerged. At the time, I knew nothing about the history of vouchers and had never even heard of economist Milton Friedman, the Nobel Prize winner who is generally given credit for first suggesting in the mid-1950s that tax dollars for education should follow the child. He argued that such competition for those tax dollars would force public schools to improve.

I'd eventually learn, though, that conservatives like Friedman were not the only ones trying to advance the idea of vouchers. By the early 1960s, others on the opposite end of the political spectrum also were making the argument that vouchers were a viable alternative for getting around the bureaucracy and ineffectiveness of many public schools. To me, vouchers just seemed like the next step in a logical progression of the struggle. Our efforts to change the system hadnt worked, and so we had to have a way for low-income parents to opt out of it. Families with means already had the freedom to choose. If they didn't like their neighborhood schools, they had the resources to move their children elsewhere. I believed poor and working-class families should have that same opportunity.

There had been a change in the leadership of the Milwaukee Public Schools with the selection of Dr. Robert S. Peterkin as the new Superintendent. He had named as his Deputy Superintendent Dr. Deborah McGriff, who had come with him from Cambridge, Massachusetts, where there was a version of parent choice within the school system. Bob and Debbie, both African American, were open to some kind of choice program in Milwaukee, and they met with a number of community leaders, both Black and white, who had been pushing for a choice program for quite a while. The meetings were productive, and Bob and Debbie actually had agreed on some broad parameters for a voucher program to allow low-income parents to access private schools that had a proven record of educating poor children. But somewhere in the process, the teachers' union got involved and interjected language that was unacceptable to the community. So, community leaders again turned to Polly and her assistant, Larry, who together drafted a bill creating the Milwaukee Parental Choice Program. Under the program, children from low-income families would receive state aid to attend non-religious, private schools.

Democrats, who controlled the legislature at the time, did not support vouchers as a party, and Polly had a difficult time even getting the measure heard during the 1989 legislative session. The chairwoman of the State Assembly's Education Committee refused to put the bill on the agenda for a public hearing, but Larry and Polly organized a campaign that included calling the chairwoman non-stop until she changed her mind. The hearing was held at the Milwaukee Public Schools auditorium, and I was involved in the organizing effort that pulled together hundreds of parents, students, and other community members, who packed the meeting room. We selected powerful speakers to represent them. Polly and others did the necessary politicking behind the scenes, but on the day of the hearing we knew we were still at least one vote short of the majority needed to move the bill out of the committee and onto the Assembly floor. But when it came time for a vote, Kim Plache, a Democrat who had not been supportive of vouchers, astonished her colleagues by voting in favor of the measure. She said that she could not in good conscience side against so many people in the community. Her critical vote kept the proposal alive. Polly then worked with State Senator Gary George, a Black legislator who represented the north side of Milwaukee, to get the new program, and financing for it, included as part of the state budget bill. It would have been impossible to get the program into the proposed budget without the support of Senator George, then co-chairman of the Joint Finance Committee, the legislature's budget writing body. I have no idea what deal Polly and Gary worked out to get his support for in-cluding the measure as part of the budget. But if the program had moved forward as a separate measure, it likely would not have passed.

Another important part of this story was the election of Tommy Thompson, a Republican who had defeated my old boss, Tony Earl, as Governor. As much as I respected Tony, I realized that if he had won re-election, I am fairly certain he would have vetoed the program. Tommy was a supporter of parent choice and over the years became a huge ally in keeping the program alive. But Polly should get the lion's share of credit for pulling together a coalition of Republicans and moderate Democrats—a group she would later call "The Unholy Alliance"—to get the program through the legislature. So, it is im-portant to note that the program, which initially involved just seven schools and 337 children, started out with bi-partisan support.

All of the Black leaders who supported vouchers, most especial-ly Polly, took a lot of abuse from critics, who made all kinds of wild claims, including that conservatives were using us to push their own hidden agenda. But I believe strongly in the concept of "interest con-vergence," which my friend, the late Derrick Bell, taught me. Derrick, a scholar and activist who had been the first Black tenured law profes-sor at Harvard University, explained that Black people in this coun-try have made progress only when our interests converged with the interests of people in power. For example, our people made progress during the Civil Rights Movement largely because of our own strug-gle, of course. But at a certain point, our interests converged with the interests of those in power, who were trying to convince the rest of the world that democracy was a better form of government than commu-nism. It was certainly hard to do that with Bull Connor siccing dogs on Black people. So, those in power moved to stop those kinds of actions. I have ALWAYS been clear that some of the people with whom I've been aligned on the parent choice issue are in the battle for very different reasons than mine. We do not share the same world view. We have a temporary merger of interests that don't necessarily extend beyond parent choice. Nevertheless, when the legislature approved the Milwaukee Parental Choice Program near the end of the 1989 legislative session for implementation in the 1990-91 school year, it was a monumental victory for the parent choice movement.

The Milwaukee movement would experience another major victory six years later when the voucher program was expanded to include religious schools. By then, Republicans controlled both houses of the legislature, and with Tommy, a Republican, still the governor, most people began to view the program primarily as a Republican-led initiative. Opponents would claim that the inclusion of religious schools among the choices for parents violated the separation of church and state, required by the federal constitution, and they challenged the program in court. The Wisconsin Supreme Court eventually would uphold the decision, and with religious schools among the options for parents, the program began to flourish. That growth would cause some serious battles down the road. There was no denying that the Milwaukee Parental Choice Program had given steam to a nationwide movement that was taking off.

In time, I would find a home in that movement. But first, my life would take a sudden and unexpected turn after Bob made a stunning announcement that he was leaving his job as Milwaukee Public Schools Superintendent at the end of his contract in June 1991 to take a position at Harvard University.

13

THE EDUCATION OF MY LIFE

Sometime before Bob's big announcement, I got a call from Deborah McGriff, his Deputy, who called to invite me to breakfast. She broke the news that her boss was leaving, and asked if I would support her to replace him. I gave her an enthusiastic YES!! She was perfect for the job—a smart, tough sister who had the credentials and the skills, and I knew she cared deeply about our children.

I'd met Debbie in 1988, soon after Bob, who had been Superintendent of Schools in Cambridge, Massachusetts, brought her from his old administration to help him in Milwaukee. To educate themselves on the city and its schools, they read old newspaper stories and talked to community leaders, who told them about my involvement in the effort to create a separate school district. As Debbie later put it, she and Bob knew all about "the crazy Black man who was trying to take part of the school district." She told me that Bob assigned her to meet with me and try to figure out what I wanted. But I clarified my intentions as soon as we met: "I don't know what you've heard about me," I told her. "But I want you to be successful." My fight against the school system had been purely about the kids and what was best for them, I explained. If she and Bob could improve the schools for the children of Milwaukee, especially for poor kids, that's exactly what I wanted. Debbie and I discussed the need for the school district and the Department of Health and Human Services to work together, and we actually became good friends. The two of us were even able to secure a shared $5 million grant between our organizations to create an innovative program that provided intervention to help keep needy families together and their children out of the foster care system. The program also set up protocols for the two systems to work together on identifying and reporting child abuse of MPS students.

By early March 1991, the Milwaukee Board of School Directors had narrowed its search for a superintendent to two people, and Debbie was one of them. Then, something unexpected happened. I learned from someone I trusted that she didn't have the votes to win. It was never clear to me exactly why, but I was told that some board members were hesitant to hire a woman for the job. It was ridiculous and sexist. I heard that one member even expressed concern privately that Debbie, who is petite in stature, wouldn't be able to break up fights, as if that is among the duties of a superintendent. When it was clear to me that Debbie could not get the votes needed to win, I started listening to some of my supporters in the community who were urging me to throw my hat in the ring. I called Debbie and told her what I had learned and that, because of it, I'd decided to seek the position. By then, she, too, had heard that the board did not plan to select her, and she was already interviewing in other school districts across the country. But it still hurt her to hear that I was going after the job. Our conversation ended abruptly, and for a few months she refused even to speak to me. It was never my intention to hurt or betray Debbie, and to this day, I think she should have gotten the job. I just knew it wasn't going to happen, and I didn't want to see someone else from outside our city become the next Superintendent. I was also intrigued by the idea of seeing if, after so many years of being a critic, I could actually make the district better for our kids. At the very least, I knew no one would work harder trying.

The problem with my seeking the job was that I had never worked as an elementary or secondary school teacher or principal. Wisconsin law required school superintendents in the state to have a minimum of three years of elementary or secondary teaching experience and a state license to work as a supervisor in the schools. That stipulation seemed unnecessary for a job that was to me about setting a vision for the district, managing high-level employees, dealing with board politics, handling relationships with the press, the community, and the unions, and most important, using the bully pulpit to fight for kids. I felt that I had been uniquely prepared for the job by my myriad roles both inside and outside of education, and so I turned to legislators with whom I'd developed good working relationships over the years to change state law. Fourteen state representatives ended up co-signing a bill that would waive the teaching and licensing requirements for a school superintendent in Milwaukee. Six senators introduced an identical bill. Soon after the measures became public, the NAACP and representatives of five Black church groups held a press conference in Milwaukee to denounce the move. The ministers not only expressed their disapproval of the legislation, but they attacked me personally. When reporters called me for comment, though, I refused to respond. I'd learned long ago not to allow this kind of criticism to creep into my soul. What mattered at the end of the day was what those who were making the decision thought. Another group of ministers held an event at a local church to publicly express their support for me, and went to Madison to testify in favor of the bill that would allow me to become superintendent. The measure passed easily through the legislature, clearing the way for the school board to interview me for the job.

I knew from the start that some board members had mixed opinions of me. Board President Jeanette Mitchell was one of them. She told me later that she had heard I was very polarizing and jumped from job to job. But she had also heard that I was a dedicated and effective leader, and so she decided to keep an open mind. I'm glad she did because she would become one of my strongest supporters. For my first interview, the board arranged a secret meeting in a private room at the Chicago airport. I was surprised to see reporters waiting with their questions as I arrived. I wore my favorite tie, a bright, colorful one with sketches of kids all over it from an organization called "Save the Children." The tie captured perfectly my priority, the children. I had spent many hours thinking of what I wanted for the children of Milwaukee Public Schools, and during the interview I laid out five specific goals that would guide me as superintendent:

> That all children become lifelong learners who maximize their intellectual, emotional, physical, and moral capabilities.

> That those who attend college immediately upon graduation do so without needing to spend their first year in remedial classes.

> That those who immediately enter the world of work have the skills and attitudes they need to secure at least an entry-level job, and receive the same rigorous preparation as those who immediately go on to college.

> That some of them develop an entrepreneurial spirit that would enable them to create jobs and wealth for themselves and their community.

That all of them engage in what Paulo Friere calls "the practice of freedom, the means by which men and women deal critically and creatively with reality and discover how to participate in the transformation of their world."

Every child has the capacity to learn and succeed, I told board members, but the school system needed to do more to prepare them. I'd never forgotten my time at Marquette when a young lady from MPS entered the Educational Opportunity Program with a 3.6 grade point average and had never taken a college preparatory course. Even with the program's support, she was not able to enroll in Marquette. The system was failing so many of our children who wanted to go to college but had no idea how inadequately prepared they were. I also discussed my plans to add technical training to the curriculum so that students who had no intentions of attending college graduated from high school at least with skills that would help them land well-paying jobs. But this would be accomplished without diluting the academic rigor of the curriculum.

The board interviewed me a second time at the school administration building on Friday, May 17, but I had no idea they would meet afterward and decide to begin negotiations to hire me. Jeanette made the surprise announcement during a press conference after the meeting. She said the board would vote on my contract at its May 29th meeting. When I walked into my house on the night after my second interview, my telephone was ringing, and there had been so many other calls that my answering machine was full and could take no more messages. Jeanette and several friends were calling to congratulate me.

On the night of the board's final vote, I first served as a deejay (one of my favorite hobbies) at a fundraiser for Mayor John Norquist, who was among the public officials who had supported my appointment as superintendent. Then, I headed to the school board meeting in time for the board's vote on whether to extend me a three-year contract. The decision was unanimous, nine to zero. A huge sense of relief and excitement rushed through me, and I jumped onto the stage of the auditorium and shook hands with each board member. I had brought with me two Milwaukee Area Technical College students who lived in the Hillside housing project, where I'd spent part of my youth. My comments to the media afterward were in part aimed at inspiring them: "I think it's significant," I said, "that someone from the projects is going to be superintendent of schools."

I had no time to waste. The new school year was just months away, and the board was already into its new budget cycle. The vote took place on a Wednesday, and I wrapped things up at the county and started as superintendent the following Monday. Even though the public vote was unanimous, it became evident to me right away that behind the scenes was another matter. During my first strategy meeting with the board shortly after the vote, I was not even allowed to speak. I sat there the entire time, ready to present my "Strategy for Change," and none of the board members asked me a single question or recognized me to say a word. The tension was thick, and I was fuming. The next day, I wrote an open letter to the board and sent it to the newspaper. In it, I threatened to quit if I were not treated with more dignity. Jeanette then convened a closed meeting for the board members and me to talk. Some of the members were downright angry that I had been selected. Jeanette told me later that I had been able to get enough votes to win primarily because I was local. Bob's departure after just three years had stunned and upset the board, and my supporters argued that I would be more invested in the system since I had grown up in Milwaukee and was a product of its public schools. That swayed enough undecided members to give me the majority, but there was lingering resentment. My opponents complained that I had tried to destroy the school system with my leadership role in the North Division and independent school district controversies and my support of parental choice. But they were outnumbered and had felt pressured by their colleagues, the community, and the media to vote for me and put forth a united front in public. During our private meeting, some of them questioned me vigorously about how my support for parental choice would play out in my role as superintendent. They would not stand for me to be out advocating for parental choice, while at the same time trying to lead the school system, they said. But I pushed back, telling them point blank that I would never denounce educational options for parents or even say that I was not supportive of choice. As a compromise, though, I agreed that since I was now the superintendent, I would not discuss parental choice publicly or advocate for it. I assured the board that I wanted what they wanted: a better public school system to help all of our children to be more successful. When the nine board members and I finally stepped out of the meeting together three hours later, some of them were wearing T-shirts bearing my photograph and the words "Join Dr. Howard Fuller in the Crusade to Save Our Children."

The shirts had been made during my time with the county when I organized an effort to get the community more involved in ending child abuse.

I moved right into my role as superintendent. The first day was full of the kind of ceremonial stuff that takes place when there's a change of administrations. But it was important to me to visit a school, and so five hours after being sworn into office at city hall, I made my way to Granville Elementary. I had visited the school in January to speak to the students about Dr. Martin Luther King, Jr., in honor of his birthday. When the students heard that I had become superintendent, they and their teacher wrote and invited me back for another visit. I decided it would be the perfect way to start my new job. From the moment I stepped into the classroom and saw the students' cheery faces, I couldn't help smiling. They reminded me of why this job was so important. They were relying on those of us in charge to make sure they were ready for a world they could barely even envision. I wish they knew how much I wanted to do my part and give them the best opportunity for success. I encouraged them to do their part by aiming high: "Each one of you can go on to college," I told them. "Each one of you can go on to be whatever it is you want to go on to be."

Visiting schools became a crucial part of my routine as superintendent. I promised my staff that I would go to every school in the entire district, and I'm proud to say I did just that. It took me four years, but I made sure that practically every week my secretary scheduled school visits into my busy agenda. At each school, I spent time in classrooms and asked staff members to point me to the worst-behaving kids in the class. Normally, I talked to them to try to get a sense of what was happening in their lives. I was always trying to find the underlying reasons for their behavior. On many occasions our conversations would end with me promising to take them to a Milwaukee Bucks game if there was improvement in the way they were acting in school. I knew that would be a huge incentive. Most of the troublemakers were boys who didn't have fathers at home who spent time hanging out with them in this way, and often their families couldn't afford such a luxury. When report card time came, I followed up with the teachers, rounded up the kids who had kept their end of the deal, and took them to a game. That's why I asked for a mini-van, instead of the standard luxury car, when the school district issued me a vehicle. On the day that I completed my pledge to visit all of the district's schools, the elementary school kids inside gathered with excitement at the window as I approached their school. I paused to touch the window, and a photographer snapped what became one of my favorite photos.

At Fernwood Elementary, on the city's south side, I went a step further, adopting a class of twenty-nine eighth-graders. I don't know what it was about that group, but I just connected with them and promised to stay in touch over the years. I was diligent about it, too, sending congratulatory notes, calling to check on them, following up with their teachers, and visiting their homes. Their real-life struggles kept me close to the challenges many of our students faced, both inside and outside of the classroom. Four years later, only thirteen of the twenty-nine students I'd first met in that eighth grade class graduated, and for each one of them—those who finished, as well as those who did not—there was a compelling story. One of my students, for example, got pregnant in high school. When she first confided this to me, I visited her at her grandmother's house, and the grandmother and I teamed up and told her we would not let her drop out of school. It warmed my heart to see her walk across the stage at graduation. But for every triumphant story in the group, there was another one like that of a young lady who, four years later, had progressed only to the ninth grade. She'd had three babies with three different dudes, and when I showed up at her home to try to talk to her, neither she nor her mother saw anything wrong with the situation. I couldn't save every kid, and there were constant reminders of that. But I would never stop trying, and touching one child's life every now and then was far superior to me than doing nothing.

About the same time that I was getting started in Milwaukee, Debbie was beginning her new role as Superintendent of Schools in Detroit. She was the first woman chosen to lead the school district, as she had been in her jobs as Deputy Superintendent in both Cambridge and Milwaukee. I was very proud of her and felt badly about how our friendship had ended. When she returned to Milwaukee one weekend to complete her move to Detroit, I called to congratulate her and invite her out for drinks after an event that we both had been invited to attend. I don't even drink, but I figured it would give us a chance to clear the air. We had a good conversation. She was thrilled about achieving her longtime goal of becoming the superintendent of a large urban school district and believed that in the end it had worked out better for her to be able to make her own mark in a brand-new place.

We agreed that it was silly for the two of us not to talk to each other. I was separated and going through a divorce. So, the next night, I asked her out to dinner. Then, for her first official day on the job, I sent her a beautiful bouquet of tropical flowers and a note wishing her well. That was the beginning of a four-year courtship. We managed to keep our relationship quiet for a few months, until a reporter spotted us out together at a Luther Vandross concert in Milwaukee on New Year's Eve in 1991 and mentioned it in the newspaper's social column.

Meanwhile, I jumped right into my change agenda. Just weeks after I arrived, I began a major restructuring of the school district. The previous superintendent had divided the district into six smaller units with about twenty-five schools and 15,000 students, each headed by a community superintendent. While the intent—to move services closer to the schools—was good, my analysis of the system showed that it just wasn't working. It added a layer of bureaucracy that was unnecessary for schools and parents. I wanted to flatten the structure and give principals more power to control what happened in their buildings, including drafting their own budgets and hiring their own staffs. Plus, I knew we needed to make some deep cuts. The business manager came to talk to me one day about the budget and drew a line in the center of a piece of paper. On one side he wrote kindergarten, music, and sports; on the other, the area superintendents. I had to choose. At first, I thought it was a joke. When I realized it wasn't, there was no other choice really. I eliminated the six community superintendents and their accompanying staffs, a total of about ninety positions. Most were reassigned back to the schools, but the restructuring resulted in a number of layoffs. I didn't take that lightly. Layoffs are never easy, but they are sometimes necessary to bring about significant change. The board approved the restructuring, and the $2.8 million in savings were redirected to the schools for their kindergarten, music, and sports programs. Because many of the principals had never controlled their budgets, some of them had no idea even how to create or maintain one. My administration provided management training for them. I also created a central office position for oversight of the principals to ensure they got what they needed quickly. And I let them know they still had direct access to me.

Another element of my change strategy was to make sure our schools were safe and orderly. I set up a task force to come up with recommendations for addressing the significant disciplinary problems.

According to data that I had seen, middle schools had reported more than 100,000 disciplinary incidents in the previous year. More than two-thirds involved classroom discipline and refusal to accept instruction. I wanted proposals that would ensure orderly classrooms but also better serve kids who needed alternative services. I realized the actions called for by the proposals might cause suspensions and expulsions to go up in the short term, but I truly believed that, in the long run, all kids would be better served.

One of the biggest safety measures I implemented was unannounced use of metal detectors in some of our middle and high schools. I hated to take that step, but it was the right thing to do. The program began in December 1991 with weapons searches at high school basketball games. There was a lot of publicity about the checks beforehand, and fortunately no one was caught trying to bring a gun into a game. I had the security check outside the school during a particular game, though, and officers found all kinds of weapons hidden in the bushes. After another game, a huge fight broke out between an MPS school and one from the suburbs. The next day, I called the superintendent of that school district to apologize for the behavior of our students. I remain convinced that if we had not implemented the metal detectors, someone would have wound up seriously hurt or killed. Once I began the random use of the equipment during the school day, a group of Black ministers organized against me, claiming this practice was going to disproportionately affect Black males. That argument was insane. I told them that the policy would disproportionately affect Black males only if Black males disproportionately brought guns or other weapons to school. This was not something I wanted to do, but I wasn't backing down or apologizing for trying to protect children. A few days after the practice began, there was a shooting outside a middle school on the south side of the city. Fortunately, no one was injured, but my administrators and I knew it involved gang activity. We decided to set up the detectors the next day at that school, and a little dude, standing no higher than my waist, tried to walk through with a loaded .32-caliber pistol. He didn't even understand what a metal detector was and had no clue that he couldn't walk through it with a gun. So, what kind of thought process would he have used when it came to firing that gun? His response to me when I asked why he'd brought the gun to school let me know that he'd never even thought about the possible consequences of his actions. He said his gang leader had told him to come to school prepared to "get them back" for what had happened the previous day.

While trying to protect the children in our schools, I wouldn't let people forget our students who were dying in our community. The early 1990s were particularly brutal years. I compiled a list of MPS students who had been killed or had committed suicide between December 1992 and December 1993, fifteen of whom were under the age of seventeen. Every time I was invited somewhere to speak, I started by reading their names. It made people uncomfortable. I knew it. I could see it in their faces. I told them I knew they were unsettled by my actions. But I also told them that as long as our children were dying in the streets, we *should* feel uncomfortable. And I was determined not to let anyone under the sound of my voice act as if this was ok. I was concerned that the public's reaction to the deaths of our children would become like what had happened during the Vietnam War era when television stations listed the body count on our screens. People got so used to it that they seemed no longer affected. I was determined not to let that happen.

The naysayers were always there, complaining about something that I had done, even when I created a childcare center in the Central Office. I noticed that school buses were dropping off elementary school kids at certain stops, regardless of whether anyone was there to pick them up. That was ridiculous. So, to ensure the safety of the children, I required school bus drivers to stop at the center daily at the end of their route to drop off children who didn't have a parent or caregiver waiting to pick them up. Some people complained that I was creating a babysitting service and that parents would take advantage, but I didn't care what they said. I was not going to put little ones in danger because of irresponsible adults. In the end, very few people took advantage of the new policy.

People often ask me what my greatest accomplishments were as superintendent. I know I did some good things. We saw third grade reading scores go up after that first year. We empowered principals and held them accountable for their schools. We also strengthened the academic curriculum by requiring all ninth graders to take algebra. The College Board, the not-for-profit organization that administers the SAT, had chosen Milwaukee as one of six pilot sites to implement its Equity 2000 program, which began in 1990 to help better prepare more minority students for college in the next millennium.

Participating school districts were instructed to remove tracking programs that often steered African American and Latino students away
from enrolling in higher-level math courses. Equity 2000 also provided supportive resources for math students and more professional
development for math teachers. When early results from the test sites
showed that more students were taking and passing algebra and ge-
ometry, I used the leverage of the program to implement the algebra
requirement for all of our ninth graders. I then eliminated all other
ninth grade math courses. Within just two years, more Black kids were
passing algebra than the total number of them who had been enrolled
in the course when I first started as superintendent. While taking
aggressive measures to prepare kids for college, my administration
also partnered with the business community to implement a "School
to Work" program to get students ready for the world of work. Our
reforms were even praised in the April 17, 1995, edition of *Business
Week*. Of course, to some people such recognition meant I was trying
to allow corporations to take over the school district.

Of all the things I managed to achieve as superintendent, what still
makes me most proud is the relationships I established with the kids.
Every group in the system had organized representatives always looking out for their interests—everyone except the kids. But the kids had
me! They came first in everything I did. Sometimes, that meant post-
poning a meeting with a board member to make time for a student.
Late one night, I was leaving a board meeting held in a south side
community when a teenager recognized me and yelled from the street:
"Hey man, I wrote you a letter."

I responded: "What about?"

"Just something I wanted to talk to you about," he replied.

When I asked the student if he had a ride home, he said he did. But
I excused myself from Jeanette, the board president who was walking
out of the meeting with me, caught up with the student, and insisted
on driving him home to find out what was on his mind. The details
of conversations like those have faded with time, but not the essence
of what it meant to me to be able to show kids they mattered to me.
That's the kind of concern I tried to demonstrate and wanted my entire administration to reflect. One of the first things I noticed when
I started the job was that the school administration building didn't
look like a place that had anything to do with kids. So, I had my staff
seek out the best student art from all of the schools, and we displayed

the pieces on the walls throughout the administration building. That practice exists to this day. I also arranged for students from various schools to perform at principals' meetings. I wanted the talent of our students on display as often as possible.

I made a point of connecting with students. I didn't want them to view me as some bureaucrat sitting behind the doors of a big office all day, making decisions about their lives without ever even talking to them. I wanted to make sure they saw me up close, even in my neighborhood. When I saw kids headed to and from school or just hanging out, I usually stopped to talk to them. "Hey, you need to walk faster than that," I'd yell out of my car window when I recognized a student trudging along to school. They talked back to me, too. Every time the first snowflake fell in the winter, my doorbell was ringing, and one the kids was standing out there, pleading: "Dr. Fuller, I know you gon' call off school today!" I liked that they knew I didn't live behind some big iron gates and that I was accessible to them. And it saddened me when they expected otherwise. Once, I was shopping in a drugstore near my house, and I overheard two girls debating whether the person shopping next to them was really me. When one of the girls pushed the other into asking, I pulled out my school identification card. Her jaw dropped. "I didn't think it was really you," she explained. "Somebody like you wouldn't be *down* here with us."

Not only did I live in the neighborhood, I sat among the parents and fans at their football and basketball games and academic competitions. Washington High School was right up the street from my house on the city's north side, and I was a regular at the girls' basketball games. The girls' team was phenomenal, winning the state championship in 1994. I got to know the team members, and I told them that if they won the championship again in 1995, I would do something really special for them. Sure enough, they won, and I was down on the floor, hugging and celebrating with them. To reward them, I arranged to use one of the business suites at the Bradley Center during a Boyz II Men concert. The three young R&B singers were huge stars, particularly among teenage girls. On the night of the concert, I arranged for a white stretch limousine to pick up the girls' basketball team from school and shuttle them to the arena. The girls were ecstatic to ride in the limo and even more so when they stepped into the suite and saw tables full of their favorite foods and soft drinks and a view of the stage that made the celebrities seem almost close enough to touch.

Afterward, I dropped off the girls at their homes. My heart sank as I watched some of them walk back into the desperate circumstances of their lives. That, I couldn't change, but for one night every one of those teammates felt like the superstar she was. In 1996, I sat in the stands and watched as my girls went on to win an astonishing third state championship in a row.

With my staff, I tried to be as accessible as I was to the kids. I wanted to demystify the position of superintendent. I made friends with some of the staff from various departments in the central office. One group of ladies played bid whist on a regular basis. Since I am one of the top bid whist players in the world, I joined them as often as possible. Once, I pulled together all of the secretaries and asked them what they would like to see done differently, and I implemented some of their suggestions. Likewise, when I identified the only guy on staff who really understood every detail of how pay plans were put together, I walked downstairs to his office, plopped down in a chair, and asked him to walk me through it. I didn't go in there pretending to know something I didn't. I suspect that gesture made him feel valued, and he saved me from embarrassment time and time again when I sought his input or he caught an error before it became public.

Connecting with students and staff in a personal way was one thing. But trying to bring true reform to a huge system entrenched in its ways was far more difficult. And unfortunately, the greatest resistance would come from within the system.

With outgoing Milwaukee Public Schools Superintendent Bob Peterkin the night I was named to replace him.

With South African human rights activist Archbishop Desmond Tutu during his visit to a Milwaukee school.

With Milwaukee public schoolchildren, who remindec me daily why the job as Superintende*t of Schools was so important.

With some of the thirteen students who completed high school
from the class of twenty-nine eighth-graders
I adopted as Superintendent.

Outside a school on my last school visit before I left the district.

I4

THE BATTLES WITHIN

From my first days as superintendent, my relationship with the Milwaukee Teachers' Education Association, the union representing teachers, got off to a rocky start. One of the first clashes occurred when I tried to assign seven African-American teachers to two African immersion schools—a middle and an elementary school. My predecessors had created the schools and negotiated everything but the personnel. When I arrived, there were seven vacant teaching positions between the two schools. It made sense to me to fill the slots with African-American teachers, given the special nature of the schools. I'd even found seven Black teachers in our system willing to volunteer to move to the schools. Because the positions were open, no white teachers would be displaced. But the union objected, vigorously.

The head of the union argued that transferring the African-American teachers to the African immersion schools would violate the teachers' contract. The contract contained language from a court-ordered desegregation ruling, which said that no school should have more than the overall percentage of Black teachers in the entire system. My proposal would have given the African immersion school ten percent more Black teachers than the total number of Black teachers who worked for the system. I tried to reason with the organization and asked the president to sign off on a Memorandum of Understanding, agreeing to the change in this one case since it was a specialty school. He wouldn't budge. The union claimed that my real agenda was to try to put only Black teachers in schools in the inner city. It was a ridiculous accusation. Even if I'd wanted to do that it was numerically impossible; there were not enough Black teachers in the system to make that happen.

At the same time that this discussion was taking place, a group of Black parents and community activists had gone to the school board to demand that only Black teachers be placed in the middle school in their neighborhood. As a show of good faith, I told the union that I would publicly oppose that request. I attended an after-school community meeting with the parents and told them that, in my role as superintendent, I couldn't go along with what they were requesting. The union president was sitting in the meeting when I talked to the group, which included some of my friends who had worked beside me on other community issues. The parents were incensed and called me every kind of traitor and handkerchief head Negro. Still, I hoped my taking that step would show the union that my intent was pure, that I just wanted to use open positions to put African-American teachers in an African immersion program, nothing more. But the union president told me his position hadn't changed. The teachers had a contract, and the organization still opposed the move. I was done trying to appease them. I moved the Black teachers anyhow, even though I knew things probably would not end well. The union sued and ultimately won. Though it took some time to work through the courts, that initial battle set the stage for what was to come.

I had been at war with the teachers' union from the days when I was fighting the system from the outside. It seemed to me that the predominantly white organization was often on the wrong side of issues when it came to what was best for children, particularly poor Black children. I had never viewed the teachers' union as a working-class organization. It was not at all like the union to which my mother had belonged or to the Local 77, for which I'd worked in Durham, fighting for the janitors, maids, and other service workers at Duke University. I had great affinity for those groups, whose struggle was often about social justice, centered on helping those true working-class people improve their lives. From where I stood, I saw a powerful Milwaukee teachers union that functioned solely in its own interests, even when those interests conflicted with the best interests of children.

I was a brand new superintendent and the school year had not even started in August 1991 when I got word that an NBC investigative television show, called "Exposé," had sent a former student into my alma mater, North Division, with a hidden camera. The student had shot some disturbing television footage, and I agreed to come to the school to watch the video. I sat at a long cafeteria table with the principal on one side of me and the union president on the other. A small microphone was attached to my clothes and a camera pointed at my face to catch my reaction as I watched in disgust at the fifteen-minute segment. The video showed one teacher nonchalantly reading a newspaper or magazine, while the class carried on in complete chaos. Another teacher did nothing while kids shot dice in a back corner of a classroom, while yet another teacher threatened to slap a student's mama. I was appalled and told the reporters right away that the three teachers visible on the video would be fired. There was no excuse for such behavior, and it wouldn't be tolerated under my watch, I said. But I happened to glance up while I was giving my fiery response on camera and caught a glimpse of my horrified staff member in the background, shaking his head "no," slicing his hands across his neck, warning me to stop. Later, my staff explained that I didn't have the authority to fire the teachers like that. What? I was the superintendent, and this type of behavior was unacceptable, I argued. What did they mean I couldn't fire anybody? It boiled down to two words: union contract. We did end up firing them, but a binding arbitration process was guaranteed by the teachers' contract. The process dragged on for a year and ultimately forced me to reinstate the teachers with back pay. It was a huge disappointment and helped to color my opinion of the teachers' unions as too protective of the status quo and as a real detriment to the kind of reform that is needed to shake up troubled school districts. It also was a clear lesson to me—I was in charge but not in control.

There were other instances, too, of the union fighting to protect teachers who had no business standing in front of classrooms with the responsibility of shaping kids' lives. One holdover case from the previous administration also landed in my lap. Bob and Debbie had fired a fourth-grade teacher for his extreme punishment of a student who misbehaved. The teacher had broken up a fight and separated the two students involved. While taking one of the students to the office, the teacher ordered the other student to stand in the corner and not move. The teacher warned that he would dunk the child's head in a toilet if the child moved. When the teacher returned, the child had moved. The teacher followed through on his threat, dragged the fourth-grader down the stairs, found a soiled toilet, and pushed the child's head in it. An arbitrator bought into the union's argument that this was a good teacher who had no other blemishes on his record, but on the day of the offense had simply had a bad day. I've always felt that if it had been my child, the teacher would have had an even worse day because he would have had to deal with me. His actions were unconscionable. Yet, I was forced to return the teacher, not only to the school district, but to the same school where the incident occurred.

Because I couldn't discuss personnel issues publicly, the parents and community members who had heard about the incidents didn't understand why I couldn't just get rid of the bad teachers. The community once picketed to protest my handling of a case involving a special education teacher. The teacher had forced a student to wear a dunce cap and allowed other students to throw things at the kid. My first instinct was to fire the teacher. But by then, I'd had some bad experiences with the arbitration process and didn't want the school system to end up paying another fat judgment. I ended up suspending him for 30 days without pay, and then he was brought back into the system.

I realize that a few bad teachers aren't representative of the entire profession. I also know most teachers care about children, work hard for them every day, and don't get nearly the respect they deserve for being substitute parents and counselors, as well as educators. But there are teachers who don't give a damn about educating our children and need to find something else to do. They are standing in the way of progress, and, worse yet, many times they are protected by well-funded, inflexible unions that have the resources and the wherewithal to go after anybody and any measure of change that they deem a threat to the way things are. The teachers' unions seem to think the system exists just to provide good jobs and benefits, and that is what they fight to protect, not in most instances what is best for the children.

Those early battles were tough enough. Then came the 1992-93 budget process. It was my first time submitting my own budget for the school system, because I had started the job after the process had begun the previous year. I believed in zero-based budgeting, starting each year with a clean slate and justifying each expense, instead of setting aside money for something just because it was in the budget the year before. I asked administrators to make the case for every budget request. At the high school level, there were many programs that weren't doing a thing to help a single student graduate. So, I proposed a major shift of about $50 million from the high school level to the elementary schools. I knew it would cause an outcry. Since eighty to eighty-five percent of the school system's budget was devoted to personnel, any significant change in funding affected jobs. But I figured that if we could pump up resources to the elementary schools and begin to address the academic deficiencies earlier, we wouldn't need so much of that kind of programming at the high schools. The teachers were incensed. They organized against me and filled every public hearing with protesters, including parents and students. At one hearing, a teenage girl, upset about the proposed cuts to her favorite program, pointed her finger at me during her testimony and said, "Dr. Fuller, you are destroying my dream!" Her words sliced through me like blades. Then on the other side of the room were the little elementary school students and their parents, carrying signs that read, "Please, Dr. Fuller, help us!" The scene was the same at every hearing, and the pressure intensified. All of a sudden, I couldn't even think straight. I had been sure I was doing the right thing, but the young lady's words kept reverberating in my spirit. *Dr. Fuller, you are destroying my dream!* It didn't matter that it wasn't true, that I spent every waking moment trying to make things better for her and her peers. Her perception was that I was destroying her dreams. And that hurt, deeply. When adults organize kids, the kids always don't know the history, background, and gray areas of an issue. But they can be effective protesters because they come across as passionate and innocent, and they attract media attention. I'd been on the other side, so I was clear about what was going on. But it didn't make the scene any less painful.

I sank into a really low place in my mind. I had trouble focusing. I could barely speak, didn't feel like eating, and couldn't leave the house for almost a week. It was the closest I had ever come to what might be characterized as a nervous breakdown. Only my most trusted staff members and close friends knew. That included Susan Mitchell, whom I had hired again under contract to help with the restructuring. Susan was always very focused, and she talked me through that difficult time, helping me to sort through all of my options and possible alternatives.

Change is difficult. I knew the board was under tremendous pressure, too, and that I likely would have to compromise. What I had to figure out was how to get some of what I wanted. In the end, as I figured, I didn't have the votes for the board to approve the funding shift, but we came up with a compromise that set a floor for per-pupil expenditures at the elementary level. That ensured that the amount of money spent on every student in the elementary schools couldn't drop below a certain amount, which increased financing for some of the schools.

It wasn't a surprise that teachers came out so vehemently against my funding proposal. In the same budget, I had proposed no raises across the board. Property taxes were the primary source of financing for the school system, and the city had been increasing the taxes on city residents every year. I knew that was not sustainable, and with salaries accounting for the bulk of the school system's budget, the only way to avoid another big tax increase was to freeze salaries. I talked to Mayor John Norquist prior to proposing my budget and got his agreement on the frozen salaries. Imagine my surprise the day after I submitted my budget to the board when I saw him prominently quoted in the newspaper, saying my budget was bogus because it did not contain raises for employees. I called him and said, "Man, I thought we had an agreement." He told me I must have misunderstood what he said. We both knew that was bullshit. It was the first of two times that he told me one thing privately and did another publicly.

The teachers' union also played a role in the defeat of a February 1993 referendum, asking city residents whether they supported in-creased property taxes that would generate $366 million to pay for the construction of new schools, the renovation of others, the reduction of class sizes, and more resources for schools. The school district was one of four governmental entities that had the authority to assess and collect taxes to raise revenue. But of the four, which also included the city, the county, and Milwaukee Area Technical College, the school district was the only one that had to ask for voter approval to raise taxes for building construction. Many voters were still angry about the announcement in 1992 that the county would build a new Milwaukee County Stadium at the public's expense, no questions asked. I knew it would be difficult to win a referendum that would raise taxes. But I could hardly fathom teachers standing in front of classrooms with big buttons, urging people to "Vote No!" on the referendum, when some special education children were attending classes in closets. I can un-derstand how confusing that must have been to average voters. Why should they vote for higher taxes for improved schools when some of the teachers didn't even want it?

The mayor had offered his support during a private conversation, but once again his word to me in private meant nothing. He back-tracked in late October, less than a week before the school board final-ly decided to put the referendum on the ballot. The mayor submitted his own plan that would not have generated nearly as much money.

But there was no way the school board was going to back down at that point. The anger against the mayor was intense, and I knew that the board and I had to move forward with our proposal. I fought my hardest for the referendum and made as passionate a case for it as I could in every corner of the city, from the Rotary Club to churches to senior citizen centers. But even some of my former allies, including State Representative Polly Williams, ended up taking a stance against it. A week before the referendum, I was supposed to debate Mayor Norquist about it on a local news show, but somehow (I still don't know what happened) Polly ended up taking his place. And Polly was... well, Polly, arguing passionately the whole time. It was the broken system that needed fixing, not the buildings, she yelled over and over. You've got to know Polly to know it really wasn't personal. She has her own style. But a couple of times I had to grip the podium and remind myself, *Howard, stay calm. Stay on point.* To this day, I don't know why Polly came out against the referendum. I hated the spectacle of two Black leaders pitted against each other so publicly on this issue. But it didn't change one bit the way I feel about Polly Williams. I love Polly, and I respect Polly.

Other elements worked against us on the referendum, as well, and the most vicious of all was racism. Milwaukee is a very segregated city, with most white people living on the south side, and Black folks on the north side. There are two overtly racist instances I will never forget. We were making a presentation on the south side when a white woman shook her finger in my face and said her community was "not going to build school buildings on the north side for the children of lazy Black women on welfare." It took every bit of mental strength I had to keep from responding. Nothing I could have said would have changed her mind; anger from me would only have assured the referendum's demise.

In another instance at a school on the south side, a young Black woman with her baby in her arms stood up and said she supported the referendum because she wanted her baby to have early childhood education. Someone in the audience shouted out, "You should not have had the damn baby in the first place." The white crowd cheered. Both the young mother and I were amazingly calm in the face of such ignorance, but neither of us ever forgot. Nineteen years later, in 2012, I was speaking at Morehouse College in Atlanta when a young woman came up to me and asked if I recognized her. Her face didn't seem familiar at first, and she then asked me if I remembered the night at the school when a woman stood up with her baby and spoke in favor of the referendum. Of course I remembered, and we simultaneously repeated what the audience member had shouted out. The young lady identified herself as the mother who had spoken that night, and she asked me to step outside to meet someone. It was the baby she had held in her arms. He was a freshman at Morehouse. What a special, special moment.

But on February 15, 1993, the night before the big vote on the referendum, all I felt was dread as I listened to President Bill Clinton give his first national address. In it, he announced that he would not be able to keep his campaign pledge of no new taxes. Whatever hope I'd tried to maintain for the referendum slipped away. I was sure the President's revelation would leave voters feeling overwhelmed by taxes. A survey by the local newspaper had showed that a large majority of white voters in Milwaukee disapproved of increasing their property taxes to upgrade schools. The same poll showed the opposite was true for Black voters. But on election day, the supporters showed up in low numbers at the polls, while incensed white voters broke records for their turnout in a February election. The referendum was trounced by a three-to-one margin. I got my butt kicked. It hurt, but I'd done what I thought was the right thing to do for the kids. As superintendent, I couldn't go and sit in a corner and pout because things didn't go my way. I ultimately sat down with the mayor to find a way to generate more money for the schools. He agreed to add money to the city's budget for maintenance that had been deferred on school buildings that the city owned.

I was exasperated, though. My friends and family were worried, especially my mother, because the stress was beginning to show. I wasn't eating well. Sometimes, my days were so hectic that I just forgot to eat. As the months passed, I was more tired than usual, and I lost twelve pounds. But I suspected something serious was wrong when I developed a dry, hacking cough that wouldn't go away. In September 1993, I went to see Dr. Geoffrey C. Lamb, an internal medicine specialist, who hospitalized me and ran a battery of tests. Dr. Lamb practiced at the Medical College of Wisconsin, a teaching hospital where doctors were always conducting innovative research. The advantage of such an environment is that there is a better-than-average chance that someone at the institution knows about even the most obscure illnesses. Tests showed that I had a large mass in one of my lungs. My doctor initially suspected a tumor or pneumonia. Further tests ruled out those possibilities and revealed a condition called sarcoidosis, then a little-known illness in which inflammation develops and poses a dangerous threat to certain organs of the body, particularly the lungs. I'd never even heard of sarcoidosis, which made the condition seem even scarier. But I immediately began doing my own research. I learned that while there is no cure, I could still live a full, productive life. I decided to go public with the news, and the local paper ran a big story about my diagnosis. I began receiving letters, cards, and telephone calls from other people throughout the country who suffered from the same illness, which helped me to learn even more about it.

One of the people who called while I was still in the hospital was the mother of the child I'd had out of wedlock decades earlier. My son wanted to meet me, she said. A mix of excitement, guilt, and fear filled me. I couldn't help thinking of the moment years earlier when my own father had come to me out of the blue. I had given a speech, and a man approached me afterward and introduced himself as Tom Fuller. By then, I was a grown man who had built a full life without a father. I felt no connection to him, no warmth, and no desire for a relationship. I'm sure that came across in our introduction, and we never spoke again. So, I had no idea how things would go with Darwin. But a short time after I talked to his mother, Darwin called. I apologized to him for not being there, and we agreed to look forward, not behind. I told my family about him and sent him a ticket to visit me in Milwaukee so that we could begin getting to know one another. About two years later, Van, as he is known to friends and family, moved to Milwaukee and stayed about seven months. He lived with me for a while, and then he and Malcolm shared a place, before branching out on their own. Over the past twenty-plus years, Van and I have built the best relationship we could under the circumstances. He is a great young man who shares my passion for education. He has earned a Doctor of Education (Ed.D.) in School Administration and Supervision and works as a Supervisor in the Newport News public schools in Virginia. I give my son full credit for bringing us together.

Meanwhile, as my health slowly improved, my mother wanted me to quit my job. She was convinced that the stress of being superintendent had made me sick. But once I realized I would be able to function normally, I didn't even consider quitting. I went back to work and eventually began taking Prednisone, a steroidal medication that helped to control the effects of the illness. There was still so much more I wanted to accomplish.

One of the primary issues occupying my mind was how to generate much-needed revenue for the system, given the referendum's defeat. In 1994, a new organization called The Edison Project expressed interest in contracting with the school system to manage two of the city's public schools. The private, New York-based company laid out a plan to operate the schools more efficiently and improve student performance. The company also pledged to pump $1.5 million in each of the two schools right away. If The Edison Project could deliver the promised results, it seemed of little importance to me that the project was a profit-making venture for the owners. The school system wouldn't have to put out a dime more, and we would get a major infusion of resources into the schools out of the deal. The project struck me as innovative and definitely worth pursuing. So I had Edison representatives to make a number of public presentations to the board and the community. Afterward, I set up a separate presentation for principals and then sent a message to them asking for their opinions. I assured them that how they felt would not be held against them in any way. Sixty-six principals said they would welcome the program. When all of the presentations were done, the critics came out. The unions and others opposed to the Edison Project began to speculate wildly and publicly that my ultimate goal was to privatize the entire school system and that Edison was just the beginning. Critics both inside and outside the school system began to spread rumors that my next effort would involve hiring outside contractors to take care of the grounds and run the cafeterias. These tactics were aimed at Black workers who held many of these jobs. It was a successful strategy that tapped into a deep reservoir of suspicion amongst many Black people and white, so-called liberals about the business community. The hysteria put extreme pressure on the board, and I knew I didn't have the support to get the project through. I expressed that to Edison's leaders, and after months of controversy, they withdrew their offer. "Given the overall climate in Milwaukee concerning this potential partnership, we do not feel it is appropriate to continue actively pursuing such a relationship for the 1995-96 school year," Edison Vice President Richard T. Roberts said in a letter.

The Edison flap became the central theme in the school board race the following year, when the teachers' union ran a slate of five candidates opposed to my reform efforts. The union pumped more than $40,000 into those candidates' campaigns, running ads and spreading literature with the same false claims that I was trying to privatize the school system. I was home alone the night of April 4, 1995, when I heard a report about the election results. Four of their candidates had won. I felt numb. I knew then what I had to do. But I spent many hours over the next two weeks, talking to my family and closest friends about my decision and reflecting. How could I continue to move forward with four of the nine board members automatically opposed to any significant reform measures I put forward? If I stayed, I would constantly have to fight for that fifth vote. How would that serve the children? I wouldn't be backed into a position of having to grovel for the board's respect. No way. I had sought this job for one reason: to make Milwaukee Public Schools better for our children. I'd poured everything I had into doing that, and I'd done so with the confidence of the board. We hadn't agreed on everything, but I knew they wanted me to succeed for the children. The election had changed that.

A couple of my fellow superintendents in whom I'd confided my plans to resign urged me to try to get the board to buy out the rest of my contract. I'd just signed a new one for two years, and while completely legal, asking the board to pay me to walk away just didn't seem right. I decided to just resign and leave with no strings attached. Before sending my letter of resignation to the board, I talked it over one last time with Debbie. By then, she had been through her own trials in Detroit and had resigned as superintendent there. More than anyone else in the world, she knew how I was feeling. She assured me I was doing the right thing.

On the night of April 19, 1995, my family, closest friends, and supporters packed the auditorium at the school board office. The media had been speculating since the election about what I would do, and I had sat down with reporters and editors from the *Milwaukee Journal* a few hours earlier to explain my plans. I would rather walk out with my head held high than die by a thousand cuts, I told them. The mood in the auditorium was a bit somber. Several parents walked over to whisper words of support and give me hugs. Others waved signs to thank me. I was calm, totally at peace with my decision. Soon after the board emerged from an hour-long closed session, it was time for me to speak. I made my way to the podium and opened by reminding people of the same five goals that had guided me throughout my tenure as superintendent. Then, I moved into the heart of my statement:

> For all of my adult life in Milwaukee, every fiber of my being has been devoted to helping this community's children achieve a better future. This will always be the agenda that guides me.
>
> It is a tribute to the resiliency and intelligence of the children and parents of Milwaukee that they have done as well as they have in spite of the neglect they have suffered.
>
> It is a tribute to the dedication of thousands of splendid individual educators and support staff in the Milwaukee Public Schools that they have done so much for our children, in spite of the self-serving vision of their purported "representatives." We have heard from these "representatives"—those who protect the forces of the status quo—that Howard Fuller wants to sell out our children to "privatization." We have heard about my supposedly "secret agenda." We have heard that I am in the hip pocket of the "downtown business interests." Indeed, these were the scurrilous messages that the Milwaukee Teachers Education Association and others spread during the recent school board campaign. These charges reflect the central strategy of defenders of the status quo: smear any effort to bring genuine reform to the system as a "plot" to destroy public education.
>
> I believe the people and the children of Milwaukee know better. I'm in nobody's pocket. People who know me understand I have been willing, and I remain willing, to sit down with anyone, anytime, anywhere to promote the interest of our children.
>
> Yes, I am supportive of a whole range of ideas to improve educational opportunity for our children and their parents. Yes, I will challenge the rigid, bureaucratic, and self-serving rules of the system, by opening the door to innovative and radical educational approaches. But in anyone's pocket? NO! For kids? YES! I will stand with anyone who puts the children and their parents first and foremost. I will oppose anyone who puts jobs, privileges, and rules before our children.
>
> My real mission has and always will be the effective education of all of our children. There are hundreds of administrators, teachers, and support staff in the Milwaukee Public Schools system who share that mission with me. They believe as I do that this system must be transformed radically if this mission is to be accomplished.

But the educational system as presently configured still is not designed to achieve this mission. Instead, our system remains fundamentally mired in the status quo. Powerful forces conspire to protect careers, contracts and current practices before tending to the interests of our children. Because of these forces, what we have achieved has too often been painfully and unnecessarily slow in coming.

Let me be blunt. Too often in the last several years, our children have suffered under the yoke of these powerful forces. The events of the last several months have created a more detrimental political environment, which now threatens to reverse the momentum we need to make major change. I now believe I will be maneuvered into a position where I would be expected to become a bureaucrat protecting the status quo, while the public is led to believe that true reform is underway.

The day-to-day management of the District will be crippled in an atmosphere where the superintendent and staff are uncertain about the depth of board support. There cannot be a running public debate about whether the board and superintendent are in harmony. The District cannot succeed if the primary question, day after day, week after week, is whether the Superintendent can "patch together five votes" to support the many actions that will be necessary to carry out a rigorous reform agenda.

For these reasons, I have regretfully concluded that I can no longer pursue my goals and mission as Superintendent of the Milwaukee Public Schools. And so, I have submitted my resignation to the Board of School Directors effective July 31, 1995.

I am eternally grateful to the people of Milwaukee, and the Board which hired me, for the opportunity to have served as your Superintendent of Schools.

Let me emphasize that for me this is not the end. Today is the first day of the rest of the struggle, for me and for all of us who are totally committed to our children. The words of William Daggett will continue to guide us:

"We must love our children's hopes, dreams, and prayers more than we love the institutional heritage of the school system."

With my son, Darwin Mills ("Van") and his wife, Tammy.

My children (left to right, Van, Kelli, Miata, Malcolm), all together.

15

THE RIGHT CHOICE

The one thing I knew for sure about my future after stepping down as Milwaukee Public Schools Superintendent was that I would continue to fight for all children to get the quality education they deserve. But I didn't want to end up sitting alone somewhere, trying to figure out the best way to do that. Great ideas usually come from a collaborative process, and so I convened a meeting of about six people whose opinions I respected to help me figure out my options. The group included former Milwaukee Board of School Directors President Jeanette Mitchell, a few close friends, and a couple of foundation executives.

We met at the historic University Club in Milwaukee, spent a few hours discussing the possibilities, and narrowed my focus to three prospects: I could become a school superintendent in another city, work for a nonprofit, or get a job at a university. Soon after that brainstorming session, a headhunter called me about the search for a school superintendent in Prince George's County, Maryland, and I agreed to interview for the position. But I realized I had no desire to be a superintendent again and would not have taken the job even if it had been offered to me. It had become clear to me that I could do more to push for the kinds of reforms I believed were best for children and families outside of a job as superintendent. As superintendent, whenever I tried to do anything, I had to get the support of so many people to make it happen, and often, the agendas of some of those people were not the same as mine. I would find a way that I could have the freedom of working outside the system but at the same time maintain my deep connections to the people still "in the room." So, I eliminated the option of becoming a superintendent elsewhere and decided not to interview with any other school districts.

I had preliminary talks with a national nonprofit and the University of Wisconsin in Milwaukee. But the best offer came quickly from Marquette University. When I met with key Marquette officials, they basically said: "Tell us what you want to do." It was the perfect scenario. They gave me wide range to define my dream job at the university, and I did exactly that. I began to envision a place that would bring together all kinds of people to work on transforming education in this country. That idea became the Institute for the Transformation of Learning, which opened at Marquette with me as director on August 16, 1995. The university agreed to pay half of my salary and to provide office space and resources support, while I committed to raise the rest through grants and donations. I was also named a Distinguished Professor of Education, and given the opportunity to teach graduate and undergraduate students. It was really a blessing to be able to return to the place that had helped to restore my sense of mission all those years ago. I'm sure many thought that Marquette would be just a soft place for me to land while I figured out my next big move. But my partnership with the university has endured longer than any other job I've ever had, and it has enabled me to do some of the most exciting work of my life.

Much of that work has been through the Institute, which received its first $200,000 grant from the Joyce Foundation in Chicago. After my resignation as MPS Superintendent, I was contacted by the foundation's Education Program Officer, Warren Chapman, who offered the grant for me to take a personal yearlong sabbatical. But when I began talks with Marquette, I asked the foundation to award the money instead to the Institute. I then assembled a varied group of about eighty-five people to help me think about what the Institute should do. My goal was to bring together people who ordinarily wouldn't wind up in the same room to talk openly about education and come up with specific projects that would enhance learning both inside and outside the traditional school setting. The group included teachers from public, private, parochial, and alternative schools, community activists, school superintendents, school board members, and business representatives. We came up with a name that captured our mission, Explorations, and met for one evening and at least two all-day sessions. Most of the programs that the Institute implemented in the first year came out of those sessions. By spring 1996, an additional $100,000 grant had come from the Lynde and Harry Bradley Foundation in

Milwaukee and another $50,000 a year for two years from the Helen
Bader Foundation to finance our ideas.

It was important to all of us who were a part of Explorations that
the Institute have a direct relationship with kids in the community.
Thus, one of the first things the Institute did was create technology
learning centers in five area churches for after-school programs. Each
of the churches set aside the appropriate space in their buildings, and
we provided fully-equipped computers, educational software, and
support staff. That enabled students to go to a safe place they trusted
in their neighborhoods to do homework, receive computer training,
and stay out of trouble. The centers helped to level the playing field
a bit for poor families that might not have had computers in their
homes or the know-how to work on them without help at the local
libraries. I loved visiting the sites and seeing kids engaged in learning
on the computers. This was tangible proof that the Institute was out
there in the neighborhoods, at ground zero, doing our best to fill in
some of the academic gaps for students.

Another of the recommendations from Explorations was that the
Institute get involved in designing new schools and strengthening existing ones to participate in Milwaukee's Parental Choice Program.
That led to the creation of the School Design and Development
Center. To lead the effort, I brought in a longtime educator and moti-
vator, Dr. Robert Pavlik. Bob had written books on literacy and spent
many years as a teacher and college professor. There is no one better
than he is at training teachers and getting them excited about helping children learn. His enthusiasm is contagious. He also is a master
thinker and organizer who can create an easy-to-follow template to
take just about any idea from concept to completion. With his leadership, the Institute helped to develop more than thirty schools from
1996 to 2005.

One new school even grew out of the Explorations group when
Dr. Christine Faltz, a member who was also head of the Upward
Bound program at Marquette, decided she wanted to create a charter school. She formed a separate committee and approached the City
of Milwaukee's Housing Authority, which was applying for a new
grant program that provided funds to renovate the Parklawn Housing
Project on Milwaukee's west side. The city agreed to include $3 mil-
lion for the school in its grant proposal. Once the grant was approved,
Christine and those of us working with her realized we did not have

enough money. She then appealed to Johnson Controls, which under-wrote a loan for the remaining funds to build what became the Central City Cyber School, a kindergarten-through-eighth-grade school built inside Parklawn. The new Cyber School won a charter from the city and was far ahead of the curve in using the latest technology to advance learning for its kindergarten-through-eighth-grade students, most of whom live in public housing. For example, every child in the school has access to a laptop.

The third component that Explorations identified as important for the Institute was research, and we quickly focused on the Milwaukee Teachers' Education Association as the subject of our inaugural project. It was clear to me from my days as Superintendent that the union contract had a huge impact on what administrators could do to improve schools. The Institute decided in late 1996 to commission a study that analyzed the history of the teachers' union contract and its impact on day-to-day school operations and educational outcomes. Two consultants whom I trusted, my friend George A. Mitchell, who was a great researcher and writer, and Michael E. Hartmann, who was director of research at the Wisconsin Policy Research Institute, spent a year looking at every aspect of the contract. The study found that, while the contract had helped teachers significantly increase their salaries and secure better medical and retirement benefits and job security, it worsened the relationships between teachers, administrators, and the school board. The contract also imposed rules so rigid that any variance or new effort required a legal agreement, called a Memorandum of Understanding (MOU). Between 1971 and 1995, for example, there were 1,700 such agreements. These MOUs had the legal standing of contractual provisions—so much so that we called them "the contract behind the contract." The union would pull them out as needed. Most superintendents and their staffs had little historical knowledge of these documents or the additional 300 rulings from arbitration and grievance hearings. All of these agreements stacked together were at times formidable obstacles to change in the district. The contract itself had grown from eighteen pages in 1964 into a dense, complex document of 174 pages in 1995. Overall, our study found that the collective bargaining process had not improved academic achievement for students and, at times, had interfered with a successful learning environment. It called for a public collective bargaining process and for MPS administrators and the union to adopt a contract that led to improved student outcomes.

The study was groundbreaking. As far as we knew, no one had ever looked at the teachers' union contract in that kind of detail, and only a few people in the entire school system even knew exactly what was in it and understood it. The report made front-page news and got lots of media attention. Of course, the union took issue with some parts of it, but we encouraged public debate. George, Michael, and I were invited to Harvard University to present our findings and participate in a discussion about unions. I was proud that we had conducted such an exhaustive, thorough study and raised issues that needed to be raised. But it didn't surprise me that not much changed in the way MPS and the union conducted their business.

While still developing the Institute in October 1995, I simultaneously accepted an appointment as a senior fellow at the Annenberg Institute for School Reform at Brown University. The project's director was Theodore R. Sizer, whom I respect enormously. His work in education reform dates back to the early 1970s, when his study of hundreds of high schools led to his eye-opening 1984 book, *Horace's Compromise*. The same year, Ted founded a movement of new schools, called the Coalition of Essential Schools. Working with him through the fellowship was a great experience that connected me with fellow school reformers throughout the country and gave me the opportunity to spend two years visiting an array of schools. It furthered my understanding of the internal workings of schools and, as Ted liked to say, "school people." My work with him and our colleagues, Dennis Litky and Deborah Meier, helped me understand the difficulty of creating and sustaining a great school. I developed a close friendship with Dennis, who is a strong proponent of project learning. He went on to create the Big Picture Company, which established a number of schools throughout the country. When it comes to working with kids, he is one of the most creative people I have ever met.

The month after I accepted the fellowship, my personal life changed again in a wonderful way: I married Deborah McGriff. After that first date, Debbie and I had continued to grow closer. She had gone on to work as Executive Vice President at Edison Schools, and we often moved in the same circles. Most important to me, she understood me and appreciated my passion and commitment to my work. She wanted a church wedding, but with our busy schedules, we couldn't figure

244 _Howard Fuller_ NO STRUGGLE, NO PROGRESS

out a time when we both would be free long enough to plan and host a wedding. I didn't want to put it off any longer, and so, while visiting New York together on November 16, 1995, we went to a courthouse and got married. Debbie deserved better than a courthouse wedding, and I promised her that I would do something to make up for it.

Our first year zipped past. As our second anniversary was approaching, I worked with two good friends of mine in Milwaukee, Thelma Sias and Cecelia Gore, both terrific event planners, to put together a surprise wedding anniversary celebration. We developed an elaborate scheme to keep it a secret from Debbie, which people who know her will attest was a monumental task. Our scheme started with my taking her to dinner at the Hyatt Hotel in Milwaukee and dropping my business card in a large fish bowl to compete for a free dinner in a random drawing. I made sure Debbie saw me drop my card in the bowl. My event planners then had the hotel send me a letter announcing that I had been selected for the free dinner. I showed it to Debbie and suggested that we take advantage of the gift for our anniversary. I started the celebration the day before by taking her and four of our children—Jacqueline (her daughter from a previous marriage), Kelli and Miata (my two daughters), and Malcolm (my younger son)—out to dinner. Our daughters all lived outside Milwaukee and had excuses for why they were in town, and so they made a big deal about being able to spend the evening with us. But they all said they had to leave the next day. I had flowers delivered to the dinner, and it was a wonderful evening. The next day, a Saturday, I took her shopping for a new dress to wear on our special night. I wore a suit and tie, and when we arrived at the hotel with our letter, we got first-class treatment. The parking attendant and staff congratulated us on winning the drawing and pointed us to the elevators. On the way up to the restaurant on the top floor, I made up an excuse for us to stop briefly on the second floor. When we stepped off the elevator, Debbie was stunned to see our children, who she thought had all left town. More than two hundred other family members and friends also were gathered in a huge open room for the surprise party. Even the mayor was there, and Gov. Tommy Thompson called later to congratulate us. I could hardly believe that I actually managed to pull off the surprise, but Debbie declares to this day she didn't have a clue.

After we got to the party, I still wasn't done. As our guests enjoyed the live band and hors d'oeuvres, Jacqueline asked her mother to accompany her upstairs to the ladies' room. While they were away, hotel workers wheeled out a wedding cake and pushed back a set of sliding doors to reveal a makeshift altar surrounded by flowers. When Debbie made it back downstairs, I was standing there with a microphone in my hand and a minister standing next to me. I asked her again if she would marry me. The crowd went wild with applause. Debbie was speechless. And trust me, that never happens. She joined me at the altar. At our courthouse wedding, she had written her own vows. This time, I recited vows to her that I had created from the hundreds of cards I'd sent her over the years. It was truly one of the most special nights of our lives.

By the time we got married I had become a full-time advocate for the parental choice movement. I was getting invitations to speak all over the country. It wasn't lost on me why this was so. I was a novelty, an outspoken Black man and former schools superintendent who supported a growing movement that was largely championed by conservative white people. Often, I was the only Black person in the room. But I was convinced that vouchers, charter schools, and other educational alternatives offered the best hope for Black children from poor and working-class families to receive the quality education they deserved. They were the ones largely trapped in schools that were failing to educate them, and they needed someone representing their interests around the tables and in the rooms where these issues were being discussed.

"This movement is never going to work if it's led only by white people," I said to a mostly white crowd gathered in D.C. one night for a formal gala sponsored by the Center for Education Reform. The organization, founded by my friend Jeanne Allen, was presenting me an award for my work on behalf of parent choice. Jeanne is one of the country's strongest fighters for parent choice and creating great schools for kids. Several others also were recognized that night, including my close friend and ally, Pennsylvania State Representative Dwight Evans, an African-American legislator who was an early supporter of parental choice. After making that statement about the leadership of the movement, the question for me became, well, who's going to do something about it? I decided then that I at least had to try.

Whenever I was invited to speak or attend functions related to parental choice, I began zeroing in on the few Black people in the room and made sure I collected their business cards. I picked up a few cards from Black supporters of choice when I testified before Congress in favor of vouchers. Sometimes my advocacy on behalf of parent choice brought me into debates with some interesting people, like the time I was asked to participate on a three-member panel at an education policy luncheon in Chicago on June 17, 1998. One of the panelists was Seymour Fliegel, whose Center for Educational Innovation first earned widespread recognition in the early 1980s by creating a string of successful small charter schools in some of New York City's poorest neighborhoods. The other panelist was a young Illinois State Senator who opposed vouchers. His name: Barack Obama. The debate was civil, but one exchange between Senator Obama and me went something like this:

> *Obama: I do think that the whole issue of vouchers is a distraction. But the reason I brought it up is that I think it does confuse the debate. Part of the reason why it confuses the debate is because it distracts from the fact that many of the benefits that we point to, not only in private schools and parochial schools, but also in charter schools, could be achievable within the public school framework. That's perhaps where I differ from Howard. He's undergone the bureaucratic battles, trying to implement some of these changes system-wide. I recognize the difficulties, politically, of implementing them. But when you think of something like instituting a little more teacher autonomy, or providing principals with more authority to hire and fire, there's nothing that tells us innately that can't be done within the public school system... My sense is that part of the reason folks put out the voucher idea is that they don't want to tackle those difficult issues—those political battles. They would rather settle for helping a certain portion of the population, the fifteen percent, twenty percent who can benefit from a choice system. I guess that I believe if we can't change the system overall, then I probably would be game to go ahead and just help those who can escape it. But maybe I just have a little more confidence that we might be able to change the entire system.*
>
> *Me: May I respond to that? First of all, I've been engaged in this battle for twenty-five years. And I think the view that those of us who support vouchers are running away from the battle is, first of all, incorrect.*
>
> *Obama: Oh, I didn't mean that.*
>
> *Me: No, but I'm telling you that when we lay stuff out like that we make these broad sweeps in order to make a point. And I'm trying to make a point that: Number one, I don't view the voucher struggle as a distraction, because there's a whole lot of discussion that's now going on*

about change in public education that wouldn't ever happen if we were not involved in the debates... Number two, a lot of people have a total misconception, in my opinion, about what constitutes public education in America. A lot of people are living in "la-la land" if they think that public education is the place where all the races and classes come together in America. In many of the schools, there ain't no coming together of all the races and classes. What's coming together are poor kids who are forced to stay in places that did not work for them, while people who have money are pontificating about the goodness of the public schools, while they themselves are putting their kids in schools that work for their children.

I talked about one of the major problems that reformers encounter when trying to implement meaningful change within the existing school—the teachers' union. And I cited examples from the Institute's study. I summed up my remarks this way:

And you sit here and claim that we can make changes in the existing system? If you can do that, God bless you. But I'm going to tell you this. Those of us who are out there fighting are not going to wait for you to do that. We're going to keep trying to find ways to help people whose kids are being undereducated, miseducated, not educated.

Barack Obama and I have not crossed paths since that day—at least not directly. I felt the pride that most African Americans felt in 2008, when we helped to elect him as the nation's first African-American president. And since then, I actually think he has done a better than solid job pushing education reform, particularly charter schools. Obviously, I wish he had a different position on vouchers. His views have not really changed. As a matter of fact, his public comments have echoed what he said during our debate back in 1993.

After that debate, I continued collecting business cards from the few Black supporters of parental choice I met at various events. When I'd collected several cards, I invited the fellow choice supporters to meet me at the Institute—all seven of them. It was a small but productive meeting as we discussed how we could generate more Black support for parental choice. For starters, we all agreed that each of us would bring five additional people to our next meeting. A short time later, about thirty-five of us met and began planning a larger event, the First Annual Symposium, which was held in Milwaukee in March 1999. It drew 150 Black participants who spent the weekend discussing the theme, "The Power of Options." When I convened the meeting, I had hoped just to create a loose network of Black people who supported parental choice. But afterward, I had discussions with a number of people, including my good friend, Armstrong Williams, who felt we needed to create an organization that would advance the cause within our community and advocate for more educational options for Black families. The following December, fifty of us met for two days at the historic Mayflower Hotel in Washington, D.C., where we established the Black Alliance for Educational Options (BAEO) and drafted its mission and general principles.

BAEO was the first Black-centered parental choice advocacy group, and word about it spread quickly. A total of 350 people attended our second symposium, held again in Milwaukee in March 2000. Ninety of us stayed afterward for an organizational meeting, where I was elected as BAEO's first President and given the authority to create a national board. On the way home, I called my friend, John Walton, and explained what we were trying to do. I had become friends with John, the son of Walmart founder Sam Walton, years earlier when we both served on the board of a group called the American Education Reform Council, whose president was Susan Mitchell. John and I began to have some deep conversations about education, poverty, and the parental choice movement, and the two of us grew close. John's support for BAEO was unwavering: "I trust you, Howard. I believe in you," he said. "Just tell me what kind of support you need." Ultimately, the Walton Family Foundation awarded BAEO a startup grant of $900,000. We formed a twenty-nine-member board and officially launched the group in August 2000 at the National Press Club in Washington, D.C. We based our headquarters there and have continued to grow into one of the organizations at the forefront of the education reform movement in this country. The difference between us and most of the other organizations doing this important work is that BAEO is run and controlled by Black people. We have maintained our original purpose of fighting to ensure that low- income and working-class Black people have the power to choose high quality educational options of their children.

I am very proud of the fact that BAEO has established itself as the premier Black organization in both the parent choice movement and the broader movement for education reform. Our annual symposium has blossomed into the largest gathering of Black education reform supporters in the nation. The annual event draws over five hundred parents, students, educators, elected officials, and community leaders. One year in Philadelphia, more than one thousand people attended. The goal each year is for participants to be informed, inspired, and empowered so that they can go back into their communities to wage a struggle on behalf of families and their children. BAEO currently has staff working in Milwaukee, Philadelphia, Louisiana, Kentucky, Alabama, and Mississippi. In most of those places, we have worked with other parental choice advocates and lawmakers to secure major victories for the movement. As a national organization, we are a consistent Black voice throughout the country in the battle for parent choice and transformational education reform.

BAEO was well underway in November 2000, when George W. Bush was elected President of the United States and later invited me and several other parental choice advocates to the White House. I started to write a newspaper opinion piece, responding to the critics who claimed I had sold out. But I decided against it. Why waste time trying to win over critics when there is so much to be done to change the horrific educational reality for so many of our poorest children? That is why I stay on the move at an often frantic pace.

Life, though, has its own way of slowing us down. I was sixty years old in December 2001, when my doctor called to say he had some very bad news. I braced myself. A routine checkup four years earlier had revealed an elevated PSA score, which is sometimes an indication of potential prostate problems. I'd been dedicated to keeping up my regular doctor visits and monitoring, but this time a biopsy had revealed evidence of prostate cancer. My doctor's words sucked all of the air out of me. The C-word is scary as hell, no matter who you are or how strong you think you are. I'd dealt with serious health issues before, but knowing that you have cancer somehow feels different, more serious, than anything else. And for the first time in my life I began to think about my own mortality. I still had so much I wanted to accomplish. Could I survive this? And if I did, would I make it through with my manhood intact? Men don't normally admit it, but the questions, the fears, are real, and they can drive you crazy if you let them.

After talking with Debbie, I called my children. Both of my daughters were on the telephone at the same time when I broke the news. Miata, who is a lot like me, instantly went to the Internet to begin researching what to do, while Kelli began to cry. All I could do was try to assure them that I would be okay, though at that moment, I wasn't even sure of that myself. But I'm a realist, and I don't like wallowing in self-pity. I gave myself a deadline to decide whether to have surgery or pursue some other course of treatment: the following Monday at 5:00 p.m. That gave me two days to feel sorry for myself, research, and do whatever I needed to arrive at my decision. I read as much material as I could find, but the more I read, the more confused I felt. What helped me was talking to several of my friends who had survived prostate cancer. Their encouragement calmed me and assisted me greatly in making a decision. By my Monday deadline, I was ready.

On January 24, 2002, just days after my 61st birthday, I underwent surgery for prostate cancer. My recovery was fairly smooth, and just weeks later, I eased my way back in the work. Before long, I was feeling like my old self, stronger than ever. It's a good thing, too, because the years ahead would bring some of the parental choice movement's toughest battles. And they would require every ounce of strength I had.

With Debbie at the surprise renewal of our wedding vows.
(Photo courtesy of Frankie Cole.)

With my mother and youngest daughter, Miata, at the marriage renewal ceremony. (Photo courtesy of Frankie Cole.)

With the family at the marriage vows renewal (from left to right, Ma, Jacqueline, Malcolm, me, Debbie, Kelli, and Miata).

With Ma.

With Debbie.

With my son, Van, and stepdaughter's husband, Michael Cooper.

Founding meeting of BAEO on December 3, 1999.

16

TOUGH TESTS

When the Bill and Melinda Gates Foundation convened a meeting in Seattle in the early 2000s to brainstorm how it should invest in education, I was among the reform advocates invited to participate. As we discussed our experiences, the conversation zoomed in on the idea of creating smaller high schools. A number of the individuals there had been involved with the development of those types of schools, folks like Ted Sizer, creator of the Coalition of Essential Schools. The discussion around the table was that smaller schools were better for kids than the mammoth secondary institutions that many children, particularly in urban areas of the country, were attending. People also cited the success of private schools, most of which had no more than one hundred students per grade at the high school level. The argument for such schools was that they provided students a more personalized education, resulting in better academic performance, less absenteeism, lower dropout rates, less violence and vandalism, better student attendance, improved student-faculty relationships, and stronger community ties. There also was a push during the meeting for multiple ways of assessing students, as opposed to using just test scores. It was my first real exposure to concepts like presentations and portfolio assessments as a way to measure student learning.

While it was important to have the reformers and researchers there, the most important person in the room was Tom Vander Ark, who had been appointed to head the Foundation's initiative. Tom had been a superintendent in the Federal Way School district, located between Seattle and Tacoma. He did not say much, but he was extremely attentive to the conversation. The meeting was one of the key elements that led Tom to make the development of small high schools the major initiative of the Gates Foundation's education work. Tom decided to pursue two methods of establishing these schools: (1) working with traditional school systems to create new schools within the district and to break up larger schools into smaller schools within the same buildings; and (2) to support the creation of smaller schools outside the district, in most cases charter schools.

One of the districts Tom decided to explore was Milwaukee. At that time the superintendent of the Milwaukee Public Schools was William Andrekopoulos, who had been a reform-minded principal when I was superintendent. He was very open to trying new ideas to help students. Most of Milwaukee's high schools were large and were not doing a good job of educating students, particularly poor Black kids. Despite my best efforts, I had made very little or no progress in changing that reality when I was superintendent, and Bill was facing the same issue.

I'd been in touch with Tom occasionally since the Seattle meeting. We arranged to meet for breakfast when he came to Milwaukee to talk to a broad group of people representing the school district, business community, and other educators and activists engaged in developing schools outside of the district. We discussed the possibility of the foundation making a major investment in the city. I also pitched Tom on awarding a grant to the Black Alliance for Educational Options (BAEO), so that we could develop some small schools led by African Americans. It turned out to be a very fruitful discussion because ultimately the foundation decided to invest in Milwaukee and BAEO.

In early 2003, the Gates Foundation held a press conference in Boston to announce some of the first recipients of its $375 million initiative to finance the restructuring of high schools across the country. I was there, along with other BAEO officials, to receive a $4 million grant to create eight new small high schools. BAEO was the only Black-run organization among the awardees and the only group that openly supported vouchers. Some of the other awardees were clearly anti-vouchers and were not supportive of our being there. I got the feeling that they felt we had crashed the party.

In July of the same year, the foundation came to Milwaukee to announce that it was investing $17.25 million over five years in a program called "A New Vision of Secondary Education in Milwaukee." (The grant period was eventually extended to seven years ending in 2010.) In the initial proposal, the grant would be used to redesign seven of

the city's existing large public high schools into multiplexes, an estimated three small schools at each site. The money also would assist in
creating forty new small, high-quality high schools through the visionary process and first two years of operations. Thirty of them would
be created inside or in partnership with Milwaukee Public Schools
and ten for students outside the district through a group called the
Alliance for Choices in Education, where I served as chairman of the
board. During the first year of the grant, its guidelines were revised
to allow for the creation of fifty new small high schools. Gates told
Milwaukee to fund the best proposals received, regardless of whether
or not they were to be operated in the public school district.

This kind of private investment in education in Milwaukee was un-
precedented. To disburse the funds, the Gates Foundation required
an intermediary group to manage the grant. The person ultimately
given that responsibility was Daniel Grego, a good friend of mine who
headed a group called Trans Center for Youth. Dan initially created
the Technical Assistance & Leadership Center (TALC) to provide
training and technical assistance to those planning to create the new
schools. After the first year, TALC took over managing the grant, as
well. I have so much respect for Dan, who had earned his reputation as
a reformer by creating a number of successful small schools in the city.
All of us who had been involved in attracting the funds to Milwaukee
were filled with hope. At last it seemed we had the resources needed
to spur radical change in our schools. But even under the best of circumstances, this degree of change is never easy. Dan and a committee he established reviewed one hundred and nine proposals for new
schools. They then selected the best among them, trained the leaders,
and slowly helped many of the high schools to open. Andrekopoulos
moved quickly to create some smaller high schools simply by breaking
up two of the district's largest schools into multiple schools sharing
the same space. North Division, for example, was divided into three
individual high schools on its old campus.

In all, forty-two small high schools were created in Milwaukee. By
2008, when the grants initially were due to expire, though, the Gates
Foundation was not impressed with the results. Only a few of the city's
schools showed improved academic performance. The results were not
much better nationwide. Despite ultimately investing nearly $2 billion
and creating 2,600 small schools in forty-five states and the District
of Columbia, the Gates Foundation announced in 2010 that it was

discontinuing the small high school initiative. Citing statistics showing the overall lack of academic improvement, the foundation found that the effort had failed. The news was, of course, disappointing, especially to my friend, Dan, who had worked so hard to help the schools succeed. Dan had data, such as dramatically improved graduation rates, indicating that the project was working, particularly in the new schools that had started from scratch. Success was much less evident in the public high schools that simply had broken into smaller schools on the same campus without adequate staff training and preparation. In media interviews, Dan said he believed the Gates Foundation gave up on the initiative too soon. Many of the newly-created high schools had difficulty generating enough money to sustain their budgets, and by the 2009-2010 school year, only twenty-three of the forty-two new schools created in Milwaukee remained operational. Only seventeen of them still existed at the time this book was published.

I could see both sides of the issue—the Foundation's hesitation to keep pouring significant money into an initiative that had not yielded the expected results and the frustration of those on the ground, doing the work, seeing things change slowly, feeling certain that more time would get them where they needed to be. But I'm a realist. The decision had been made, and I try not to linger on any feelings of disappointment. Before I allow bad news to cripple me, I'm on to the next question: How can I fix this? What do I do now? And one particular school, C.E.O. Leadership Academy, needed my undivided attention to survive.

The school had been created by a group of ministers in 2004 with support from the Gates Foundation funds and TALC. I had helped to bring ministers together a year or two earlier to rally around parental choice when I heard that People for the American Way, a liberal group founded by Hollywood screenwriter and producer Norman Lear, was coming to town to organize opposition to Milwaukee's school voucher program. The group was bringing Jesse Jackson, Jr., to headline an anti-vouchers event in conjunction with some local pastors. But through my community activism, I had a good working relationship with a number of other pastors in the city and planned a counter-meeting on the same day and time. Our meeting drew a couple hundred supporters, including many Black parents and children, and it received good media coverage, overshadowing the smaller, mostly white People for the American Way event.

The ministers who had come together for our meeting represented a cross-section of denominations and wanted to maintain their
alliance. They formed the Clergy for Educational Options and began holding regular meetings. Among the issues on their agenda was
whether or not to create a high school that would become a feeder for
church-based elementary-middle schools, either schools that already
existed or new ones that could be formed. Once I realized there was
support for the school, I hired a woman named Denise Pitchford as
a Fellow in my Institute at Marquette. Denise had gone through the
Compton Fellows program, which I had helped create to train and
place non-traditional minorities in Milwaukee Public Schools as middle school teachers. She had completed the program and had spent a
couple years as a public school teacher in Milwaukee. I knew she was a
dedicated educator, and I believed she would be a good person to lead
the development of the school and become its first Principal. Her sole
responsibility as a Fellow was to organize the school. She had nine
months to get it done. She pulled together a design team, developed
the board, and submitted a proposal to TALC for a planning grant to
help pull it all together.

There was some talk of naming the school after me, but I did not
like that idea, nor did some of the ministers. So, fortunately we did
not do it. I think it's a mistake to name a school after someone who is
still alive. As crazy as I am, I didn't even want to think about the possibility of someday saying or doing something that somebody could
find offensive and then have to endure the debate over whether the
school's name should be changed. So, the ministers agreed to name the
school after their organization, and it opened in Fall 2004 as C.E.O.
Leadership Academy, with Denise as the principal. The school was a
participant in the Milwaukee Parental Choice Program, and so the
financial support for operations was primarily the per-pupil allotment from the state, based on the numbers of students enrolled in the
school. The school did get some additional support from TALC in the
form of an implementation grant, but those resources had to be primarily used for professional development. So, enrollment of students
was the critical factor to determine the continuation of the school.

After the school opened and the board was formed, I turned my
attention to other local and national work. I was surprised in May
2005, when Denise called and asked me to attend a crisis meeting at a
local bank, where one of the board members worked as president. The

meeting revealed some shocking news: The school was broke. It had run out of money and was operating at a loss. The financial problems stemmed from the fact that on the first day of school only thirty-three students had shown up. That was a major problem because the budget was based on an enrollment of 125 students. More students came after that first day, but the number only rose to sixty-seven students. Yet, the school had made no significant budgetary adjustments and now faced the possibility of closure. I sat there thinking, *Oh my God! Oh my God!...* But no matter what I'm feeling inside, I try to maintain outward calm. I didn't want the school to fail. After examining the situation, I talked privately with the board's chairman, Rev. Archie Ivy, pastor of New Hope Missionary Baptist Church, and we agreed that he should resign and that I should take over the role so that I could begin to address the problem immediately. One of the issues was that the school operated in an education building that had been built as an attachment to his church, and the church was owed $50,000. I had enormous respect for Pastor Ivy, who had been my mother's pastor a long time. I knew that he was in a very difficult position, and so we moved quickly to make the change. The rest of the board agreed, too, and I immediately went into battle to save the school. One of the board members who became a co-partner in making the decisions that needed to be made was Rev. John W. McVicker, Sr., pastor of Christ the King Baptist Church, one of the larger churches in Milwaukee. He was the type of clear-thinking person I needed to help me stave off disaster.

One of the first things I did was to hold a meeting with the staff to let them know what was going on and to assure them that, despite the fiscal situation, they would get paid. To maintain a sense of security and stability in an organization, staff members should never have to worry whether they will get their paychecks. It is important to respect their work and to honor it by paying them on time. I awarded the school a grant from the Institute to help cover the payroll. I then went to a close friend, Andy Fleckenstein, and tried to get a grant from his foundation. Andy declined, but he used his influence to get us a $100,000 loan from a bank where he had a strong business relationship. Susan Mitchell, my consultant friend, also stepped up and allowed the comptroller from her education reform organization to come in and help us set up appropriate financial systems. The actions we took moved us away from the brink, but there was still a lot to be done.

We pulled the staff together and made it clear that, for the next school year, we needed to have a minimum of 115 students enrolled. The staff and students began an "all hands on deck" recruitment effort. They went into the neighborhoods and churches to talk to families one-on-one about the school—a tactic that I had used back in my community organizing days in North Carolina. The recruiting effort paid off big time, helping us to enroll 125 students the following school year. The increase in students brought in more state dollars under the voucher program and bought us more time.

As chairman of the board, I took a hands-on approach, meeting regularly with Denise and the board to ensure that we were making sound fiscal decisions and operating smoothly. And, as always, it was important to me to get to know the staff, students, and their families. I showed up at the school practically every day that I was in town. I began teaching a Black History class, attending some staff meetings, and sometimes sat in on meetings with parents. I even deejayed the prom a time or two. I got to know my kids' stories so that when I talked about the school, I was talking about something I knew intimately. I also got to know how tough the work was that our teachers, dean of students, and principal were doing every day because I was there; I saw it. I knew that, for some of our kids, it was no small feat for them just to make it to school, given their lives outside school. We had one kid whose mother made him bring several bags of marijuana with him into our school building because she was a drug dealer and feared getting caught with it at home. She figured he was a minor and would face a lesser penalty, if caught. He indeed got caught during an unannounced locker check by teachers and administrators. Our school has no security personnel because we have tried to create a strict but loving environment where officers are not necessary. But as required by law, our staff immediately called police. We also called the mother, and when she and her son were interviewed separately it quickly became clear what had happened. We didn't want to punish the child for the mother's unimaginable behavior, but this is the kind of pressure that many of our kids face every day in their neighborhoods and homes.

Many of them have never traveled but a few miles beyond their own communities, and so even now, I try to expose them to the wider world and show them the possibilities for their lives. Every year to this day,

I take a group of them and staff chaperones to San Francisco, at no cost to them or the school. We eat dinner in China Town, ride the cable cars to Fisherman's Wharf, walk across part of the Golden State bridge, and, most important of all, visit Stanford University and the University of California at Berkeley. I want them to see the schools that attract people who intend to run the world.

We also take them to BAEO Symposia, held annually throughout the country, and bus trips to colleges, including Historically Black Colleges and Universities. I have tremendous respect for the roles these institutions continue to play in educating primarily Black students, including, in some cases, those who have the potential but not necessarily the standardized test scores to get into other schools. With a college education, these students are able to change their lives. As a result of such travels, our students have been to New York, New Mexico, Philadelphia, Washington, D.C., New Orleans, Orlando, and Atlanta. And many of our graduates have become students at schools we visited. I eventually would like to emulate what the well-regarded, college preparatory schools that are part of KIPP Academy have done—take students outside of the United States. I particularly want to take a group to a few countries in Africa.

For many of the students who travel with us, it is their first time riding on a plane. When I take them to nice restaurants, I encourage them to try foods they have never had. I try to show them that there is life beyond Milwaukee and that they can find their place in the world if they make good choices and stay in school. One of our kids was definitely falling prey to the streets. He is at heart a really good kid, but the pull from the street is great. I invited him to join me on of one of the trips to San Francisco. He was startled to get the invitation and could hardly believe he was going until he was on the plane. I knew his dream was to become a chef someday, and so we took him to a famous culinary school, Le Cordon Bleu in San Francisco, and the school accepted him as a student on the spot. But once he got back home, we could not raise the money that would have allowed him to go back to San Francisco to attend. It really set him back because he had his heart set on going to that school. But like many of our kids, his ability to continue in school beyond high school is almost an impossible dream because of financial obstacles. He did graduate from high school, an accomplishment that he had never even imagined for himself. But he still struggles to find a permanent job, and it will require extraordinary strength for him to keep pushing back against the pull from the streets. I know without a doubt, though, that without the school, he would have had no shot at all.

That's the frustrating thing about schools like ours. If you look just at our raw test scores, it is not yet a "high performing" school. But if a student comes to us, as many of our students do, with an ACT score lower than an eleven or twelve, and we push him to increase that score to sixteen or seventeen, we still aren't considered a high-achieving school. But with a minimum ACT score of a sixteen or seventeen, decent grades, grit, and determination, a young person can get into college somewhere and change the trajectory of his or her life. I've seen it happen time and time again. The perennial challenge is how do we as a school deal with the reality of our students' lives while holding them to the same high standard that they will be judged against in the outside world? Some of our board members have argued that we should recruit more students who are at or above grade level. That, of course, would be wonderful because our overall academic performance would be better. But I believe we have to have some high schools that accept kids who come in with low scores and commit to working with them to get them to a point where they at least have a chance at making it legitimately in the wider world. This is a huge challenge that some schools are indeed meeting. We still have a ways to go to become one of those schools.

There are no easy answers. But the kids are the reason I got in this fight in the first place. They are the reason I stay in it. And they are the reason I will continue to give each new struggle all that I've got.

With the staff of the C.E.O Leadership Academy in Milwaukee.

With C.E.O. students on a trip to San Francisco.

At a C.E.O. high school graduation ceremony.

With Milwaukee Collegiate Academy (formerly C.E.O.) students at
Stanford University.

17

THE STRUGGLE CONTINUES

Every few years, a new battle emerges in the ongoing fight to preserve the Milwaukee Parental Choice Program, the country's oldest state-financed system of school vouchers. And I have found myself in the middle of many of them.

Just after the start of the school year in October 2005, the Wisconsin Department of Public Instruction announced that the choice program had reached the enrollment cap that legislators had placed on it a decade earlier. No more than fifteen percent of the students enrolled in the entire school system were allowed to participate. Republican legislators had fought for three straight years, during the spring legislative sessions in 2003, 2004, and 2005, to lift the cap. But each time that they managed to get legislation approved, the state's new Governor Jim Doyle, a Democrat, vetoed it.

By the fall of 2005, 14,750 students were already in the program, but based on the school system's enrollment, that was 250 more students than allowed by the cap. That meant 250 children faced the possibility of losing their slots, and no new students would be admitted. There was talk of rationing slots, allotting a certain number to each school in the program, but that seemed ridiculous to me. It was time for me to go into battle again to get the cap lifted. Since Governor Doyle already had vetoed such legislation three times, I knew my colleagues and I were in for a tough fight.

Supporters of the program pulled together our resources and organized a powerful "Lift the Cap" campaign in advance of the 2006 legislative session. We ran radio and television advertisements featuring parents and children. We staged daily demonstrations at the capital that included hundreds of parents and children enrolled in the program. The kids filled the rotunda at the state capitol and stood there silently, wearing T-shirts and carrying signs calling for lawmakers to

"Lift the Cap." My school, C.E.O. Leadership Academy, was among those that participated. It was amazing to see kids so engaged in the process. We spent a significant amount of time educating them about the issue, and so they understood perfectly what was at stake.

Our protest got Governor Doyle's attention, and in the heat of battle, he agreed to a compromise that kept the cap in place and raised the number of participants to 22,500. The agreement also included a requirement for participating private schools to go through an accreditation process, and my Institute for the Transformation of Learning was designated as one of the organizations that could accredit the participating private schools. The deal was a big victory for those of us who supported parental choice, but one of the things I regret is that we didn't give Governor Doyle enough credit for his willingness to negotiate. Sometimes, in these political fights, you don't look at the other side. There were many Democrats upset with Governor Doyle for signing off on the deal. We supporters took the credit for forcing his hand. But at the end of the day, he didn't have to agree, and the deal wouldn't have happened without him.

We were reminded of that in 2008, when the worst fears of those who supported Milwaukee's voucher program were realized. Statewide elections put Democrats in control of the General Assembly *and* the Senate, and Governor Doyle, a Democrat, also retained his office. While a few Democrats always had broken ranks with the rest of their party to support the program, it had been protected in past years by either a Republican governor, a Republican-controlled legislature, or at least a Republican-controlled General Assembly. With Democrats now in control of the executive and legislative branches, supporters of the voucher program worried that it would be in grave jeopardy during the 2009 legislative session. The Democrats had long complained that there was no accountability for the participating private schools and teachers. Others simply wanted to end the program. But choice advocates had fought attempts to kill the program and/or weigh it down with the kind of rules and regulations that had stifled change and innovation in the traditional public school system. Sure enough, when Governor Doyle submitted his initial budget to the Joint Finance Committee, it contained a list of new regulations aimed mostly at tightening the controls on participating private schools and teachers.

Again, parental choice advocates went into battle. But this one would be bloodier than ever, splitting the movement over a strategy decision, and even ripping apart a longtime friendship. The confusion started when the governor sent a back door message to us through mutual friends that he wanted some changes to the Milwaukee Parental Choice Program but was willing to talk. He was clear, though: If we went after him like we had done in 2006, he was prepared to entertain that fight. But he promised that this time, the results would be very different. He was likely still angry about our lack of appreciation for his willingness to compromise the last time. But he made a strong point: We couldn't win. For the first time since the program began, we were in the extremely precarious position of needing Democrats to protect the program. I saw no way that could happen unless we could convince Black Democratic legislators from Milwaukee to step up and protect a program that most of them and their party did not support.

There was a problem, though: Susan Mitchell, who had been the key strategist for our side, didn't agree. She wanted an all-out battle. It was the first time Susan and I had been on opposing sides of a strategy argument. At some point, she and I had a telephone conversation about it. Then, each of us brought our supporters to a later strategic meeting that included about thirty-five parental choice advocates. We took turns explaining our positions. When it was Susan's turn, I was stunned when I heard her say something like: "I couldn't trust Howard to tell the truth. That's why I taped him!" She had recorded our telephone conversation without my knowledge. Susan had been one of my closest, most trusted friends and allies in the movement, and I was extremely disappointed that she felt it necessary to tape our conversation without my knowledge. Even some of her supporters seemed taken aback. I don't even recall what I'd said during the conversation she taped. I just knew for sure that I would never be able to trust her again and that our longtime friendship had come to an abrupt end. Susan and I have not spoken since that day.

Nevertheless, I began reaching out to the Black legislators. Among the first was Senator Lena Taylor, who was a member of the Joint Finance Committee, where the state budget originated and changes to the voucher program would be hashed out. When I approached her, she said something like: "By all rights, I shouldn't even be talking to you." I understood completely. I had been involved in a coalition of parental choice supporters that had campaigned against her, running advertisements that called her a slumlord when she ran for the Senate against one of our favored candidates. But to her credit, she was willing to talk to me. In fact, we talked for three hours, and I left kicking myself that I had not had that conversation with her sooner. She agreed to support the program if we were willing to accept some accountability measures. I came to know and trust Lena, and today I count her as a close and trusted friend.

After I had reached out to the seven Black legislators, I planned a meeting at my house, a session that became known as the famous "pound cake meeting" because I served my mother's delicious, homemade pound cake. Six of the seven legislators showed up, and we met for an intense two and a half hours, trying to work out legislation that would be agreeable to both the Democrats and parental choice advocates. The legislators agreed that Lena would take the lead in the Senate and that her counterparts in the State Assembly would do their part. That was the beginning of an alliance and a strategy that I think ultimately rescued the program. With the support of the Black legislators and their influence on their colleagues, we were able to defeat some of the more restrictive measures that would have imposed tougher standards on private schools in the program than existed for the regular public schools. But the Democrats were successful in placing some accountability measures on the private school participants, cutting the per-pupil allowance for the participants by $165 to $6,442, and freezing the payments at that rate for two years.

I saw the changes as reasonable, considering the damage that could have been done during that session. And many of us who supported the vouchers program viewed it as a victory. Needless to say, though, some fellow parental choice advocates viewed my working with the Democrats as a betrayal. That schism never has been repaired. Both Lena and I lost friends because we worked together. But, I can honestly say that effort was one of my proudest moments because, as Black people who deeply care about our children, we were able to put aside our differences and work to find common ground.

Soon, though, I would find myself engaged in a whole new fight over the program. When newly-elected Republican Governor Scott Walker took office in 2011, he proposed completely lifting the income cap, which had preserved the program for poor and low-income families. It seemed to me an outrageous attempt to steer the program from its original intent, which had been to provide educational options for poor and low-income families with children stuck in failing schools. To open the program to anyone who wanted to apply could eventually squeeze out those who most need the help. Opponents of vouchers have long suspected that the true intent of many conservatives who support Milwaukee's voucher program is to provide a state-financed alternative for families who already have the resources they need to afford a private alternative for their children. I couldn't just sit back and quietly allow this to happen, even if it meant taking a stand against many who had been my allies.

At a statewide budget hearing on the legislation, my testimony caught some state lawmakers by surprise. But I told them that their proposal was egregious. It undermined the very reason I had pushed for vouchers in the first place. Then, I issued a warning: If the proposed changes were adopted, "this is where I get off the train." I meant it. Before I could even make it out the door of the hearing room, two Republican lawmakers rushed over and followed me out of the room. The legislators and the governor eventually agreed to a compromise that I had proposed, which raised the income limit to the same standard used to allow people to participate in Badger Care, a statewide health insurance for low- to moderate-income people. This compromise would allow more people with slightly higher incomes than were acceptable under the previous guidelines into the program, but it was a change I could accept. And I appreciated the willingness of the governor and the Legislature to compromise on that issue.

That was another battle behind me. But one of the things that I have come to understand about the tough work of education reform—or any battle for social justice in this country, for that matter—is that a new battle, a new issue, a new problem is always on the horizon. There are no permanent victories and no permanent defeats. And so, to stay in the fight for the long term, you've got to stay ready, stay informed, and you've got to know where your line is in the sand. Better yet, you've got to know clearly why you drew that line in the first place.

I'm clear about my line. It is, as it always has been, on the side of the least fortunate among my people. They are the ones suffering disproportionately, in part because of this country's failure to educate our children. With the time I have left to make a difference, working in the area of education gives me the best chance to make an impact on the individual lives of poor children and their families.

I remain Director of the Institute for the Transformation of Learning at Marquette, where our mission is to support exemplary options that transform learning for students, while empowering families, particularly those with low incomes, to choose the best schools for their children. The Institute will continue to advocate for the Milwaukee Parental Choice Program, charter schools, and other educational reforms that benefit low-income and working-class families, particularly in Milwaukee. The Institute also will continue to operate a summer reading project started by a group of committed Black leaders in 2010. Milwaukee has some of the worst reading scores in the United States for Black children on the National Assessment of Education Progress (NAEP) tests. The project, which serves struggling readers in second, third, and fourth grades, is showing some very positive results. Research shows that, for children who do not learn to read by the third grade, the chances of finishing high school are pretty dismal. And without at least a high school diploma, a life of struggle is almost guaranteed. The hope is to be able to expand the program to operate during the school year so that children are affected all year long.

Much of my national work is focused on the Black Alliance for Educational Options (BAEO), which is still the only Black-led organization that is a constant unapologetic voice for low-income and working-class Black people in the parental choice movement. It is also one of the few Black-led organizations participating in the broader education reform movement. Since its founding in 1999, BAEO has established itself as a viable organization. The organization, led by President Kenneth Campbell, will continue its advocacy work in states like Louisiana, where the Louisiana Scholarship Program that provides financial support for poor children statewide to attend private schools is in constant jeopardy. That is so because a court decision set up the financing in a way that forces the state legislature and governor to allocate funds for the program and vote on it apart from the state budget each year. In addition, the U.S. Department of Justice has entered the battle, putting in jeopardy the ability of eligible families to exercise their choice. The Department claims that the vouchers have had a negative impact on integration, but the program's impact on integration is so small that the argument is practically meaningless. In any case, the Department of Justice is fighting the wrong battle at the wrong time in history, and BAEO is doing all we can to intervene and fight back on behalf of the state's children.

BAEO also will continue its support of education reform in New Orleans, which presents a different set of challenges than in other parts of Louisiana. The charter school movement has made great strides in New Orleans, where most schools were transformed into charter schools after Hurricane Katrina. After the hurricane left most of the city's schools devastated in 2005, the state assumed control of them through its Recovery School District, which the legislature had created two years earlier to take over schools in crisis throughout the state. The results have been promising, with the charter schools showing the state's strongest academic growth for Black children for the past five years. However, some Black residents are angered by what they see as white outsiders coming into their community and leaving them out of the decision-making process. BAEO will work to make sure that Black people in New Orleans are engaged and that they have a voice in what is happening with education reform. But at the same time, BAEO will not shy away from its support of reforms that are making a difference for students, or allow race to be used as a cover to block change that would greatly benefit the city's children.

Anyone who thinks the school children of New Orleans are not better off today than they were before Katrina is highly delusional. Yet, there will continue to be contention over state control of the city's schools, as some in New Orleans are pushing to return the command of the schools back to the Orleans Parish School Board, like in the pre-Katrina days.

In neighboring Mississippi, BAEO helped to get a charter schools law passed, but our work still is not done. We will continue pushing to strengthen the law so that it will include areas of the state that are currently exempt from it. The exempt areas have some of the lowest-performing schools and large numbers of poor children who need the kind of academic innovation that good charter schools can offer.

I also believe that it is important for BAEO to work to make sure that some high-performing schools are created and led by Black people. BAEO plans to expand its work into Tennessee and continue the fight in Kentucky to get a charter school law passed. We will also continue to be a voice for Black people in the national debates about reform issues, such as the Common Core, which BAEO supports. The initiative, initially called for by the National Governors Association Center for Best Practices and the Council of Chief State School Officers, seeks to establish a clear set of standards for English Language Arts

and math that are uniform across all states. While every public policy has an upside and a downside, we believe the potential benefits of
Common Core outweigh the legitimate concerns of some of its critics.
BAEO is excited that the Common Core standards strive to eradicate
geography as a factor in the quality of education a child receives. The
standards also better equip parents by providing them information
about what their children should be learning at certain benchmarks.
I do not take lightly the additional work that this may require for individual schools in the forty-five states that so far have adopted the
program voluntarily. Our children are worth the effort.

I remain chair of the board at my amazing school, which in 2011
changed its name to the Commitment, Excellence, and Opportunity
Leadership Academy and reopened as a charter school authorized by
the City of Milwaukee. Two years later, in September 2013, we moved
into a more spacious and modern building and renamed the school
the Milwaukee Collegiate Academy. Academically, our school is still
trying to hit the benchmarks set up by our local authorizer and those
required by the state of Wisconsin, as well as our own internal standards, which are even higher than both of those. And we won't stop
trying to get there.

We have transitioned to a blended learning curriculum, utilizing
the latest technology to access the best in online content as part of
our regular learning. We also remain relentlessly focused on fulfilling
our mission of getting our scholars into and through college. I remain
amazed by the strength and resiliency shown by many of our students,
who are dealing with extremely difficult circumstances in their families and in their communities but refuse to quit. Many of them come
into high school well behind where they should be in their academic
preparation, particularly in reading and mathematics. But our job is
to take them from where they are to where they must be to have any
chance to be college-ready when they leave us. Our current principal,
Rashida Evans, is a dedicated educator who cares deeply for our students and has the leadership skills and the knowledge base that serve
our scholars and our school well.

It remains to be seen if we can continue to raise the money that is
needed to operate the school. It is not possible to operate a high-performing charter school with only the per-pupil allotment from the
state. One of the critical issues for charter schools in some states is the
difference in funding versus traditional public schools. In Milwaukee,

charter schools receive more than $5,000 less per student than the traditional public schools. It is not enough to support the human and physical resources needed to create a great school. I've had to call on philanthropist friends, including Christy Walton, the wife of my friend and Walmart heir, John, who has bailed us out financially more than once.

I really love our school. I love our kids. Some people my age are scared of these kids and don't want to be around them. But they are just young people who have been through things and have seen things that no teenagers should have to see or experience. And, despite their tough exterior, they just want somebody to love and care for them and help them get better, even when they make bad decisions.

Everything I do is with them in mind. If a school can't provide the kind of solid education that will give these young people what they deserve, it needs to go out of business. It shouldn't be a permanent fixture guaranteed to continue for generations, whether or not it is doing what is expected. The promise of charter schools is just that simple: If we don't do what we are authorized to do, we go out of business. And we must live up to that promise.

The question that we as educators and reformers must answer is primarily one of time. How much time is enough to determine whether a school with promise is meeting the mark? It would break my heart to see my school shut down, but what would break my heart more is to fail to provide our kids with what I know they need to have a chance in this world.

As I look ahead at the work to be done, I am deeply grateful to the foundations, organizations, and individuals who have supported my work through the years, I have always been up front about where BAEO, the Institute, the Academy, and other organizations affiliated with me get their financial support. I realize that my critics will continue to make assertions about the fact that many of those supporters are aligned with so-called conservative causes and/or individuals. I remember one time a group of young people came to visit me in Milwaukee. As we sat in a circle talking, they criticized me for accepting money from the Lynde and Harry Bradley Foundation. It wasn't the first time I'd heard that criticism, and I'm sure it won't be the last. But I'll say here what I said to the students—yes, I'm well aware that the Bradley Foundation has long supported ultra-conservative causes and that the Foundation itself even provided financial support for the highly controversial book, *The Bell Curve*. That book tried to use research to make the ridiculous assertion that Black people are genetically inferior intellectually to other races. But as I see it, my accepting money from the Bradley Foundation is poetic justice, because everything I do is predicated on the fact that Black children are inferior to no one. Poor Black children, especially, just have far more obstacles to overcome to even be able to compete. But, if we somehow try to level the playing field and help provide them the tools and opportunities for them to be successful, they can be successful, and I am confident they will do just that. So, just as the students who criticized me needed the financial support of the Rockefeller Foundation to do what they considered important, I need financial support to do work that I believe is important to me and my community. I find it a complete waste of time to debate which people and organizations are considered acceptable donors and which ones are not. My criteria for accepting financial support is that it must allow the organizations with which I am most intimately involved to stay true to our mission. I have always said that BAEO, the Institute, and even the school must be willing to go out of business if we cannot be who we say we are. But I can honestly say that no one has ever come to me and said, "Take this money to do this work this way." It has always been the other way around, where I'm the one out there, trying to find resources to support my work. I'm just extremely grateful that there have been people willing to finance it. Without resources, you can have all the great ideas in the world, but they will remain just a bunch of ideas that go nowhere and help no one.

I realize that my work, and that of many others involved in the parental choice movement, is more of a rescue mission than a fight for broad societal change. But every time we create policies that empower low-income and working-class families to choose better learning environments for their children, I consider that a positive move forward. When we are able to create new learning environments through more effective use of today's technology, I consider that an important breakthrough for the students who are able to benefit. And every time we help a young person, who had every reason to fail, to graduate from high school and go on to college or into a job with a viable skill, I am reminded of why I got into this work.

With fellow protesters during the "Lift the Cap" campaign.

At the 2005 BAEO Symposium with former U.S. Department of
Education Secretary Rod Paige and
Pennsylvania State Representative Dwight Evans.

With Lawrence Patrick III, former BAEO President,
at the 2005 Symposium.

Dancing with Debbie at a BAEO party.

With gospel recording artist Marvin Sapp after a 2013 BAEO event.

With my grandson, William.

With my granddaughter, Zoe.

CONCLUSION

In November 2013, I traveled back to Durham, North Carolina, to participate in the 50th anniversary celebration of the historic North Carolina Fund. As I talked at several events about our groundbreaking antipoverty work in the 1960s and '70s, the memories were bittersweet. I couldn't help thinking about the many dear friends and fellow warriors who are no longer with us on this earth. Ben Ruffin, George Esser, Minnie Fuller, John Edwards, Charsie Hedgepeth, Joan Burton, Arch Foster, Reggie Durante, Dewitt Sullivan, Kwame McDonald, Joyce Nichols Thorpe, Osendi Hadari, Lonnie Wilson, Pat Rogers, and Thelma Jean Miller (T.J.), all gone too soon. There are others, but unfortunately the list is too long to cite completely. As I talked at the reunion that day, I felt myself being lifted spiritually and encouraged by them. And I felt a responsibility to tell our story for them.

For me, looking backwards, as that celebration and this book have pushed me to do, is very difficult. I'm not ordinarily a person who spends much time looking back. I'm always more focused on the present struggles and the ones that lie ahead. While I see so much that I want and need to do, I have to admit that education reform is the toughest work of my life. At the end of each year, when I finally slow down long enough to reflect on what I've done and set goals for the coming year, I often have to fight off despair. I struggle with whether my efforts are making a difference. You can't be in this struggle for as long as I have, look out and see that for such a large part of our community nothing seems to have changed, and not be disheartened. Sometimes, that fact makes it tough to figure out the road ahead and to keep going.

Many years ago, famed Black psychologist Kenneth B. Clark visited Marquette and stopped by my office to chat. I will never forget the image of him standing at the window, staring out solemnly, questioning the value of all the work he had done. This was the same Dr. Kenneth Clark, noted scholar, researcher, and author, whose famous doll experiment had been used to support the case to end school segregation in the *Brown v. Board of Education* decision by the U.S. Supreme Court.

Dr. Clark's research wasn't beyond reproach, and I've expressed the issues I have with parts of the argument in the Brown case. But there is no debating that the work of Dr. Clark, and his wife and fellow psychologist, Mamie, helped changed the course of history and knocked down doors that had been closed to our people. Many of us benefitted. Yet, in his later years, he felt the same frustration I feel when I look at the conditions today for so many of our people.

I recently read Dr. Clark's book, *Dark Ghetto: Dilemmas of Social Power*, first published in 1965, in which he describes the desperate conditions in Harlem and other Black communities throughout this country. The tragedy is that, in many of the descriptions he cited, you could replace the year 1965 with 2014, and his depictions still would be true. That reality is hard to face. I didn't get into this struggle nearly fifty years ago just so that my life and my own children's lives would be better. Of course I wanted that, but I had always hoped to help make life better for my entire community. There is no denying that life indeed is better for many of us. Even in the 1960s and '70s, while we were engaged in the struggle for basic human dignity, we saw improvements that made life better for some people. Yet, when I travel around the country today, it becomes clear just how intractable poverty is. For the poorest segment of the community, conditions actually seem worse than ever. Perhaps that seems so because the gap between Black people with education and resources and those without appears wider than ever. It also seems that more Black people are adopting the notion of "race fatigue," distancing themselves from those in their racial group who are less fortunate.

For me, the whole idea of "race fatigue" is not, never has been, and never will be an option. How do you do that anyway, just declare yourself tired of being seen as Black, and tired of caring about your people? I literally ache when I think about how my people have been treated throughout history. I wake up most days thinking about what I can do to make the horrible conditions that I see better. It haunts me when I walk into schools, talk to children, and hear stories that remind me what so many poor, Black kids are up against just to survive. In some cases, the first big hurdle they have to get over is their parents, individuals who are ill-equipped to nurture and guide anyone, least of all impressionable, defenseless children. And if the kids are able to overcome unstable homes with their sanity intact, they still have to navigate their way through neighborhoods where violence and the worst of human behavior are a regular part of life. These are the nurting children who show up in our schools. I see them. I talk to them on a regular basis.

The challenge all schools face is that they must find a way to educate the most vulnerable children and equip them to be academically competitive in spite of these issues. For most of our traditional public schools, mountains of red tape and rules and regulations, as well as overly powerful unions, stifle the kind of creativity and innovation needed to help these children leap over the high hurdles inherent in their lives. That is why I fight for poor parents to have a wide range of educational options. Historically, Black people have fared better as a group when we have more than one option in all aspects of our lives, including education.

While I have discussed some specific plans for the Institute, BAEO, and the Milwaukee Collegiate Academy in this book, we have to make sure that we stay mission driven. We have to be careful not to get committed to any particular strategy or tactic to the point that we ignore the purpose for our actions. Reformers must always be committed to purpose and not to the method used to get to that purpose. We cannot get so committed to any particular governance structure or school reform initiative that we ignore its impact on the intended purpose: educating students. We should support reforms only to the extent that they enable us to ensure that our kids are effectively educated. Those of us who get committed to method, instead of the purpose, could ultimately run the risk of becoming what we are fighting against, protectors of the status quo.

I am under no illusions about the role that education plays in our society. As I often tell our students, "Getting an education in America guarantees you nothing, but I guarantee you, you will have nothing without an education." Focusing on education does not mean I do not understand how other institutions and policies impact the lives of our children. Nor do I think schools alone can solve the problems that impact our children before they ever get to school. In fact, we have children who should get a medal for just showing up at school, given what they are dealing with in their homes and communities. And I'm always in awe of those who, despite the incredible odds against them, somehow make it out and succeed. Far more times than not, they are able to do so because they have help—a teacher, a neighbor, a church member, a friend's parent, someone who offers a hand along the way.

That's why I can never just throw my hands up in surrender. I wouldn't dare. To do so would be unconscionable.

I have always believed that those of us who have achieved some level of success—an education, a job, a somewhat comfortable life—have a responsibility to reach back to help others improve their status in life. It doesn't mean that doing so won't get challenging or frustrating. But in those times, I think about how difficult life is every single day for those who don't have the necessities, the extras, the breaks in life that many of us so easily take for granted. That helps to renew my strength and focus. I think, too, about my grandmother, who died in 1976, and my mother, who passed away in 2010, and I recall the sacrifices they made to educate me and support my dreams, whatever they were at a given time. I'm glad my mother got to see much of my evolution, her son fighting for poor, Black people in North Carolina, her son fighting for children, particularly poor, Black children in Milwaukee, her son fighting for children and families across this nation. In her final days, I hired a home health care agency to come in a few days a week and help care for her. My mother, then eighty-eight, suffered from chronic obstructive pulmonary disease, which I believe was caused by her constant exposure to lint in the factory where she had worked for many years. The agency sent a representative, who, as part of assessing her condition, including her memory, began asking a battery of questions. One question was something like, "What was your proudest accomplishment in life?" She sat up in her chair, turned and pointed to me. Few other moments in my life have made me feel as grateful and proud.

When I first landed in North Carolina nearly fifty years ago, I truly believed I could help end poverty. That youthful naiveté vanished long ago, but not the belief that I MUST do something to change the conditions and the life chances of our poorest citizens. Without a doubt, education offers the best route out of poverty for individuals, and for me, putting poor children on that path is today's most urgent struggle. Until my time runs out, I will spend my days launching rescue missions, trying to save as many kids as I can, as often as I can, no matter how hard the struggle.

This I know for sure: *If there is no struggle, there is no progress.*

A NOTE ON SOURCES

A memoir is, by its very nature, an imperfect snapshot of a moment in time. This one is based primarily on my recollections, but because so much of my life was lived in public, I was able to use various sources to make sure that my accounts are as historically accurate as possible. In the two years that my co-writer, Lisa Frazier Page, and I worked on this book, we spent much time poring over old newspaper clippings and photos, particularly those of the *Carolina Times, Durham Morning Herald, Charlotte News & Observer, Greensboro Daily News, North Carolina Anvil, Duke Chronicle, Milwaukee Journal,* and *Milwaukee Journal Sentinel.* We also visited the Wilson Library at the University of North Carolina at Chapel Hill, where we were able to go through the North Carolina Fund Records, which are archived there as part of the Southern Historical Collection. We found valuable details, facts, and figures to help flesh out the memories of my time with the North Carolina Fund, as well as the Foundation for Community Development, one of the three spinoff groups that received the Fund's remaining financial assets when it disbanded in 1968.

In addition to my own voluminous files, we are thankful for the meticulous record-keeping of Dr. Faye Coleman, who was instrumental in forming Malcolm X Liberation University and shared her notes and memories. Her husband, Milton Coleman, a former editor at *The Washington Post* and a student of history, also helped to add valuable historical context, particularly in the chapter on Milwaukee, his hometown.

Interviews with family, friends, and former co-workers also were a tremendous asset in pulling this project together. In 2011, I gathered in Durham with a group of fellow warriors from my time with Operation Breakthrough to reminisce for the book about some of our experiences together. I'm so fortunate that the group included Joyce C. Thorpe Nichols, whose fight against public housing officials in Durham set a landmark precedent. She died the following year. Others who gathered included Ann Atwater, Rubye D. Gattis, Nathaniel and Louise Balentine, Fred and Sylvia Rebenson, Lottie Hayes, Bruce Bridges, Patricia Sutton, Shirley Thompson, and Marc Lee, the son of my successor at the Foundation for Community Development, Jim Lee.

Lisa and I also are grateful to have been able to interview Thelma Jean Miller (T.J.) before her death in 2013. Other interviews included Nathan Garrett, Walter Aaron, Doug and Judy Irvin, Bishop R.J. Burt, Sr., and Dr. Deborah McGriff, as well as several students and faculty members at the former C.E.O. Leadership Academy. As needed, many other people were called to confirm and/or clarify my recollections.

HOWARD'S ACKNOWLEDGMENTS

I could write another book full of just names if I listed every single person who encouraged, guided, or supported me along this journey. I'm grateful for each act of kindness and encouragement. As I attempt to single out at least a few of the people who have helped to make my work and this book possible, I do so knowing that this list is incomplete.

I owe much of who I am today to my mother, Juanita Smith, and my grandmother, Pearl Wagner, who poured their all into making sure that I was not only educated but also a decent human being. For much of my life I was fortunate to have the guidance and mentoring of the late Wesley Scott, the late Kwame McDonald, and Nate Harris. I feel blessed to have such a supportive family, beginning with my wife, Dr. Deborah McGriff, who has been my love, my closest adviser, and my most trusted critic at precisely the right times. My children—Kelli, Miata, and Malcolm Fuller, Darwin Mills, and his wife Tammy, my stepdaughter and her husband, Michael and Jacqueline Cooper—and my grandchildren, Zoe Cooper and William Fuller Rhatigan, are a constant source of joy and strength.

When I moved to North Carolina in 1965, my life changed forever. The people who struggled beside me during my work for Operation Breakthrough, the North Carolina Fund, the Foundation for Community Development, and Malcolm X Liberation University helped to shape the person and the activist I became. To this day, I draw upon the lessons I learned from them. Many of their stories are told, too, in this book, and I thank them all from the depths of my heart and soul.

I have benefited from having the kind of friends who are there with you during the good times and the hard times. I am thankful to Walter and Barbara Aaron and Viola Plummer and my lifelong friends from Carroll, Doug and Judy Irwin and Bill and Carla Mullen, for always being there. I will also be forever grateful to my friend, Irie Grant, who gave me a job and a chance to rebuild my life when I moved back to Milwaukee and had nowhere to turn.

I would not be able to do this work without the tremendous backing I have gotten from Marquette University. Marquette has played a major role at critical junctures in my life, beginning in the 1980s, when I was hired to work for the Educational Opportunity Program. I will always be grateful to Dr. Arnold Mitchem for giving me that chance, to my friend, Dr. George Lowery, who recommended me for the position, and to Dr. Robert Lowe, who has helped me immensely throughout my career. I also gained so much from the students in the program, including Anthony Bradford, Shree Robertson, Kathy Green, Lee Bean, and countless others. Their perseverance and hard work were an inspiration, and it was a privilege to serve them.

When I resigned as Superintendent of Milwaukee Public Schools (MPS), Marquette also enabled me to create the Institute for the Transformation of Learning (ITL), which has provided a home for much of my work in the parental choice and education reform movements since 1995. I owe so much to the staff members, who, over the past nineteen years, made ITL just what I envisioned it could be. They include Dr. Robert Pavlik and Jeannie Fenceroy, who were among the first employees, as well as longtime staff member Cindy Zautche. I can't say enough about Judith Romelus, whom I watched grow and flourish while working with me for fifteen years. My new assistant, Cheryl Olp, keeps the place functioning while I am out doing the work. There are so many others who have made ITL a joyful and productive place to work over the years.

Given my long connection to the university, it just feels right that Marquette University Press is publishing this book. I owe a heartfelt thanks to Dr. Andrew Tallon, Director, and Mrs. Maureen Kondrick, Manager, who have guided me through the process and turned this dream into reality.

The Black Alliance for Educational Options (BAEO) is, too, an offshoot of ITL, because the idea to create such an organization came out of a symposium sponsored by ITL in 1999. I could not have imagined then the important work that BAEO would do or the longevity it would have. As chair of the board, I am honored to represent our organization and extremely proud of how far we have come. I can only thank the individuals who founded it and have supported it over the past fourteen years. That includes all of the former board members, people like T. Willard Fair, Jackie Cissell, Dwight Evans, and the two remaining long-term board members, my wife Deborah McGriff and

Vernard Gant. I am thankful also to Kevin Chavous for his two-year service as chair of the board. We also owe much to the past presidents, Kaleem Caire, Lawrence Patrick III, and Gerard Robinson, and our long-serving Director of National Advocacy, Shree' Medlock.

As I plan to transition from my position as chair of the board in the months ahead, I am confident the organization will be led in the right way by the next generation of leaders, including Darryl Cobb, Mashea Ashton, Kevin Hinton, Dawn Chavous, our President Ken Campbell, and his leadership team—Shree, Tanzi West, Tiffany Forrester, Monique Pittman, Offiong Bassey, and Tracie Craft. I am also proud of all of our folks who are doing important work in the states and providing various levels of administrative support for our organization.

There are many special people and organizations that have made it possible for BAEO and ITL to function and for me to carry out my work. I must always begin any such discussion with the name John Walton. He was a very special individual, a wonderful friend, and a true supporter whom I miss greatly. I will forever be in debt to him for his generosity. Since his sudden death in 2005, his wife, Christy, has stepped into his place in my life, and I thank her for her friendship and ongoing support.

I have also been blessed over the years to have a very special relationship with the Walton Family Foundation, in particular staff members Jim Blue, Ed Kirby, Abby Schumwinger, Sherman Whites, Naccaman Williams, and Buddy D. Philpot, each of whom has been instrumental in helping me to obtain continued funding of my activities.

Several other foundations also have made possible the work of BAEO, the Institute, and the Milwaukee Collegiate Academy. Those organizations include, the Fisher Foundation, the Fleck Foundation, the Joyce Foundation, the Challenge Foundation, the Helen Bader Foundation, the Doris and Donald Fisher Fund, the Laura and John Arnold Foundation, Bill and Melinda Gates Foundation, the Lynde and Harry Bradley Foundation, and the American Federation of Children.

I am particularly grateful to Bill Oberndorf, John Kirtley, and Andy Fleckenstein, each of whom has been there with support at the most crucial moments in the lives of BAEO and the Milwaukee Collegiate Academy. I appreciate the friendship of Tim Sheehy, the president of the Metropolitan Milwaukee Chamber of Commerce, who has been a supporter and confidant through many storms over the years in the fight for education reform.

I am thankful, too, for so many good friends in Milwaukee who have had my back in this work for so many years, including Ralph Hollmon, Danae Davis, Jeanette Mitchell, Thelma Sias, Daniel Grego, Cory and Michelle Nettles, Martha Love, Elmer Anderson, Rose Massey, Dr. Archie Ivy, Rev. Harold Moore, Pastor John McVicker, Bishop Ricky Burt, Bishop Cheryl Brown, Rueben and Mildred Harpole, Mikel Holt, Michael McGee, Sr., my main man Eugene Bonner, and the late Barbara Horton. And I will always be grateful to former State Representative Polly Williams for her courage.

I am encouraged when I see bright young people coming into education through Teach For America, founded by Wendy Kopp, or the Big Picture Company, founded by my friend Dennis Littky. I marvel at the commitment and high academic performance that Mike Feinberg and David Levin have been able to generate with the Knowledge is Power Program (KIPP) schools. It warms my heart to know that both men give appropriate credit to master teacher Harriett Ball, the Black woman who trained them when they were eager, young Teach For America participants, and that her ingenious teaching techniques live on through the KIPP schools. I appreciate my long friendship with Joe Williams, who leads Democrats for Education Reform, and I am learning so much about organizing from Mark Frailey, whose advice and support the past few years have been invaluable.

I am lifted by the many white-led organizations that, while bringing resources, time, and energy into this struggle to educate our children, appreciate the value of connecting to the communities they serve. They are helping to create a diverse new generation of academic leaders. Their leaders include: Julie Jackson, an African-American woman who was the principal and a math teacher for Uncommon Schools and now trains educators throughout the world; Kendra Ferguson, who is the chief of schools for KIPP Bay Area schools; and Chastity Lord, the chief external officer for the Achievement First network of charter schools.

Other innovators include Roblin Webb, founder and director of Freedom Preparatory School, a charter school in Memphis; Laura McGowan, executive director and founder of Crown Preparatory Academy in south Los Angeles; and Nina Gilbert, founder of Ivy Preparatory Academy in Gwinnett County, Georgia. These three young leaders were prepared for their roles as fellows for the Boston-based Building Excellent Schools, created by a great friend, Linda Brown, one of the most tenacious reformers I have ever met.

On the organizing side, there are strong fighters and leaders, like Sharhonda Bossier, who, as deputy director of Families for Excellent Schools, works with high-performing charter schools in New York, New Jersey, and Connecticut to help mobilize parents around education reform; Shannel Dunns, who works for Education Reform Now in Newark, New Jersey; Jamilah Prince-Stewart, who works for ConnCan in Connecticut; and, of course, my man Darrell Bradford from New Jersey.

I am pleased to know Darrell Allison, President of Parents for Educational Freedom in North Carolina, who is one of the most effective organizers in the country. I am also proud that my youngest daughter, Miata Fuller, and my stepdaughter, Jacqueline Cooper, are a part of the movement. Miata works as chief of staff through the chief executive officer for New Leaders for New Schools, and Jacqueline is executive director of BAEO. Also, my oldest daughter, Kelli, works as an office manager for the Roseville Community Charter School in Newark.

There are also those courageous Black legislators who at times have had to fight against their own political parties to support the choice movement, people like Representative Alisha Morgan in Georgia, Senator Anthony Williams in Pennsylvania, Representative Chuck Espy in Mississippi, and Representatives Patrick Williams and Austin Badon in Louisiana, as well as former elected officials Ann DuPlessis in Louisiana and Jason Fields and Willie Hines in Wisconsin.

I am working with five young people in Milwaukee, who named themselves the "Fuller Torch Fellows." They meet with me monthly and shadow me as I give speeches and attend meetings around the country. Shawn Sprewer, Gabrielle Gray, Jarett Fields, Curtis Sails and Nikotris Perkins are teaching me, even as I try to pass on some of what I have learned to them. An extra thanks goes to Jarett for the many hours spent reading the early drafts of the manuscript and offering very helpful feedback.

I am, of course, inspired by the students, staff and board of the Milwaukee Collegiate Academy, particularly our principal, Rashida Evans, who is a excellent young education leader, absolutely committed to the students we serve.

This book was made possible with the financial support of Ellen Alberding, the president of the Joyce Foundation; the Walton Family Foundation; Bill Oberndorf; Andy Fleckenstein; and Dan Bader.

I also am so appreciative of those who volunteered many hours to read my manuscript and offer critical editorial suggestions and advice, most notably Bowie State University professor Karima Haynes, and my longtime friends and fellow warriors, Milton and Dr. Faye Coleman. I especially thank Milton for getting this book project going in the first place when he introduced me to my collaborator, Lisa Frazier Page. Her skill and commitment are the reason why this book was completed. I cannot thank her enough for her friendship and tenacity to make sure we finished.

LISA'S ACKNOWLEDGMENTS

I thank my Lord and Savior, Jesus Christ, for every chance to do the work that I love. I'm grateful to Dr. Howard Fuller for choosing me as a collaborator and for his openness and introspection, even as we explored the most painful parts of his incredible journey. Howard, I remain inspired by your independence, dedication, and perseverance.

To my husband, Kevin, thank you for the love, trust, and support that enable me to do this work. And to my children—Enjoli, Danielle, Kevin Jr., and Kyle—I love you more than you can imagine. I appreciate your patience throughout this project.

I was blessed with amazing parents, Clinton and Nettie Frazier, who have always supported my dreams, and I inherited another beautiful set of parents in my in-laws, Richard and Miriam Page. My father-in-law passed away just before the completion of this book, and it still doesn't feel quite real. But he let me know often that he was proud to have a daughter who wrote books, and I believe he is now one of my guardian angels.

I owe a special thanks to my friend and former supervisor at *The Washington Post*, Milton Coleman, for introducing me to Howard, reading the manuscript, and offering superb editorial advice. I'm also grateful to Milton's wife, Dr. Faye Coleman, and my dear friend, Karima Haynes, a Bowie State University journalism professor, for their keen insight and suggestions on the manuscript. Thanks, too, to Melody Guy for her brilliant editing early in the process and to Jarett Fields for his excellent editorial skills and ideas. All of their contributions made this book better.

Finally, to every family member and friend who encouraged me and helped to keep me sane throughout this process, I appreciate you.

With co-author Lisa Frazier Page.

INDEX

Forman, James, 176
"For Whom the Bell Tolls" (film),
    56–57, 73
Foundation for Community
    Development (FCD), 79,
    83–85, 91–92, 96, 97
Foust, Robert, 58, 70–71, 72
(FRELIMO). *See* Mozambique
    Liberation Front
    (FRELIMO)
Friedman, Milton, 204
Fuller, Howard Lamar
    arrests of, 53, 86–89, 108
    back injury of, 44, 163, 166
    Barack Obama and, 246–47
    Black Alliance for Educational
        Options (BAEO) and,
        248–49, 256, 272–74
    childhood in Milwaukee, WI,
        16–24
    childhood in Shreveport, LA,
        13–16, 20
    in Cleveland, OH, 44–46, 51–56
    continuing work of, 184, 281,
        282–83
    Darwin "Van" Mills (son) and,
        91, 233
    death threats against, 91, 155
    Deborah McGriff and
        dating relationship of, 215–16
        marriage of, 243–45, 249
    as deejay, 212, 261
    depression of, 43, 229
    discreditation of, attempted, 176
    doctoral work of, 175, 192, 193
    in Durham, NC, 61–79, 87,
        88, 89–90, 91, 93, 97,
        99–110, 156–58
    education of
        at Carroll College, 24–25,
            37–49
        in Milwaukee, WI, 18–19
        in Shreveport, LA, 15

        at Western Reserve University,
            43–44
        extramarital affair of, 90–91
        father of, 14–15, 233
        in Guyana, 111
        illness of
            cancer, 249–50
            in Mozambique, 135, 138, 143
            sarcoidosis, 232–34
        Kelli Pilar (daughter) and, 73,
            131, 132, 170, 171, 244,
            249
        in Kenya, 121–22
        Malcolm Marcus Lamar (son)
            and, 95–96, 132, 169, 244
        marriage to Claudetta Wright,
            173–74, 189
            ending of, 199
        marriage to Deborah McGriff,
            243–45, 249
        marriage to Viola Williams, 56–
            57, 72, 91, 95–96, 124,
            132, 146
            ending of, 156, 159, 169
        Marxism and, 154–55, 156–57,
            158–59
        Miata (daughter) and, 112–13,
            132, 170–71, 244, 249
        Milwaukee, returning to, 159,
            163
        with the Mozambique Liberation
            Front (FRELIMO),
            123–46
        North Division High School and,
            19–20, 171–73, 188
        as Owusu Sadauki, 112
        police brutality experienced by,
            52–53, 87–88
        returning Martin Luther King,
            Jr., Humanitarian Award,
            195
        sports and, 19, 20–22, 131, 141
            basketball, 20–21, 24, 40–41,
                44

Index 303